Picture Yourself Learning Corel® PaintShop™ Pro X4

Diane Koers

Course Technology PTR

A part of Cengage Learning

COURSE TECHNOLOGY
CENGAGE Learning™

Australia, Brazil, Japan, Korea, Mexico, Singapore, Spain, United Kingdom, United States

COURSE TECHNOLOGY
CENGAGE Learning™

**Picture Yourself Learning Corel®
PaintShop™ Pro X4**
Diane Koers

**Publisher and General Manager,
Course Technology PTR:**
Stacy L. Hiquet

Associate Director of Marketing:
Sarah Panella

Manager of Editorial Services:
Heather Talbot

Marketing Manager:
Mark Hughes

Acquisitions Editor:
Heather Hurley

Project/Copy Editor:
Karen A. Gill

Technical Reviewer:
Elaine Marmel

Interior Layout:
Shawn Morningstar

Cover Designer:
Mike Tanamachi

Indexer/Proofreader:
Kelly Talbot Editing Services

APR 2 4 2012

For product information and technology assistance, contact us at

**Cengage Learning Customer and Sales Support,
1-800-354-9706.**

For permission to use material from this text or product, submit all requests online at **cengage.com/permissions.**

Further permissions questions can be emailed to **permissionrequest@cengage.com.**

Library of Congress Control Number: 2011933245
ISBN-13: 978-1-4354-6059-1
ISBN-10: 1-4354-6059-6

Course Technology, a part of Cengage Learning
20 Channel Center Street
Boston, MA 02210
USA

Cengage Learning is a leading provider of customized learning solutions with office locations around the globe, including Singapore, the United Kingdom, Australia, Mexico, Brazil, and Japan. Locate your local office at **international.cengage.com/region.**

Cengage Learning products are represented in Canada by Nelson Education, Ltd.

For your lifelong learning solutions, visit **courseptr.com.**
Visit our corporate website at **cengage.com.**

To Spencer Ford,
With lots of love and dreams for your future.
Look ahead and smile!

Acknowledgments

IN A BOOK SUCH AS THIS ONE, IT'S HARD TO KNOW WHERE TO START. There are so many people working behind the scenes, each one as valuable as the next. First, I'd like to thank Heather Hurley for believing in me enough to let me write this book again. To Karen Gill, whose patience, support, and sense of humor (not to mention her wonderful grammatical skills) kept me going through the process. To Elaine Marmel, my marvelous dear friend, who kept me on track and had fun in the process! To Shawn Morningstar, for exercising all her outstanding layout talents in making this a beautiful book. To Kelly Talbot, Mike Tanamachi, and all the others working madly behind the scenes to get this book into print. To all of you, thank you from the bottom of my heart.

There were a number of people who provided the photographs you see in this book. It was often difficult for all of them because I frequently needed "less than perfect" images to work with, which sometimes is easier said than done. A special thank you to all photograph and creation contributors.

And finally, a huge note of appreciation goes to my husband of almost 43 years. Vern, thank you for your patience and understanding of the many late-night hours, for fending for yourself or both of us at supper time, and for keeping me encouraged and supplied with Diet Coke and working chocolate. I love you.

About the Author

DIANE KOERS owns and operates All Business Service, a software training and consulting business formed in 1988 that services the central Indiana area. Her area of expertise has long been in the word-processing, spreadsheet, and graphics areas of computing, as well as providing training and support for Peachtree Accounting Software. Diane's authoring experience includes more than 40 books on topics such as PC security, Microsoft Windows, Microsoft Office, Microsoft Works, WordPerfect, PaintShop Pro, Lotus SmartSuite, Quicken, Microsoft Money, and Peachtree Accounting, many of which have been translated into other languages such as Dutch, Bulgarian, French, Spanish, and Greek. She has also developed and written numerous training manuals for her clients.

Diane and her husband enjoy spending their free time fishing and RVing around the United States and playing with their four grandsons, their Yorkshire Terrier Sunshine, and their cute little guinea pig Ginger.

Table of Contents

Chapter 3
Becoming More Organized 35

Chapter 4
Making Selections

Chapter 5
Making Quick Fixes

Chapter 6
Manually Editing Images............................ 115

Chapter 7
Understanding Color 155

Chapter 9
Adding Effects, Filters, and Deformations 213

Chapter 10
Discovering Drawing Tools

Chapter 11
Constructing Vector Objects

Chapter 12
Editing Vector Objects 287

Chapter 13
Working with Text 301

Chapter 14
Printing and Sharing Images 319

Introduction

DESIGNED FOR ANYONE INTERESTED IN GRAPHICS, PHOTOGRAPHY, OR PHOTOGRAPHIC CREATIONS, this book came into existence to show you how you can put the incredible power of Corel PaintShop Pro X4 into play.

This book cuts right to the chase of the PaintShop Pro X4 tools that are best used when working with photographs and creating your own graphic elements. You will learn about photographs and how to correct and enhance them, making them better than they appeared out of your camera. There's even a chapter dedicated just to color and understanding how it works.

You'll learn about using layers to make adjustments, such as brightness, hue, color contrast, and many others. This book covers the often-misunderstood topic of resolution and how it applies to your monitor, your images, and your prints. Also, you will look at the PaintShop Pro RAW lab, where you can process your camera's RAW images, getting just the look you want.

It's not all work, though. You'll also learn about many of the fun things you can do with your photographs, such as creating digital scrapbook pages or 3-dimensional images with them. Discover how you can make composite images, retouch and repair damaged photographs, and create works of art with the special effects provided with PaintShop Pro X4.

The best way to absorb a feature is to jump in and try it. Taste is relative. What you like about an image may be completely different from what the person next to you likes. I am confident that as you make your way through this book, you will gain a good feel for the awesome power of PaintShop Pro X4.

Assumptions

I make a couple of assumptions about the readers of this book. First of all, and most obviously, since you're reading this right now, I assume that you want to know more. Okay, I am going to try and fill you with knowledge. Second, I assume that you know the basics of working with a computer, such as using the mouse, making menu selections, and opening, saving, and closing a file. If you know those basics, you can find your way around PaintShop Pro X4.

Book Structure

This book is divided into 16 chapters that cover a wide realm of PaintShop Pro topics beginning with getting acquainted with the PaintShop Pro basic tools and ending with printing and scrapbooking. Of course, there are numerous chapters that discuss managing and manipulating photographs, including adding filters and working with the various output functions. There are also two appendixes, the first of which lists all the PaintShop Pro keyboard shortcuts available in the Edit workspace. The second lists many useful websites pertaining to PaintShop Pro. The book also includes a glossary with explanations of common PaintShop Pro and general graphic terms.

Throughout the book, I've also included various tips and notes designed to alert you to special considerations.

Author Competence

You'll quickly determine, as you delve into this book, that I'm not a professional photographer. Even calling me an amateur would require a stretch of the imagination. I am, however, a teacher and a writer, a computer geek, and a PaintShop Pro enthusiast. With those tools and a lot of help and research, I have written this book with the intention of helping you get the most you can out of PaintShop Pro X4. I hope you enjoy learning from it as much as I enjoyed writing it.

If you have any comments about this book, please feel free to contact me at diane@thepeachtreelady.com.

—Diane

Companion Website Downloads

You may download the companion website files from www.courseptr.com/downloads. Please note that you will be redirected to our Cengage Learning site. From the Cengage Learning site, click the Film, Digital Photography & Printing link and look for this book. The website offers hundreds of useful items, including graphics, photographs, fonts, and lots of other free, fun stuff. You'll also find a variety of demo programs you can install to try some of the PaintShop Pro add-on filters.

1

Getting Acquainted

PICTURE YOURSELF VIEWING A COLONY OF ARTISTS—artists who draw, artists who paint, artists who photograph. Visualize them standing outside in the sunlight with their sketchpads, easels, and cameras, each enjoying the serene beauty of nature. Now picture yourself in the midst of them. Do you see it?

If you can't see yourself in their company because you don't draw, paint, or photograph, don't give up hope. There's another artists' colony around, and you can, with the aid of the fabulous Corel PaintShop Pro software program, join right in—even if you're allergic to sunlight. This colony consists of artists using PaintShop Pro, where you can create electronic works of art from your digital photographs.

This chapter shows you the basic instructions for maneuvering around in PaintShop Pro and introduces the various screen elements and tools. You probably already know about the process of opening and saving files, but we'll review them and perhaps show you a few shortcuts along the way.

This is a great time in our history to work with digital images. Relax. You're just a few mouse clicks away from releasing your inner creativity.

Getting Started

PAINTSHOP PRO IS AN UNPARALLELED image organizing and editing software package, designed to give you the wide range of features required when working with digital images. Its abundance of impressive features allows you to easily share, organize, and edit your digital photos. Do you want to learn how to build amazing slide shows or get into digital scrapbooking? How about organizing the thousands of digital images stored on your computer hard drive, camera, or memory card? To accomplish those tasks, you need software like PaintShop Pro. Let's take a brief look at some of the specific things you can do with PaintShop Pro:

▶ Fix common photographic flaws such as red-eye, scratches, color, contrast, or lighting.

▶ Crop unwanted image areas, allowing you to zoom in on the subject of interest.

▶ Convert your favorite color image to black and white or sepia to give it an old-fashioned appearance.

▶ Twist, warp, or stretch your images to create surreal scenes.

▶ Stylize your photos with special effects, and combine elements from different photos on multiple layers to create artistic composites or panoramas.

▶ Change or erase photo backgrounds or remove unwanted portions (such as your ex-brother-in-law).

▶ Allow your images to tell a story in colorful, decorative scrapbook pages by adding text and shapes. Go one step further and add sound and transitions to create dynamic slide shows you can view on your computer or television.

▶ Organize and manage your stored digital photos by sorting them by folder, date, name, size, format, and more.

PaintShop Pro History

There's an old saying that if you want to know where you're going, you have to look at where you've been. So before we trudge forward into all the wonderful features of PaintShop Pro, let's take a look at where the product has been.

PaintShop Pro, through Jasc Software, made its debut way back in 1991. Although it was a good product in its time, its main function was helping Windows users view and convert various formats of image files. PaintShop Pro also included basic color adjustments, image filters, and manipulations, as well as basic screen capture capability.

The folks at Jasc developed PaintShop Pro over time by listening to their users and adding new functionality with each new release of the software. The company released PaintShop Pro version 2 in 1993 and, over the next 11 years, upgraded the product a number of times with powerful new features in each subsequent version.

At the end of 2004, Corel Corporation acquired Jasc Software. The acquisition brought new and additional resources to the PaintShop Pro team, and the product evolved to a focus on photo editing. To better reflect the photo-editing focus, in 2006, PaintShop Pro was renamed Corel PaintShop Pro Photo. Now, in 2011, another version has arrived with even more focus on photo editing and again sporting a minor name change. The newest product is called PaintShop Pro X4.

Starting PaintShop Pro

Before you can begin using PaintShop Pro, you must, of course, start the program. Like many software programs, you can use three methods. All three methods provide the same access; you simply find the method you like best.

> ▶ When you installed PaintShop Pro, an icon was probably placed on the desktop. If so, simply double-click the Corel PaintShop Pro X4 icon to launch the program on the screen.

> ▶ If you have a Quick Launch toolbar displayed in the Taskbar at the bottom of the screen, as seen in Figure 1-1, you may see an icon for PaintShop Pro there as well. Launching PaintShop Pro from the Quick Launch toolbar involves just a single click.

> ▶ If you don't have an icon on your desktop or on the Quick Launch toolbar, you can launch the program through the Windows Start button. Choose Start ❯ All Programs ❯ Corel PaintShop Pro X4 ❯ Corel PaintShop Pro X4.

Sometimes programs don't open in a window that takes up the full screen. If they don't, you can maximize the window manually by clicking the Maximize button.

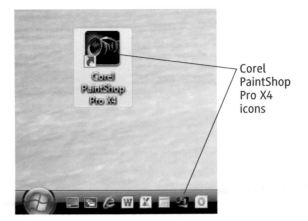

Corel PaintShop Pro X4 icons

Figure 1-1
Starting PaintShop Pro X4.

When you first open the program, you see the File Format Associations dialog box. This controls whether PaintShop Pro should open when you double-click an image on your computer. Click None if you want to decide which program opens an image, or click All if you want images to always open in PaintShop Pro. If you don't want to see this dialog box every time you open PaintShop Pro, click the Don't Show This Again check box. Click OK to close the dialog box.

Maximize the Window

You can tell PaintShop Pro to always open in a maximized window. Right-click the icon you use to start the program and choose Properties. On the Shortcut tab, change the option in the Run line to show Maximized. Click OK. This option is available for any program or document shortcut.

Next, you see the Getting Started window. This window also appears every time you launch PaintShop Pro, but again, if you don't want it to automatically appear, click the Don't Show This Again check box in the lower-left corner.

For now, click the Close button on the lower right. We'll discuss the Getting Started window later in this chapter.

Understanding Digital Workflow

BECAUSE DIGITAL PHOTOGRAPHY gives you the freedom to shoot many photos, you'll quickly develop a large number of digital files. You can then identify the photos that you want to keep and go on from there. Let's begin by looking at the creative journey you take with photographs. Called the digital workflow, these steps are not written in stone, but rather a series of typical steps.

The first step is, of course, taking the picture with your camera. Many digital photographers prefer to shoot their images in RAW mode, which gives them the equivalent of a digital negative. Chapter 6, "Manually Editing Images," has a section about RAW images and how PaintShop Pro processes them. However, whether you use RAW mode or just a point-and-shoot camera with standard JPG images, you still have to take the picture.

The next step is to bring the image into PaintShop Pro. You can transfer photos from your digital camera, memory card, or other storage device to your computer. You can also access scanned images.

After that, you'll probably make an adjustment or two to the image, perhaps to brightness, saturation, or color. Maybe you want to crop or straighten the image to better bring the subject into focus, or you want to remove something distracting from the image. You discover these types of enhancements in Chapter 5, "Making Quick Fixes," and Chapter 6.

When the picture is exactly the way you want it, you might want to share the image, either by printing it, uploading it to a website, or emailing it to someone. See Chapter 14, "Printing and Distributing Images."

PaintShop Pro manages all these steps for you—except for taking the photograph, of course! You accomplish the transfer process, the editing processes, and the sharing process through one of the three PaintShop Pro workspaces. Let's take a look.

Viewing the Screen

A *WORKSPACE* IS AN ENVIRONMENT that facilitates complete photo project management. Each of the three PaintShop Pro workspaces—the Manage workspace, the Adjust workspace, and the Edit workspace—contains many tools to assist you. Each of the three workspaces appears as a tab along the top title bar.

Using the Manage Tab

The opening workspace that appears when you start PaintShop Pro is called the Manage workspace. From the Manage tab, you can locate, sort, tag, and do other tasks related to organizing your images. And since most of us have thousands of digital images stored here, there, and everywhere, organization becomes such an important feature.

In fact, it's so important that all of Chapter 3, "Becoming More Organized," is dedicated to the Manage workspace. But let's take a brief look at it now.

Manage In Figure 1-2, you see the Manage workspace, which has four main window panels, three of which Corel calls *palettes*. Palettes display information and help you select tools, modify options, manage layers, select colors, and perform other editing tasks. The palette on the left is the Navigation palette. The first time you launch PaintShop Pro, the Navigation palette displays folders on your computer and by default looks in your Pictures and other folders and displays thumbnails of all images in those folders and their subfolders.

Navigation palette

Preview panel

Getting Started Close button

Info palette

Organizer palette

Figure 1-2
The opening screen.

The pane on the bottom is the Organizer palette. Here you can see thumbnails of the images in the selected folder—in this example, the Pictures folder.

The palette on the right is the Info palette. It's where you can enter and view information about your currently selected image. It also includes camera settings used when the image was taken.

Finally, the middle pane, called the Preview panel, is where you can see a selected image in a larger view than the thumbnail view. You can get an image into the Preview panel by clicking it once from the Thumbnails palette.

See Figure 1-3, where I clicked an image, causing it to appear in the Preview panel. You also see, in the General palette, information about the image. From here you can open and edit the image in either the Adjust or Edit workspace.

Figure 1-3
An image in the Organizer palette.

Accessing the Adjust Workspace

The Adjust workspace is the workspace you use for quick editing. It's where you can fix and enhance your photos using common tools for editing, viewing, and managing them. You can fix red-eye, exposure, color, sharpness, and noise problems as well as make speedy touch-ups to the people and objects in your photos.

Adjust From the Manage tab, select the image you want to edit and then click the Adjust tab. The image appears in the Adjust workspace, which you see in Figure 1-4.

Like the Manage workspace, the Edit workspace has several main components:

▶ The Preview panel displays the currently selected photo.

▶ The Adjust palette contains tools you use to make image adjustments. See Chapter 5 for information on making adjustments.

▶ The Organizer palette is the same one you see in the Manage workspace. Here you can see thumbnails of the images in the selected folder—in this example, the Pictures folder.

Adjust palette   Preview panel   Organizer palette

Figure 1-4
An image in the Adjust workspace.

Examining the Edit Workspace

The third workspace, and the one I use most often, is the Edit workspace. The Edit workspace is composed of different objects, each with a specific purpose for assisting in creating and editing images. You'll learn more about each of these objects as you read this book.

The Edit workspace groups many objects into two categories: toolbars and palettes. Toolbars display buttons for the most common tasks, and palettes, which I mentioned earlier in this chapter,

display information and help you select tools, modify options, manage layers, select colors, and perform other editing tasks.

Edit From either of the other workspaces, you open the Edit workspace by clicking the Edit tab. If you have an image selected in either of the other workspaces, the image opens in the Edit workspace.

Figure 1-5 illustrates the default PaintShop Pro Edit workspace.

Tools toolbar   Standard toolbar   Tool Options palette   Learning Center palette

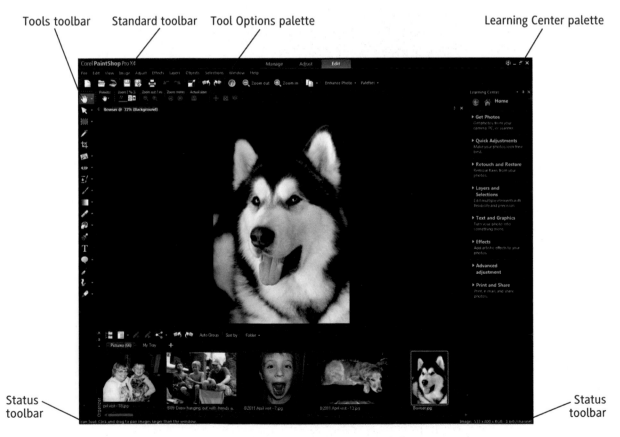

Status toolbar   Status toolbar

Figure 1-5
PaintShop Pro screen objects.

Let's look at each object.

► **Standard toolbar**: Displays tools to manage files and commonly used menu functions.

Tool Descriptions

Pause your mouse pointer over any toolbar button to see a description of the tool.

► **Tools toolbar**: Displays image-editing tools.

► **Tool Options palette**: Displays options for the currently selected tool.

► **Learning Center palette**: Contains a series of helpful guides using PaintShop Pro.

► **Status toolbar**: Displays image details such as a description of a tool or cursor coordinates.

► **Organizer palette:** This Organizer palette is the same palette seen in the Adjust and Manage workspaces.

Note

PaintShop Pro includes additional toolbars and palettes that are not displayed by default. Throughout this book, we will use these other toolbars and palettes.

Create Empty Canvas

To easily work with the remainder of this chapter, you should have an image or a blank canvas on your screen. If you want a blank canvas, choose File ❯ New, and then click OK. You'll learn more about the options in the New Image dialog box in Chapter 2, "Working with PaintShop Pro Files."

Manage

Adjust

From the Edit workspace, click the Manage tab to easily return to the Manage workspace, or click the Adjust tab to display the Adjust workspace.

Exploring the Learning Center Palette

On the right side of your screen, as shown in Figure 1-6, you see the PaintShop Pro Learning Center palette. The Learning Center contains a series of guides you can use to get started with various project types. Available only in the Edit workspace, the Learning Center includes both simple topics, such as retrieving photos from your computer or camera, and more advanced topics, such as creating photo collages or applying filters.

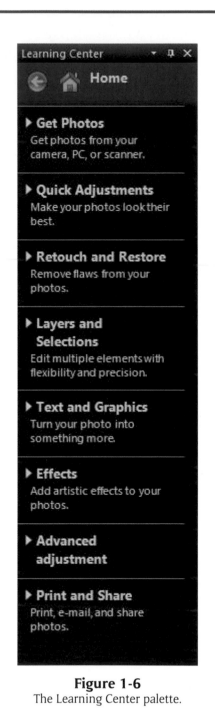

Figure 1-6
The Learning Center palette.

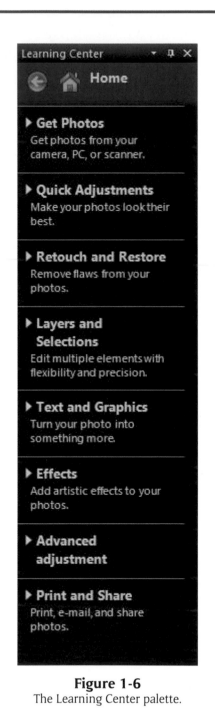 You'll work with the Learning Center in Chapter 5. For now, to maximize our screen working space, I would like you to close the Learning Center. Click the Close button, press F10, or choose View > Palettes > Learning Center.

Modifying the Screen Appearance

NOW THAT YOU'VE LEARNED what automatically appears on the PaintShop Pro screen, you can modify it to better suit your needs. Those needs may change, depending on your current project. That's okay, because you can easily change the screen options as your work demands it.

Hiding and Displaying Toolbars and Palettes

As you work with your projects, the toolbar or palette you need might not be visible, or you might want to free up screen space by hiding objects you don't want. You can easily hide or display toolbars and palettes. In fact, PaintShop Pro provides several methods for doing so. In Figure 1-7, you see a list of available toolbars on the left and a list of available palettes on the right. Any option with a check mark next to it indicates that the feature is already displayed. Clicking the checked option turns off the check mark and hides the feature. Conversely, clicking an item with no check mark turns on that feature. Palettes work the same way. A check mark means the option is already displayed; no check mark means it's hidden.

Choose the toolbar or palette you want by going to View ❯ Toolbars or View ❯ Palettes. As you choose to display several toolbars and palettes, they appear in the middle of your screen, often in an inconvenient place. Fortunately, you can easily move them wherever you want them. Simply drag the title bar across the top of the object until it's where you want it. Then release the mouse button.

Also, if you drag and drop a toolbar to the edge of the workspace window, it falls into the workspace frame. You can place palettes in the Palette Bin on the right side of the screen. Take a look at Figure 1-8. You see the Photo toolbar lying directly on the image, and on the right, you see the Materials and Layers palettes.

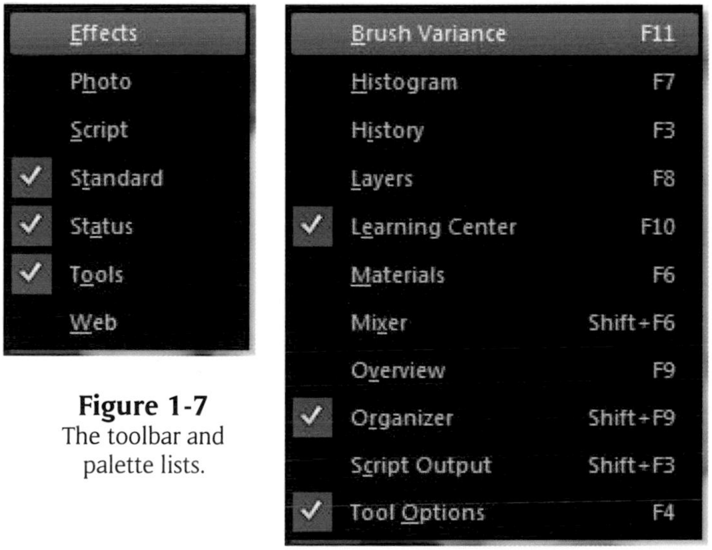

Effects
Photo
Script
✓ Standard
✓ Status
✓ Tools
Web

Figure 1-7
The toolbar and palette lists.

Brush Variance	F11
Histogram	F7
History	F3
Layers	F8
✓ Learning Center	F10
Materials	F6
Mixer	Shift+F6
Overview	F9
✓ Organizer	Shift+F9
Script Output	Shift+F3
✓ Tool Options	F4

Photo toolbar   Materials palette   Layers palette

Figure 1-8
Position toolbars where they are most convenient for you.

Viewing the Rulers, Grid, and Guides

PaintShop Pro includes several tools to help you align elements as you work on them. A horizontal and a vertical ruler help you align image elements to the physical page, and a nonprinting grid made of equally spaced vertical and horizontal lines on the screen can assist in aligning objects to each other as well as to a specific page location.

You can turn the ruler display on or off as needed by choosing View ❯ Rulers or pressing Ctrl+Alt+R. Both rulers appear or hide as needed. By default, the ruler shows measurements in *pixels*, which stands for picture elements, but you will see in the next section how you can change that to other units of measure, such as inches or centimeters. To hide or display the grid, choose View ❯ Grid or press Ctrl+Alt+G. Figure 1-9 illustrates an image with both the rulers and the grid display activated. The grid, by default, is 10 pixels, but PaintShop Pro allows you to easily customize these settings.

Rulers   Grid

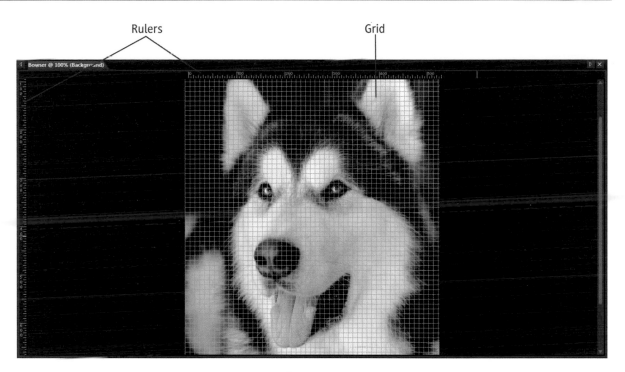

Figure 1-9
Viewing the rulers and grid.

Another element provided to aid you in precisely positioning objects are guides. *Guides* are nonprinting vertical or horizontal lines you can place at specific positions on your image. You'll find guides useful for precise work, such as straightening, cropping, and moving objects.

You must have the rulers (View ➤ Rulers) displayed to use a guide and have the Guide option activated (View ➤ Guides), which it is by default. To lay down a vertical guide, drag to the right the line located at the top of the 0-inch mark on the left side ruler. The mouse pointer turns into a double-headed arrow. As you drag the mouse cursor right, a vertical line appears. To set a horizontal guide, drag the line down, at the 0-inch mark of the top ruler. See Figure 1-10.

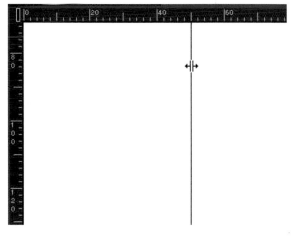

Figure 1-10
Setting a guide.

Figure 1-11 illustrates a blank canvas with both horizontal and vertical guides. If you need to reposition a guide, click and drag the guide handle until the guide is where you want it.

Guide handles

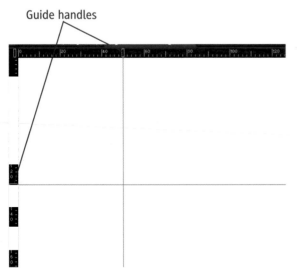

Figure 1-11
Added guides.

Create Multiple Guides

You can display multiple vertical or multiple horizontal guides.

To remove or adjust a vertical guide, drag the line from the horizontal ruler to the left side of the screen. To remove a horizontal guide, drag the line from the vertical ruler to the top of the screen.

Snapping to the Guides

Another feature related to the guides is the *snapping* function. By leaving the snapping option active (View ➤ Snap to Guides), items you draw, paint, or move automatically jump to the nearest guide. If you want to position an object at a location other than a guide, you need to turn off the snapping feature.

You control grids, guides, and snapping options through the Grid, Guide & Snap Properties dialog box. Choose View ➤ Change Grid, Guide & Snap Properties. The Grid, Guide & Snap Properties dialog box appears in Figure 1-12. From this dialog box, you can change the grid size, unit of measure, and grid line color. You can also change how close an object must be before it snaps to a grid, or from the Guides tab, how close it must be before it snaps to a guide. The Guides tab also allows you to set a color choice for your guides.

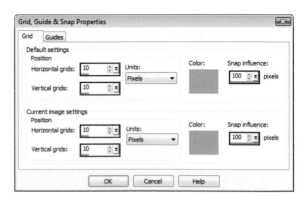

Figure 1-12
Setting grid and guide options.

Setting PaintShop Pro Preferences

PAINTSHOP PRO INCLUDES a number of dialog boxes where you instruct PaintShop Pro how to handle various aspects of your image-editing needs. You can specify how PaintShop Pro should handle the Undo command, units of measure, warning messages, and a plethora of different preference options.

Choose File > Preferences > General Program Preferences. The Preferences dialog box shown in Figure 1-13 appears.

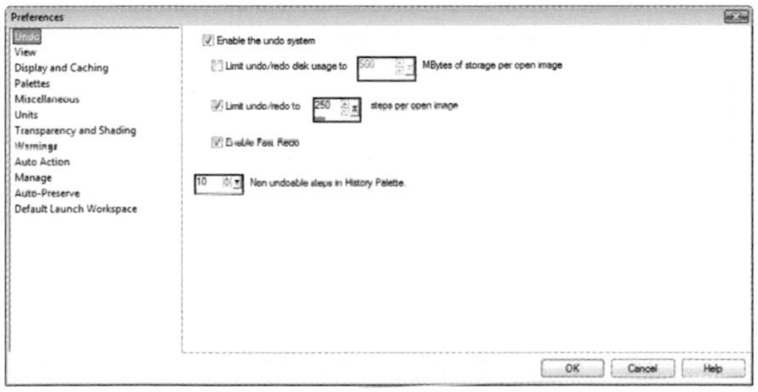

Figure 1-13
Setting program preferences.

On the left side of the dialog box are 12 categories, each providing settings for different PaintShop Pro settings. You can click each to see its applicable options:

▶ **Undo**: As you work with your images, you will want to occasionally reverse your steps. These preferences control how the Undo function works.

▶ **View**: These options control how PaintShop Pro reacts when you zoom into an image. Chapter 10, "Discovering Drawing Tools," discusses zooming in and out of your images.

▶ **Display and Caching**: These options control the appearance of tool cursors, reset the scaling quality of the zoom, and set thumbnail sizes for the Effect Browser. See Chapter 9, "Adding Effects, Filters, and Deformations," for more information on the Effect Browser.

▶ **Palettes**: Earlier in this chapter, you reviewed the PaintShop Pro palettes. These options control how those palettes behave on your screen.

▶ **Miscellaneous**: Use these options to determine how many recently used files you want listed, what PaintShop Pro should do with information you copied when you exit, as well as whether to show the PaintShop Pro opening screen.

▶ **Units**: These settings allow you to set the units of measure and other options for your rulers.

▶ **Transparency and Shading**: Use these options to control the screen display when cropping images and when using grids.

▶ **Warnings**: These options let you control whether you want PaintShop Pro to warn you if you take an action that may result in lost information or one that you can't perform in the current situation.

► **Auto Action**: Similar to warning messages, the Auto Action preferences control how PaintShop Pro behaves when certain steps are required to proceed. You can have it *never* take the steps automatically, *always* take the steps automatically, or prompt you before taking the steps.

► **Manage**: In Chapter 3, you learn about the PaintShop Pro Manage workspace, which helps you track and categorize the images stored on your computer. These options control the Manage workspace behavior.

► **Auto-Preserve**: Use this option to tell PaintShop Pro whether to save a copy of the original unedited image when you edit an image and attempt to save your changes. See Chapter 2 for more information.

► **Default Launch Workspace**: From here, you can select which workspace you want to view when you open PaintShop Pro.

Using the Help System

ALTHOUGH I HOPE YOU'LL get most of the answers to your questions from this book, I just couldn't cover everything. Therefore, this section shows you how to use the Corel Help system. It's far reaching and covers every PaintShop Pro topic.

The PaintShop Pro Help is web-based, so you must have an Internet connection to use it. You launch the Corel Help screen by clicking the Help menu. Then choose an option from the list seen in Figure 1-14.

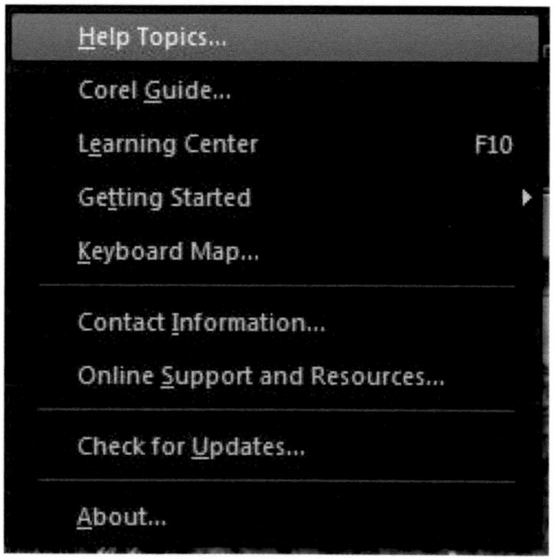

Figure 1-14
The Help menu.

Choosing Help ❯ Help Topics takes you to the Internet-based Corel Help window. On the left side of the window are two tabs: Contents and Search. From the Contents tab, scroll through the choices until you find the topic with which you need assistance. Click the topic to reveal the subtopics underneath. If you click a subtopic, the reading pane on the right side of the window displays the topic Help, like that shown in Figure 1-15.

Across the top of the Help reading pane are icons to assist you. You can browse through previous and next topics or print the current topic.

If you click the Search tab, a search text box appears that lets you search the full text of Help for a particular word or phrase. Enter a word describing the topic you want and click the Go button. A list of topics appears, as shown in Figure 1-16. Click a topic, and the reading pane on the right displays the Help information.

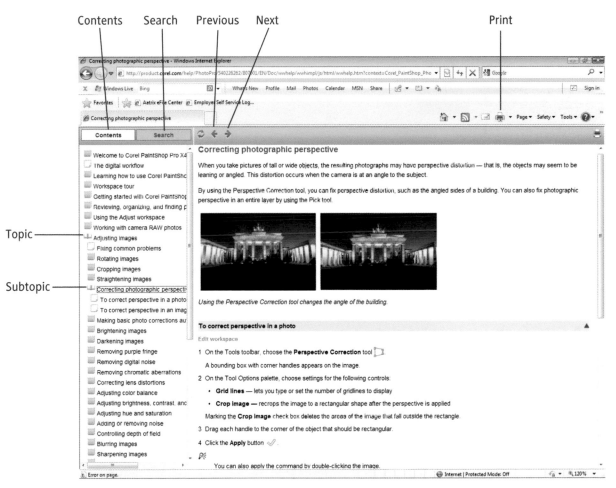

Figure 1-15
The Help Topics window.

Search by Phrase

To search for an exact phrase, type the phrase and enclose it in quotation marks.

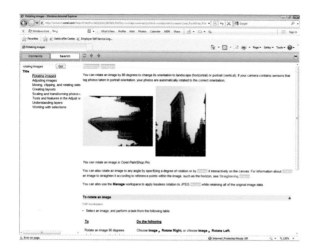

Figure 1-16
Searching for a Help topic.

Other topics under the Help menu include these:

▶ **Corel Guide**: Similar to the Learning Center option, this displays Corel Guide, where you can discover more about topics such as digital workflow, organization, and capturing and applying editing.

▶ **Learning Center**: Displays a series of helpful guides using PaintShop Pro.

▶ **Getting Started**: This displays a menu with choices that result in the same Getting Started window that appeared when you opened PaintShop Pro. From here, you can choose options to view the newest PaintShop Pro features and get general information about each of the workspaces.

▶ **Keyboard Map**: This option displays a list box (seen in Figure 1-17) that shows menu choices and shortcut keys. Click the Category drop-down list to see a different menu option. You can also refer to Appendix A, "Keyboard Shortcuts."

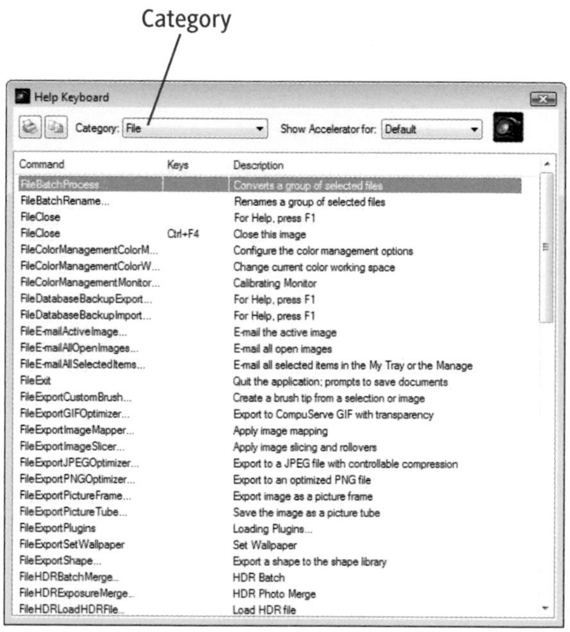

Figure 1-17
See keyboard shortcuts.

▶ **Contact Information**: This option provides you with a webpage containing a link to Corel.com, where you can access information on support services available for PaintShop Pro.

▶ **Online Support and Resources**: Choosing this option displays the Corel.com support page. From here you can obtain assistance from Corel pertaining to orders or support.

▶ **Check for Updates**: Select this to have PaintShop Pro automatically link to the Corel.com website and check for any program patches and fixes.

▶ **About**: This option provides information as to which version of PaintShop Pro you are currently using as well as other general information such as licensing information. If you call Corel about needing tech support for PaintShop Pro, you may be asked to view this window.

Working with

PaintShop Pro Files

PICTURE YOURSELF WANTING TO RECORD your family information, which might include photographs or other documents. Obviously, you have at least one paper with information on it or you wouldn't have any information to record. If you don't have a blank piece of paper, you must get one to begin with the first element you want to record. You'll need a place—probably a folder—in which to save all the papers you accumulate over the process. When you're tired of working on them, you'll want to put the papers away and get them out another day. It works the same way with computer images.

Very shortly, you'll be creating a new image file or working on one that was previously created. As you arduously work with your image and make changes to it, you will need to stop periodically and do something else— take a break, call clients, eat lunch, pay bills, walk the dog, and so forth. You need to save your file so that you can return to it whenever you're ready. Saving your file stores it on your computer storage drive, not just in the computer's temporary memory, and files it away for the future. This chapter is about working with those files.

Working with Files

IF YOU'VE USED OTHER software programs, you'll find much of this chapter a review for you since PaintShop Pro manages files similarly to other software packages. However, since PaintShop Pro works with images instead of documents, you may notice some slight differences. Let's take a look at creating a new file, saving, opening, and closing a file.

Creating a New File

Unlike some programs you use, PaintShop Pro doesn't automatically begin with a blank canvas ready for you to use. You might want to begin with an existing photograph or image, or you might want to create a drawing from scratch. If you want to create a new image, PaintShop Pro first requires several pieces of information.

Choose File ❯ New, press Ctrl+N, or click the New button on the Standard toolbar. Any of those methods brings up the New Image dialog box you see in Figure 2-1.

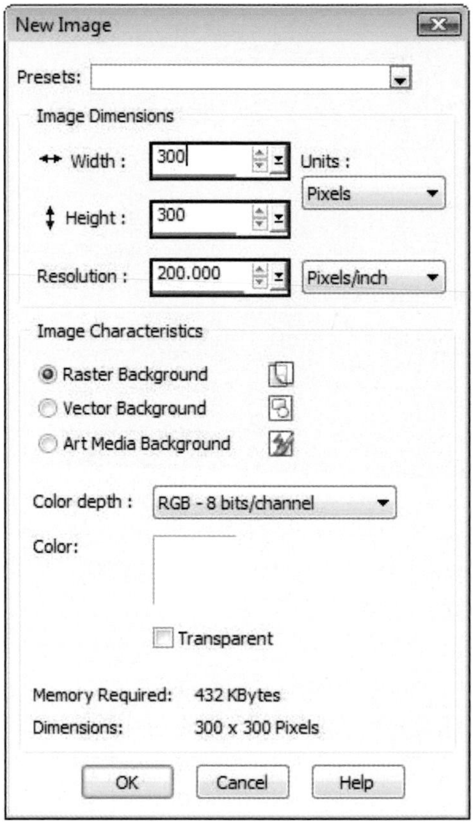

DETERMINING IMAGE SIZE

PaintShop Pro requires you to predetermine the size of the new image. You can determine the size in inches, centimeters, or the default: pixels. *Pixels*, which stands for picture elements, are the individual squares (or dots of light) that make up an image—in particular, a raster image.

Figure 2-1
Enter information about the new image.

You'll learn about raster images in later chapters. In terms of measurement, a pixel is the smallest element that can be assigned a color. Most graphics artists prefer to work in pixels.

Web Image Size

If you're going to use your image for the web, you shouldn't create it larger than 600 pixels wide or 440 pixels tall. This ensures that everyone who sees the web image can see it in its entirety. As an example, if you're designing a webpage headline, you might want to make it a maximum size of 600 pixels wide × 175 pixels tall so that it doesn't take up the entire screen height.

DETERMINING IMAGE RESOLUTION

One area in which you should familiarize yourself is resolution. Resolution measures the number of pixels in a specific unit of measurement; the higher the resolution, the more detail that's displayed. The resolution you need depends on the purpose of the image.

Here's a general rule of thumb: if you're designing a graphic for onscreen use or for posting to the web, set your resolution to somewhere between 72 and 100 pixels per inch (PPI). That's the resolution of most web browsers and email applications. If you're going to print the image, go with a higher resolution, such as 600 pixels per inch or 1200 PPI, depending on your printer.

Change the current resolution to the desired resolution. The new measurement replaces the existing one.

Note

Large image dimensions combined with high resolutions can result in large file sizes and longer loading time.

Change Unit of Measure

If you're working in units other than pixels/inch, click the Resolution down arrow and select a different unit of measurement.

DETERMINING IMAGE CHARACTERISTICS

Next, you need to decide what type of background you want for your image: raster, vector, or art media. Basically, raster graphics use pixels to store information about the image, whereas vector graphics store graphics information in a mathematical format. Art media backgrounds are somewhat similar to raster graphics. You should choose an art media background if you're planning to use the Art Media tools. See Chapter 10, "Discovering Drawing Tools."

You'll learn about working with each type of graphic as you progress through this book, beginning with raster graphics. The following steps show you how to set the image characteristics:

1. Select the background type you want. Raster is the most commonly used.

2. Click the down arrow next to Color Depth and choose a color depth option. For working with photographs, you'll probably use RGB–8 bits/channel. For more information on color depth, see Chapter 7, "Understanding Color."

3. Select a background color option. Typically, the background color, which is the color of the drawing canvas, is white. However, other selections are available:

   - If you don't want color for the background of your image, click the Transparent check box.

   - If you want a different color, texture, or pattern, click the background of the Color box. The Material Properties dialog box shown in Figure 2-2 opens. You can select your color from the predefined color box or click anywhere in the color circle to select a more precise color.

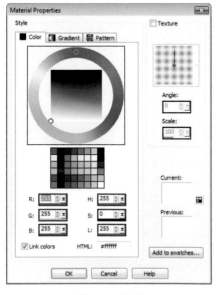

Figure 2-2
Select a color from the Materials dialog box.

More About Materials

You'll learn lots more about the Material Properties dialog box in Chapter 7.

4. Click OK. The Material Properties dialog box closes.

5. Click OK. The New Image dialog box closes, and you're ready to begin creating an image.

Saving a File

Saving a file in PaintShop Pro is identical to saving a file in most Windows applications. Don't make the mistake of waiting until you've finished working on a project to save it. Save your file early in its creation. Saving your work early and often can prevent lots of grief if your computer locks up or a power failure occurs. And, please believe me—those things *do* happen!

SAVING A FILE THE FIRST TIME

When you create a file, it has no name, so the first time you save it, PaintShop Pro prompts you for a filename and a folder in which to store the file. Once saved, the name you give the file appears in the title bar at the top of the screen.

 1. Choose File ➤ Save, press Ctrl+S, or click the Save button on the Standard toolbar. The Save As dialog box appears (see Figure 2-3).

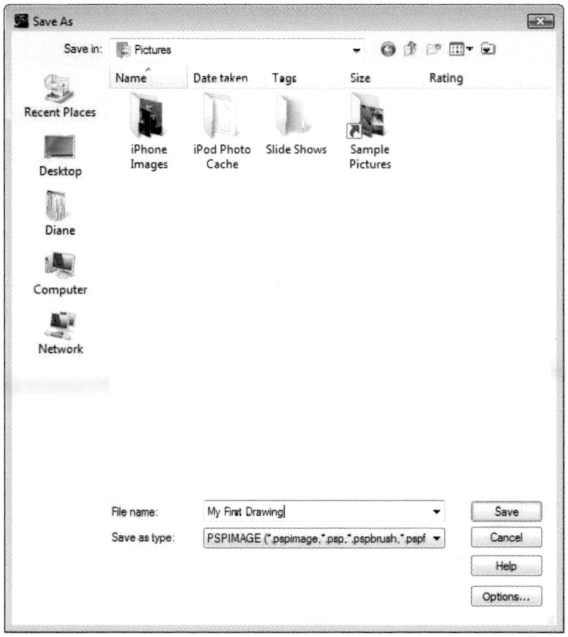

Figure 2-3
Saving a new file.

2. Enter a name for the file.

3. Choose the folder where you want to store the file. The default location is the Pictures folder located in your User Profile folder.

Note

The Save In drop-down list box displays folder options where you can save the file. Click the down arrow to browse for a different folder, or click one of the shortcut locations displayed on the left side of the dialog box.

---

4. Select a file type in which to save your image. PaintShop Pro allows you to save your image in many different file types, including web-type formats such as GIF, JPG, or PNG. However, it's usually best to save the file as the default PaintShop Pro (PSPIMAGE) format until you're finished with it. Then if you need a different file format, you can resave it with the new format. See the next sidebar titled "Comparing File Formats" to determine the best format for your image.

5. Click Save. The image filename now appears at the top of the PaintShop Pro window.

As you continue to work on your file, you should resave it every 10 minutes or so to help ensure that you don't lose your changes. If you've made changes to a file but not yet saved those changes, PaintShop Pro displays an asterisk (*) next to the filename in the title bar. You resave a file just like you did the first time. Either click the Save button, choose File ❯ Save, or press Ctrl+S. However, once a file has a name, PaintShop Pro doesn't stop and prompt you for more information. It simply saves the updated file on top of the previous file.

SAVE A FILE WITH DIFFERENT SETTINGS

If you want to save the file with a different name, in a different folder, or as a different file type, choose File ❯ Save As. The Save As dialog box prompts you for the new name, folder, or file type. If you choose to save the file with the same name, in the same folder, and as the same file type, PaintShop Pro advises you that the file already exists and asks whether you want to replace it. See Figure 2-4.

Figure 2-4
Replacing an existing file.

If you change any of the options (name, folder, or type), the original saved file remains as well as the new one and no prompt appears concerning replacing the image.

Other Save As Options

Optionally, open the Save As dialog box by pressing F12 or by clicking the Save As button on the toolbar.

Comparing File Formats

In the film world, *format* refers to the size of the film you use, such as 35mm or APS. In the digital realm, there are many file format types. A *digital format* refers to the way digital images are stored on the disk. File formats are identified by the three- or four-letter extension at the end of the identifying filename: filename.ext. Each format has its own characteristics, advantages, and disadvantages. Digital cameras offer different save file formats. Here are some of the more popular ones:

▶ **JPEG** (Joint Photographic Experts Group) is one of the most common file formats. JPEG files can be used on both Macs and PCs and are most commonly employed for images appearing on webpages or in email. JPEG operates on a lossy compression scheme, which means it throws away some of the graphics data every time you save your file using the JPEG format. There are varying levels of compression with varying loss of detail. With a higher compression, unwanted noise begins to appear on the image, giving a substantial loss of quality. The highest compression (lowest quality) can reduce files sizes to about 5% of their normal size. Merely opening a JPEG file, as on the Internet, does not result in a loss of data.

▶ **PNG** (Portable Networks Graphic) is a format similar to JPEG, but it produces higher-quality pictures and supports transparency and other features. PNG is still a relatively new format. If you're putting a PNG image on a website, the visitor must have a newer web browser. Also, PNG files are typically a little larger in size. Like JPEG, PNG formats use a lossy data compression for color images, with varying levels of compression and varying loss of detail. Generally, however, any loss is milder than using a JPEG format.

▶ **TIFF** (Tagged Image File Format) is another widely supported file format for storing images on a computer (both PCs and Macs). TIFF graphics can be any resolution, and they can be black and white, grayscale, or color. In addition, TIFF files use a nonlossy format so that no data is lost when you save and resave files in a TIFF format. Files in TIFF format end with a .tif extension. TIFF files also tend to have a large file size.

▶ **GIF** (Graphics Interchange Format) is a web standard file format that typically is small in size and therefore quick to load. GIF images also support transparency. GIF files use a lossless compression scheme and retain all the image information, but they store only 256 colors, so the prints might look rough, blotchy, jagged, or banded because they don't include enough shades of color to accurately reproduce an image. GIF is not a good choice for color photographs, but GIF files do support animation.

▶ **RAW** file format, although the largest in size, includes all information regarding a photograph, sort of a "digital negative" containing all the original information gathered by your camera with no compression or other processing. While every camera takes an image in a RAW format, you might need special software from your camera vendor to save an image in RAW format on your computer. Although RAW files are the largest, they are the most accurate representation of your image in terms of white balance, color, sharpening, and so forth.

▶ **BMP** (Bitmap) files consist of rows and columns of dots. The value of each dot (whether it's filled in or not) is stored in one or more bits of data. For simple monochrome images, one bit is sufficient to represent each dot, but for colors and shades of gray, each dot requires more than one bit of data. The more bits that represent a dot, the more colors and shades of gray that can be represented. The density of the dots, known as the resolution, determines how sharply the image is represented. This is often expressed in dots per inch (dpi) or simply by the number of rows and columns, such as 640 × 480. To display a bitmapped image on a monitor or to print it on a printer, the computer translates the bitmap into pixels (for display screens) or ink dots (for printers). Bitmapped graphics are often referred to as *raster graphics*. Bitmapped graphics become ragged when you shrink or enlarge them. They're not a good choice for photographs or web graphics.

▶ **PSPIMAGE** is a proprietary format native to PaintShop Pro. Although you can open, save, and close the PSPIMAGE file without losing special features, you can only open the file with the PaintShop Pro program. Therefore, it probably won't be the final format in which you save your file, but it's a great format to use while working on an image, especially because the image can contain layers with which you can continue to work. You'll work with layers in Chapter 8, "Developing Layers."

Opening Files

Opening an image file puts a copy of that image into the computer's memory and onto your screen so that you can work on it. If you make changes, be sure to save the file again. You can open files you've created and saved, files you've downloaded from the Internet, files you've downloaded from your digital camera, or files you've scanned from a scanner.

OPENING AN EXISTING FILE

To work on a previously created file—whether it's a file you created from scratch, a photograph, or a piece of art from another program—you can use the Open dialog box to locate your file. You can also open multiple files and easily switch between them. The following steps show you how to open an existing file:

1. Choose File ❯ Open. The Open dialog box appears (see Figure 2-5).

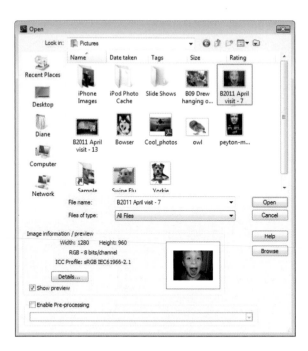

Figure 2-5
Open an existing file.

Other File Opening Methods

Other methods to display the Open dialog box include pressing Ctrl+O or clicking the Open button on the Standard toolbar.

2. Locate and click the image you want to open. The filename is highlighted. If your file is in a different folder than the one displayed in the Look In list box, click the drop-down arrow to navigate to the proper folder.

Open Multiple Files

To open multiple files at the same time, hold down the Ctrl key and click each file you want to open.

3. Click Open. The image appears on your screen, ready to edit.

OPENING A RECENTLY OPENED FILE

PaintShop Pro tracks the previous ten files you've worked with, making it easy to select one of them through the File menu. If you want to change the number of recently used files from ten to something else, you can do so in the Preferences dialog box. See Chapter 1, "Getting Acquainted," for more information on setting preferences.

As seen in Figure 2-6, choose File ❯ Recent Files to display a submenu of your recent files. Then click the filename you want to open. The image file opens on your screen, ready for you to edit.

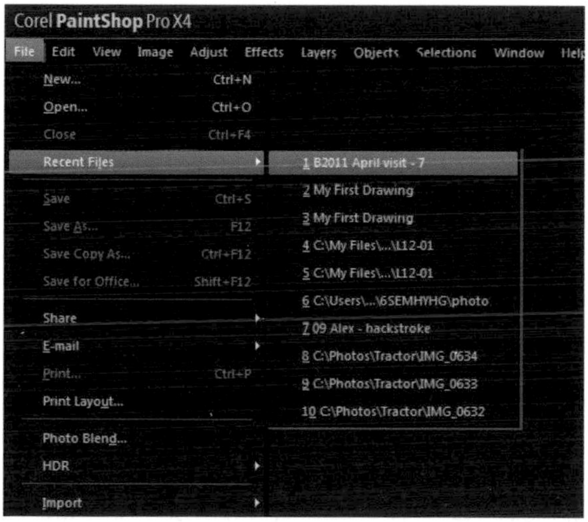

Figure 2-6
Open a recently used file.

Protecting Your Images

Your photographs are precious. You may have captured a once-in-a-lifetime moment, and you certainly don't want to mess it up and lose the image. Fortunately, PaintShop Pro includes several features you can use to protect your images from your mistakes. One is to make a backup copy of all your photographs. You'll learn about backups in Chapter 3, "Becoming More Organized." Let's take a brief look at three other PaintShop Pro methods to protect your images.

USING AUTO-PRESERVE

In most software, whenever you open an existing file, change it and resave the file, the original document is overwritten by the modified version. PaintShop Pro can do that, too; however, just in case you want both the original and the modified version, PaintShop Pro includes a feature called Auto-Preserve. As the name implies, it can automatically preserve your original image for you.

You can instruct PaintShop Pro that when you choose the Save command, PaintShop Pro should always additionally save a copy of your original unedited photograph. It stores the original in a folder named Corel Auto-Preserve, which is located in the Pictures folder. PaintShop Pro then stores the edited image in the folder you choose, which, by default, is the Pictures folder.

After choosing File ❯ Save, the Auto-Preserve Original dialog box that you see in Figure 2-7 appears. If you want PaintShop Pro to save a copy of the original as well as the edited version, make sure the Yes option is selected, and then click OK. If you don't want to save the original, click the No option and then click OK. Both files retain the same filename, but they are stored in separate folders.

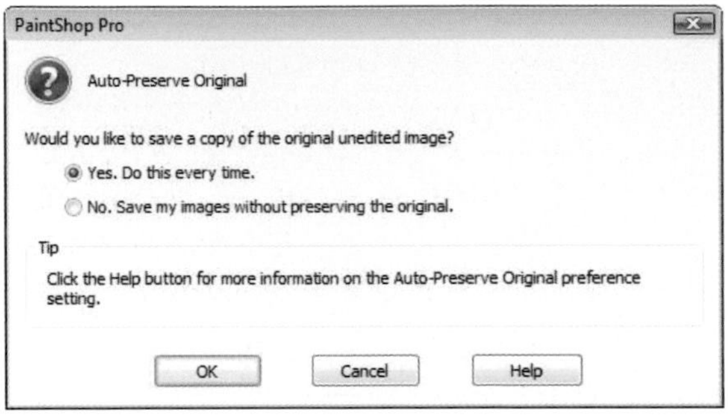

Figure 2-7
Using the Auto-Preserve function.

Auto-Preserve Behavior

To control the automatic behavior of the Auto-Preserve feature, choose File > Preferences > General Program Preferences. Click the Auto-Preserve option on the left side of the resulting dialog box.

SETTING AUTOSAVE

PaintShop Pro has a feature called Autosave that periodically saves your document for you at predefined intervals and as you move between tasks. For example, if you make some edits in the Adjust workspace and switch to another photo or workspace, PaintShop Pro automatically saves the changes. I do suggest, however, that you use caution with the Autosave feature. If you're just practicing and want to start over and you have Autosave activated, you might have changes to your image you don't want. To protect yourself, make sure you also enable Auto-Preserve if you enable Autosave.

Follow these steps:

1. Click File > Preferences > Autosave Settings. The Autosave Settings dialog box shown in Figure 2-8 opens.

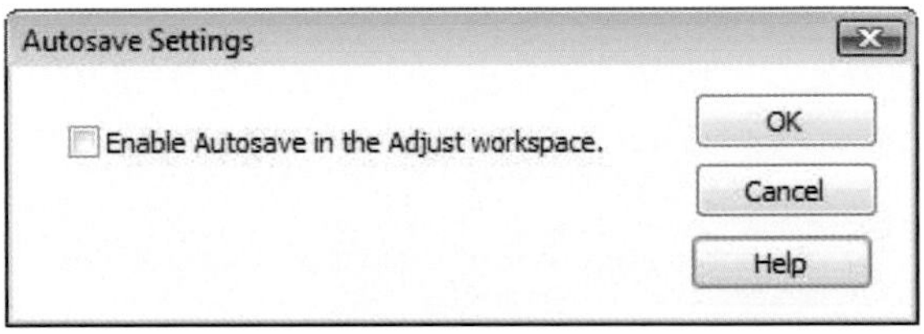

Figure 2-8
Enabling Autosave.

2. Click Enable Autosave in the Adjust workspace. The option appears with a check.

3. Click OK to close the Autosave dialog box.

DUPLICATING A FILE

Another method you can use to protect your original image is the Duplicate command. For example, if you have a file you would like to practice with, but you don't want to risk damaging the original file, use the PaintShop Pro Duplicate command, which opens another window with an exact duplicate of the currently open window. You can then close the original and practice on the duplicate.

> ### Note
>
> The duplicate file has no saved filename. If you want to keep it, you must save it.

Duplicate Recommendation

As you practice correcting your photographs, I *strongly* recommend that you duplicate the image and work on the duplicate.

With the image that you want to work on open in the PaintShop Pro window, choose Window > Duplicate. A second window, an exact copy of the first, appears. By default, PaintShop Pro displays each image in its own tabbed window. To display the images side by side as you see in Figure 2-9, choose Window > Tabbed Documents, and then choose Window > Tile Vertically. Notice the original file is still open. If you don't intend to work on it, close it.

Duplicate image   Original image

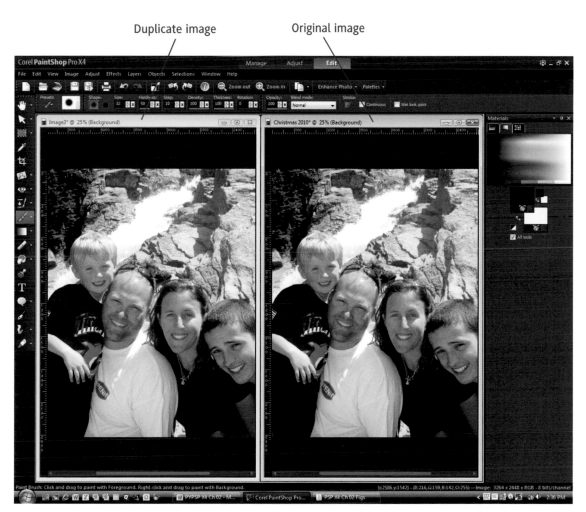

Figure 2-9
Duplicating an image.

Closing Files

When you're finished working on an image, close it. Closing is the equivalent of putting it away for later use. When you close a file, you're only putting the file away, not closing the program. PaintShop Pro is still active and ready to work for you. If you attempt to close a file with changes that haven't been saved, PaintShop Pro prompts you with a message box.

 Choose File > Close, or click the image Close button. If you haven't saved your file, choose Yes to save the changes or No to close the file without saving the changes.

Optionally, if you're working with multiple graphics image windows, you can close them all at the same time. Instead of following a prompt to save each file individually, PaintShop Pro provides a window where you can check which of the open files you want to save. Just follow these easy steps:

1. Choose Window > Close All. A Close All Files dialog box like the one you see in Figure 2-10 opens and lists any files that haven't already been saved. By default, each unsaved filename has a check indicating that you want to save the file.

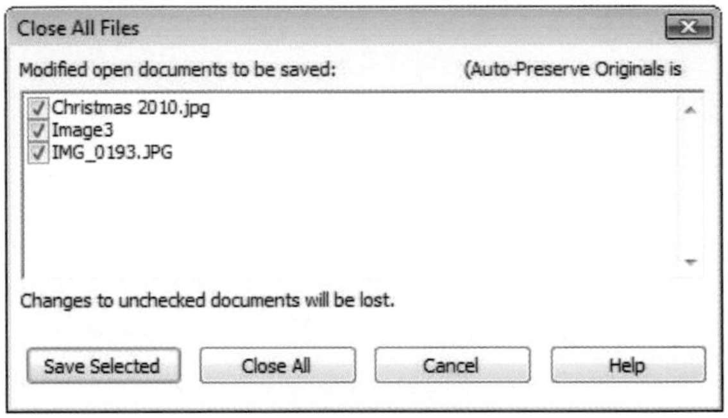

Figure 2-10
Saving modified files.

2. Remove the check from any file you don't want to save the changes for.

3. Click Save Selected. PaintShop Pro then saves the remaining checked files. Alternatively, click Close All to close all open files without saving any open ones.

The PaintShop Pro application remains open. To exit the application, choose File > Exit or click the PaintShop Pro window Close button.

Becoming

More Organized

PICTURE YOURSELF PACKING YOUR POSSESSIONS, getting ready for the moving van. You carefully wrap each of your dishes in bubble wrap and newspaper, taking extra time to protect each treasure. Next, you carefully organize and mark each box so the movers know what room it goes in. After spending so much time looking after your valuables, you would be devastated if the antique vase that Aunt Mary gave you became chipped or cracked or—even worse—lost.

Well, what about your digital photographs? If you're like most digital camera users, you have hundreds, probably thousands, of priceless memories stored on your computer. You could spend an enormous amount of time looking for that one photograph—you know, the one where your brother has the really funny grin on his face. Consider also that one bad lightning storm could crash your hard drive and permanently obliterate your entire photographical history.

So far in this book, you have discovered the basics of working with PaintShop Pro. But an equally and even sometimes more important feature in PaintShop Pro is the Manage workspace. Through the Manage workspace, you can view thumbnails of all images on your hard drive and catalog them so you can quickly search for them by folder, date, keyword, caption, or other image information. In addition, you'll find the Manage workspace a great work flow system designed to keep your projects on track. The folks at Corel call the Manage workspace a "one-stop image-management center."

This chapter is all about managing and protecting those precious image memories.

Working in the Organizer

In Chapter 1, "Getting Acquainted," you took a brief look at the Manage workspace. The Manage workspace automatically appears when you open PaintShop Pro. You'll use this workspace to import, group, and preview your images. From here, you can also rename or delete unwanted images, mark your favorites, and caption your photos and videos. It's also a launching point to edit your images, whether you want to make simple modifications through the Adjust workspace or more comprehensive edits through the Edit workspace.

Whether you're a novice or a professional, think of the Manage workspace as Image Management Central (see Figure 3-1).

Manage If you don't see the Manage workspace, from either the Adjust workspace or the Edit workspace, click the Manage button along the top of the PaintShop Pro window.

General Info panel

Navigation palette

Preview panel

Organizer palette

Figure 3-1
The Manage workspace.

Resizing Workspace Panels

The Manage workspace has four main areas: the Navigation panel, which displays the Navigation palette; the Organizer palette, which holds the thumbnail images; the Info palette, and the Preview panel. You can resize any of the areas to better meet your needs.

Position your mouse over the edge of the Preview panel left, right, or bottom side. When you get to the gray border, the mouse pointer changes from a white arrow to a double-headed black arrow with two bars inside of it. With the mouse pointer as the black arrow, drag the gray Preview panel line until the window reaches the size you want. As you can see in Figure 3-2, dragging the bottom edge of the Preview panel up decreases the size of the Preview panel but increases the size of the Organizer palette.

Border line   Mouse pointer

Figure 3-2
Resizing the panels.

Browsing Folders for Images

The first time you launch Corel PaintShop Pro, the Manage workspace automatically looks for thumbnails of all images in your Pictures folders (both private and public) and Videos folder (both private and public), including any of its subfolders. But what if you have images stored in other folders? That's not a problem, because you can easily add them to your Navigation palette. You can also exclude any specific file types or folders that you don't want included in the Navigation palette. The following steps show you how to add folders to your Organizer:

1. From the Navigation palette, click Browse More Folders. The Browse for Folder dialog box appears.

2. Locate and click the folder containing images you want to browse (see Figure 3-3).

Browse More Folders

Figure 3-3
Locating the folder with additional images for the Navigation palette.

Create New Folder

If you want to create a new folder on your computer, click the Make New Folder button.

3. Click OK. PaintShop Pro adds the selected folder to the folder list, and the images appear in the Organizer palette, as you can see in Figure 3-4. Be patient. If the folder contains a lot of images, the first time you display them may take several minutes.

Newly added folder   Additional images

Figure 3-4
The Organizer palette after adding images.

Removing Folders from the Organizer

If you have a folder in the Navigation palette that you don't want included, right-click the unwanted folder and choose Remove from List. Removing a folder from the list does not delete it from your computer; it only removes it from the File folder section.

View Organizer Thumbnails

You might be wondering, once you have your images displayed in the Organizer palette, what you can do with them. Well, you can open them for editing, view them, view information about them such as the date they were taken, sort them, tag them, group them, delete them, rotate them, email them, and quite a few other things.

Let's begin by looking at the images. From the Navigation palette, click the folder containing the images you want to view. The images in that folder appear as thumbnail representations. The Organizer palette provides several common controls that let you specify how thumbnails are displayed. In Figure 3-5, you see the Organizer palette toolbar.

Figure 3-5
The Organizer palette toolbar.

Specifying Manage Workspace Preferences

You can control the Manage workspace behavior by choosing File > Preferences > General Program Preferences and clicking on the Manage option. From the Preferences dialog box seen in Figure 3-6, change any desired settings:

> ▶ **Show Ratings with Thumbnail Images**: With this option checked, the Organizer palette can show the photo ratings next to the filename under the thumbnail image.

> ▶ **Show File Name with Thumbnail Images**: Checked by default, this option displays the filename under the thumbnail image.

> ▶ **Allow Cataloging to Complete After Exiting the Application**: By checking this box, when you exit PaintShop Pro, it reviews the folders for any image updating. Doing so speeds up the display of thumbnails the next time you start PaintShop Pro. This option is checked by default.

> ▶ **File Format Exclusions**: Click this button to display and choose any file format you do not want included in the Manage workspace. For example, if you don't want to see PNG or JPG format images, check those options.

> ▶ **Uncataloged Folders**: Click this button to specify folders you want to exclude from cataloging into the Manage workspace. By default, PaintShop Pro lists a variety of folders, such as the Recycle Bin folder and the Program Files folder. If you want to add a folder to the list, click the Add button and then use the Browse for Folder dialog box to select the folder.

If you want to remove a folder from the Uncataloged Folders list, select the folder from the list and click Delete. To reset the list of ignored folders to the PaintShop Pro default list, click the Reset to Default button.

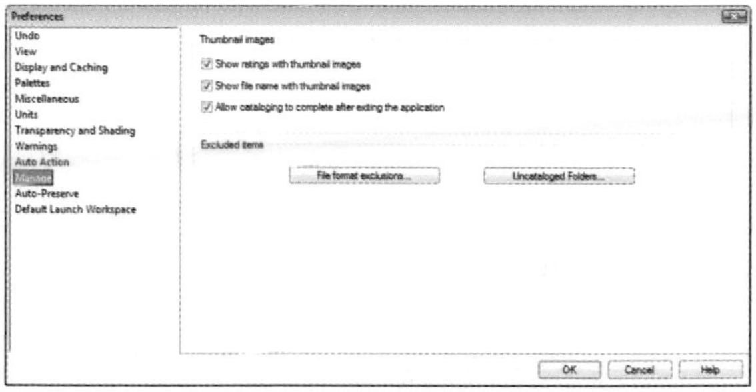

Figure 3-6
Setting the Manage workspace preferences.

Click the OK button when you are finished setting the Manage workspace preferences.

Changing Views

The Manage workspace has two display modes: Thumbnail mode and Preview mode. By default, the Preview mode is active; it shows the larger Preview panel in the middle of the screen. The other mode, Thumbnail mode, closes the Preview panel and displays multiple thumbnail-size images in the middle of the screen.

There is no menu command for changing the display mode. Instead you use the two small buttons at the top right of the screen, right under the Minimize, Restore and Close buttons. The button on the left displays Preview mode, and the button on the right displays Thumbnail mode. The button of the currently active mode is grayed out. In Figure 3-7, you see the Manage workspace in Thumbnail mode.

Figure 3-7
Organizer Thumbnail mode.

Working with Images

Now that you have your images easily accessible in the Organizer palette, you can quickly locate the image you want and adjust, edit, delete, sort, rotate, or even rename it. Use the scrollbars at the bottom of the Organizer palette or click on any image in the Organizer palette and use the right and left arrow keys to scroll through the images.

Sometimes you want to take a good look at an image without opening it, and thumbnails don't provide a large enough view. In that situation, you can use the PaintShop Pro Quick Review. Quick Review allows you to view images in a full-screen format. The images can consist of photographs, videos, and other illustrations—all standard graphics formats.

You can view the images in a full screen by double-clicking an image in the Organizer palette. In Figure 3-8, you also see two scroll arrows on the control bar that appears along the bottom of the screen. Click the arrows to view the other images in the Organizer palette.

Figure 3-8
View images in full screen.

 The control bar across the bottom disappears after a few seconds. Place your mouse along the bottom edge of the image and the control bar reappears. From this control bar, you can delete the current image by clicking on the trash can, or you can rotate the image by clicking on either of the rotation symbols.

Click the image while in full screen to zoom in on the image. Click again to restore to a full screen size. You can also drag the Zoom slider on the control bar to increase or decrease the zoom.

Press the Esc key on the keyboard to return to the standard Manage workspace.

Rotate Organizer Images

To rotate an image from the Organizer palette, select it and, from the Organizer toolbar, click the Rotate Right button to rotate the thumbnail image 90 degrees clockwise, or click the Rotate Left button to rotate the thumbnail image 90 degrees counterclockwise.

OPENING IMAGES

Before you can work on an existing image, you need to open it into the PaintShop Pro workspace. In Chapter 2, "Working with PaintShop Pro Files," you saw how to open an image by choosing File > Open or by pressing Ctrl+O. However, if you want to open an image from the Manage workspace, PaintShop Pro provides an easy method. Simply click the image you want and click either the Adjust button, which opens the image in the Adjust workspace, or the Edit button, which opens it in the Edit workspace.

If you want to work on multiple images, you can have PaintShop Pro open them at the same time. If you want to select a contiguous range of images, click the first image you want, hold down the Shift key, and click the last image you want. Not only are the first and last images you selected included, but all images between those two. You can then click the Adjust button or the Edit button, and PaintShop Pro opens all of them ready for editing.

If you want to select a noncontiguous range of images, click the first image you want, hold down the Ctrl key, and then click on each subsequent image. Again, when you have selected all the images you want, click the desired workspace button to open them. Figure 3-9 illustrates selected multiple, noncontiguous images.

Finally, if you want to open all the images in the Organizer palette, right-click any image and choose Select All or press Ctrl+A. Then click the Edit button. Don't try to open too many images at once, or you might run out of computer memory.

Selected images

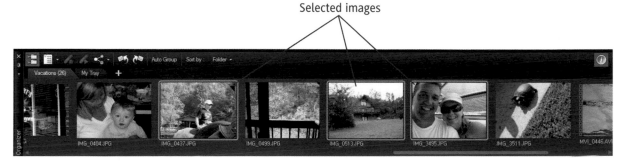

Figure 3-9
Selecting multiple images.

DELETING IMAGES

If you have an image you want to delete, you can do that through the Organizer palette. As with other Windows applications, deleting a file, in this example an image file, sends it to the Windows Recycle Bin.

To delete an image, follow these easy steps:

1. From the Organizer palette, click once on the image you want to delete. If you want to delete multiple images, you can use the Ctrl-click or Shift-click methods described in the previous section.

2. Either press the Delete key or right-click the image and choose Delete. A confirmation dialog box like the one in Figure 3-10 appears.

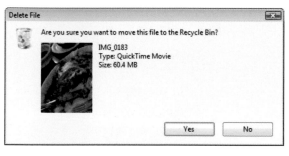

Figure 3-10
Deleting images through the Organizer palette.

3. Click the Yes button to delete the file. The file is removed from its folder and stored in the Recycle Bin.

Note

You cannot use the Undo function to restore a deleted image. You must restore it from the Recycle Bin. If you have not already emptied your Recycle Bin, you can restore the image by opening the Recycle Bin, right-clicking the image, and choosing Restore, which restores the image to its original folder.

SORTING IMAGES

If you open the folders on your hard drive, you'll probably find many, many, images stored in various folders. After you have the images included in the Organizer palette, you can sort them in a number of ways. The ability to easily sort your images makes locating the ones you need much quicker and easier. By default, the images are sorted by the folder as listed in the folder list section.

 To change the sort order, click the Sort By drop-down list button on the Organizer toolbar (the currently selected sort order appears on the face of the button) and select a sort option (see Figure 3-11). Sort options include these:

▶ **Date Created – Newest**: Choose this to sort the thumbnail images by the date on which the photo was taken, with the newest images appearing at the top. Images are grouped by dates.

▶ **Date Created – Oldest**: Choose this to sort the thumbnail images by the date on which the photo was taken, with the oldest images appearing at the top.

▶ **Date Modified**: Choose this to sort the thumbnail images by the date on which the image was last modified. If the image was never modified, the date taken is used.

▶ **Folder**: Choose this to sort the thumbnail images alphabetically by their folder name. This is the default option.

▶ **Filename**: Choose this option if you want to sort the thumbnail images by their filename.

▶ **Rating**: Choose this if you want to sort the thumbnail images by their image rating. You'll see shortly how you can rate your images from 1 to 5.

▶ **File Format**: Choose this to group the thumbnail images alphabetically by filename extension such as .pspimage, .jpg, or .tif.

▶ **File Size**: Choose this to sort the thumbnail images by their file size from smallest to largest.

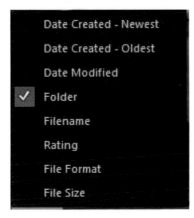

Figure 3-11
Sorting your images.

RENAMING IMAGES

As you just discovered, you can sort your images by their filename. Sometimes an image, especially one you download from your camera, has an unusual name, such as DSC01695, 100_0015, or MVC-372S. An ambiguous name can make it difficult for you to identify what the image represents. You can rename images through Windows Explorer, through the PaintShop Pro batch process (which you'll discover later in this chapter), or through the Organizer palette. The following steps show you how to rename a single image through the Organizer. Renaming a file through the Organizer palette changes the actual filename, not just the thumbnail image name.

1. Right-click the thumbnail you want to rename, and choose Rename. The Rename File dialog box shown in Figure 3-12 appears.

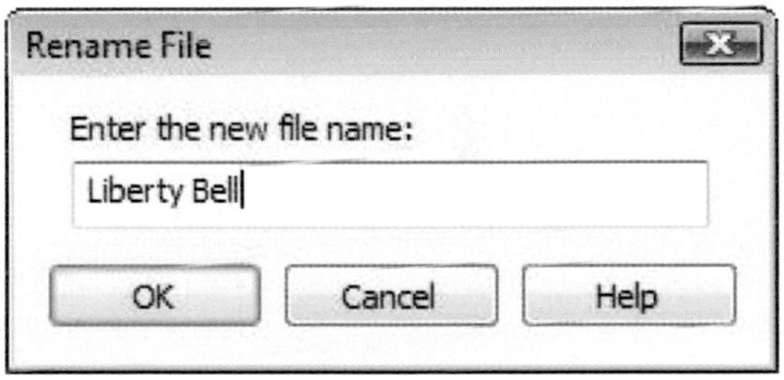

Figure 3-12
Renaming images.

2. In the Name box, type the new filename.

3. Click the OK button. The dialog box closes, and the file appears in the Organizer with the new name.

MOVING FILES

As with file renaming, you can move files by using Windows Explorer, or you can easily move your images into different folders by using the Organizer and Navigation palettes. Select the thumbnail image you want to move and drag it onto the folder where you want to store it. When you release the button, PaintShop Pro moves the image into the selected folder both in the Navigation palette and on your disk drive.

Create New Folder

To create a new folder, from the Navigation palette, right-click on an existing folder and choose Create New Folder. Type a name for the new folder, and press the Enter key.

PLAYING VIDEOS

The Manage workspace can also include video files such as AVI, WMV, or MPG. You can view the videos on the Preview screen. As you can see in Figure 3-13, video file thumbnails look a little different from image file thumbnails. The video file thumbnails have a strip running down the sides that resembles a movie film.

When you click a video in the Organizer palette, a Play button appears in the Preview panel. To play the video, click the Play button, which then turns into a Pause button.

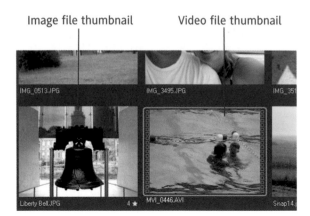

Image file thumbnail   Video file thumbnail

Figure 3-13
Video file thumbnails display differently from image file thumbnails.

After you start the video play, an additional icon appears on the preview image. It's the Capture button (see Figure 3-14).

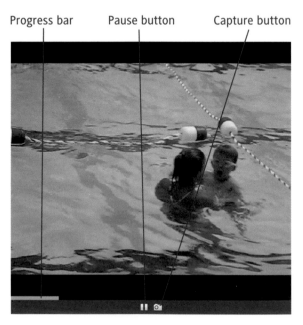

Progress bar   Pause button   Capture button

Figure 3-14
Playing video files.

By default, the video thumbnail representation displays the first frame in the video. As the video plays, a progress bar runs across the bottom of the thumbnail. You can drag the progress bar back and forth to rewind or fast-forward through the video. If you want to temporarily stop the video play, click the Pause button.

Additionally—and this is a feature I really like—you can pause the video at any frame you want and then save that particular frame as a standard image file that, of course, you can then print or manipulate in PaintShop Pro. When you reach the frame you want, click the Pause button and then click the Capture button, which displays the Save As dialog box shown in Figure 3-15. Give the image a filename and a folder location. You can also choose the file type you want. Choices include JPG, PNG, or BMP formats. Click the OK button after you've made your choices. The single image appears in the Organizer in the folder you specified.

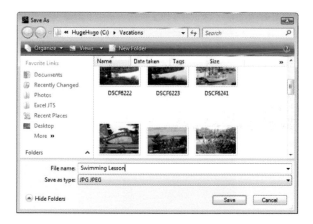

Figure 3-15
Saving a video frame.

Reviewing Image Information

Many image files contain more than just the image. They may also contain information called *metadata*, which is data about data. In the context of a camera, in which the data is the photographic image, metadata would typically include the date the photograph was taken and details of the camera settings, such as the manufacturer, model, compression, exposure time, F-stop settings, exposure, aperture, color space, and much more.

Although there are different forms for the metadata, the two most common are EXIF and IPTC. EXIF stands for Exchangeable Image File, and IPTC is an abbreviation for International Press Telecommunications Council. The data contained in these data packets depends on your individual camera and only works with still images, not video files.

In PaintShop Pro, you can view, add to, and edit some of the image metadata. You can also add captions to your images and apply ratings on a scale of 1 to 5 to your photographs. Having this information makes it easier to organize and locate your images. For example, adding a descriptive caption to an image lets you search for that image by typing text from the caption.

You view and edit the image information through the Info panel. Follow these steps:

1. From the Organizer palette, click the image about which you want to view information.

2. From the Info window, you see basic information such as the filename, date, rating, size tags, and caption (see Figure 3-16).

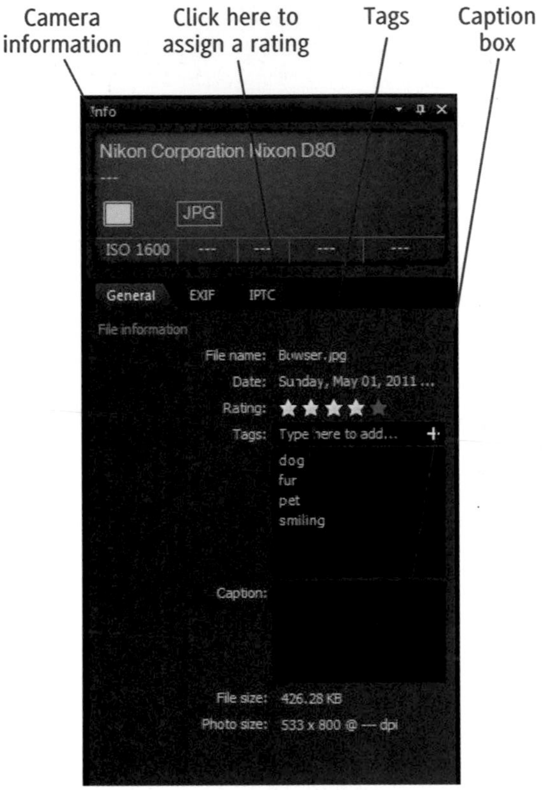

Camera
information

Click here to
assign a rating

Tags

Caption
box

Figure 3-16
Viewing basic image information.

3. As with movies, you can rate your photographs from your favorite to your least favorite, and you can perform searches based on ratings. Click the number of stars you want to assign to the image. The rating you assign is displayed in gold stars.

Assign Tags

You can assign tags to the image. See the later section titled "Using Tags" for more information.

4. Optionally, add a caption to the image. Click inside the Caption text box, and type the caption you want to apply. If you want to delete a caption, highlight the caption text and press the Delete key. Captions can appear on the images when you create slide shows.

5. Click the EXIF tab. The Info panel now displays additional information about the image, including camera model, exposure settings, aperture settings, and other EXIF and IPTC information. You need to scroll down to see additional information (see Figure 3-17). Not all information is available for all photographs, depending on the camera settings.

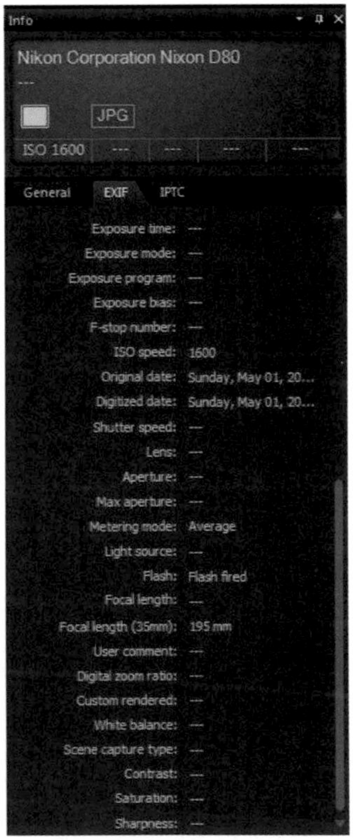

Figure 3-17
Viewing advanced image information.

Searching for Images

YOU'VE SEEN HOW EASY IT IS to view images in a specific folder by clicking the desired folder from the folder list in the Navigation palette. However, what if you have dozens or hundreds of photos in a folder? Looking through them can be time consuming. Fortunately, PaintShop Pro provides a search function to help you quickly locate just the images you want. You can search for specific images by image name, tag, or rating.

Performing a Simple Search

One simple and fast method for searching for images is using the Find text box located on the Navigation palette. This method searches for images based on all or part of the text you type.

To locate specific images, follow these easy steps:

1. Click the folder in which you want to search. If you want to look through all your images, click the Folders folder.

2. In the Find Photos text box at the top of the Navigation palette, type all or part of the data you're searching for. As you type the characters, the Navigation palette performs real-time filtering by searching through the filename, including the extension, folder, tag, caption, or metadata for the letters you type, and it displays any matching images. In Figure 3-18, I've typed the characters *Danny*, which displays only images with the word *Danny* in the name.

Find Photos text box   Find Photos button

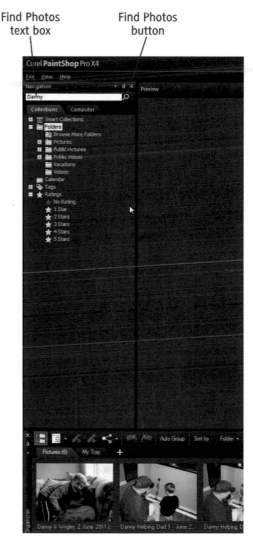

Figure 3-18
Using the Find Photos text box.

47

To redisplay all the folder images, delete any characters from the Find Photos search box.

Using Smart Collections

PaintShop Pro includes a number of predefined Smart Collections, which are simply saved search instructions. For example, locating images created in 2011 is only a mouse click away. T. You can edit and customize the Smart Collections, rename them, or even delete them.

At the top of the Navigation palette, click the plus sign next to Smart Collections to display a list of ten predefined Smart Collections. Click any collection name to quickly display images in the Organizer palette that meet the collection rules. To review or edit the rules in any collection, right-click the collection name and choose Edit. The Smart Collection dialog box appears. In Figure 3-19, you see the rules for the Smart Collection called Last 12 Months. Notice that the rule was set up to search for images with a date within the past 365 days.

Click here to expand or collapse
the Smart Collections

Figure 3-19
Reviewing predefined Smart Collections.

Finding Images Using the Calendar

One other method provided in the Organizer to help you locate images is using the Calendar. For example, you know you want images created on a specific date or range of dates. The Calendar search function makes this easy. Begin by clicking Calendar from the Navigation palette. The Calendar Search window seen in Figure 3-20 appears.

Dates shown in red indicate images created on that date. You can click any date to view images in the Organizer palette with that date. As you choose dates, the Organizer palette updates to display images created on that date or range. In addition, you can do any of the following:

▶ Click the Previous Month, Previous Year, Next Month, or Next Year button to review other months.

▶ Select a sequential date range by clicking on the first day you want and then, holding down the Shift key, clicking on the last day you want.

▶ Select a nonsequential date range by clicking on the first day you want and then, holding down the Ctrl key, clicking on each additional day you want.

Click the Close button when you are finished and want to close the Calendar window.

Previous Year   Previous Month   Next Month

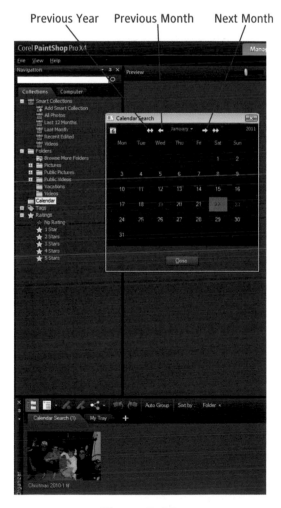

Figure 3-20
Choosing images by date.

Using Tags

ALL THROUGH THIS CHAPTER, you've seen tags mentioned. *Tags* are keywords for people, such as Tommy; events, such as Bob's Wedding; or places, such as Our Trip West. You assign one or more tags to your images so that you can easily locate and organize them. PaintShop Pro includes a huge variety of predefined tags; however, you can also create an unlimited number of new tags. After you assign a tag to an image, you can quickly find the image by clicking on the tag name in the folder list section.

Managing Tags

You create and assign tags in the Navigation palette. To view any currently listed tags, click the plus sign next to Tags in the Navigation palette section. The Tags item expands to display a list of your tags. See Figure 3-21 to view my tags.

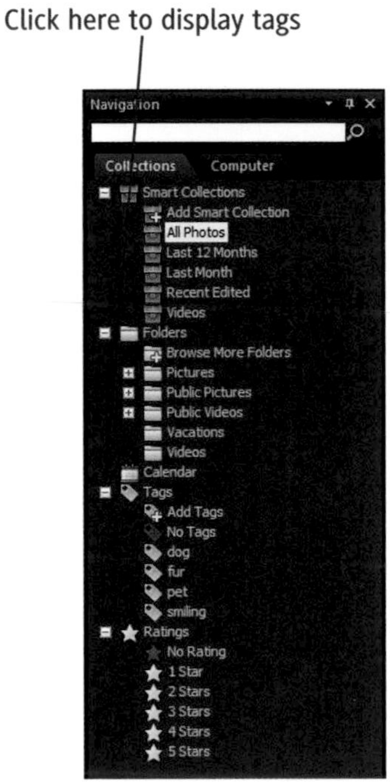

You may not see tags when you first begin using the Navigation palette, or you might see a list of tags that were attached to your images by other sources, such as Windows. You can modify the tag list so that it more appropriately matches your needs. You can add tags, rename existing tags, and delete tags:

▶ **Add**: To add a tag, click the Add Tags tag. An Add Tag dialog box appears. Enter the name of the new tag, and click the OK button. The new tag now appears in the tag list.

Click here to display tags

Figure 3-21
A sample list of tags.

▶ **Rename**: To rename a tag, right-click the tag and choose Rename. The Rename tag dialog box appears. Type the new tag name and click the OK button. The tag is renamed, and any images associated with the tag also show the new tag name.

▶ **Delete**: To delete a tag, first remove the tag from any associated images. (See the next section, "Assigning Tags.") Then right-click the unwanted tag and choose Delete. The tag is removed from the tag list.

Assigning Tags

After you create your tags, you can associate a photograph and a tag. Remember that images can have more than one tag associated with them. For example, suppose that you create and attach tags called *Niagara Falls* to the images you took from your last vacation. You might have another tag for your individual friends or family members, such as *Mom* or *Uncle Joe*. Images can have multiple tags. The picture of Mom standing close to Niagara Falls could have both the *Niagara Falls* tag and the *Mom* tag.

You can assign tags one at a time to individual photographs, or you can select a group of images (such as all the Niagara Falls trip images) and assign them all the same tag. The Manage workspace provides a couple of different methods to attach tags to photographs:

▶ Drag the tag from the tag list until it's on top of the image you want in the Organizer palette. When you release the mouse button, PaintShop Pro assigns the tag to the image. In Figure 3-22, I'm dragging the *Northeast Trip* tag onto one of the images. Using this method, I'll need to drag the tag to each image.

▶ Drag the images from the Organizer palette onto the tag on the Navigation palette. Using this method, you can select and drag multiple images to the tag (see Figure 3-23). When you release the mouse button, PaintShop Pro assigns the tag to the images.

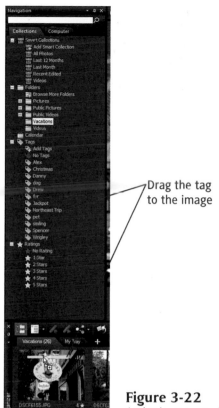

Drag the tag to the image

Figure 3-22
Assigning tags to images.

Drag the images to the tag

Figure 3-23
Assigning images to tags.

If you want to remove a tag from an image, you can also use the Info panel. Select the image, and in the list of image tags, click the tag assignment you want to delete. Then click the Delete tag button. Repeat this for each tag assignment you want to delete (see Figure 3-24).

Finding Untagged Images

To quickly display all thumbnails not yet assigned a tag, from the Navigation palette, click the tag called No Tags. Any thumbnail image without an assigned tag appears in the Organizer window.

Delete tag

Figure 3-24
Deleting an image tag.

Applying Editing to Multiple Photos

AS YOU ARE SORTING through your images, you'll probably open some for quick editing in the Adjust workspace or more advanced editing with the Edit workspace. From the Organizer palette, you can select all the changes made to an image and apply them to as many images as you want. You can capture the image edits for the current session only. PaintShop Pro automatically deletes all captured edits when you exit the program.

Follow these steps to save yourself lots of editing time:

1. Select the first image you want to edit, and make your changes either through the Adjust workspace or the Edit workspace.

2. Save the image with its modifications.

3. Display the Manage workspace and select the image thumbnail whose edits you want to capture. A pencil icon appears next to the image thumbnail, which indicates the image has edits (see Figure 3-25).

4. From the Organizer palette toolbar, click the Capture Editing button.

Edits icon

Figure 3-25
A thumbnail depicting edits.

5. Select the image thumbnails for which you want to apply the captured edits.

6. From the Organizer palette toolbar, click the Apply Editing button. A progress box appears showing the process. A batch process window appears illustrating the progress. You'll learn about batch processing later in this chapter.

7. When the process is finished, click OK.

Alternative Method

Optionally, capture the edits by right-clicking the selected thumbnail and choosing Capture Editing.

Editing RAW Files

You cannot apply captured edits of a regular file to a RAW file; conversely, you cannot apply captured edits of a RAW file to a regular file. See Chapter 6, "Manually Editing Images," for information about RAW image files.

Creating Trays

LIKE MOST OF US, YOU PROBABLY have numerous photos in the Pictures folder and various other folders. Often when working on a project, you want to work on a number of different photos, but you don't want to view all the images in the folder, just the ones you'll use in the project. Rather than manually creating another folder for the project images, you can create a tray. Think of a tray as a temporary folder. In PaintShop Pro, you can have several trays. Trays appear in all three PaintShop Pro workspaces, and you can manage the trays from any of the workspaces.

In a tray, you gather the images you need, whether from one folder or many folders, and place them in the tray. The images remain in their original folder, but you see a thumbnail of the image in the tray. The tray thumbnails are shortcuts to the real images. You open an image in the tray as you would from the standard Organizer palette.

You click it and then click either the Adjust button or the Edit button. In fact, the Organizer palette is really an automated tray! The default tray displayed in the Organizer palette is named after the currently selected folder.

PaintShop Pro automatically creates a blank custom tray called My Tray; however, you can add additional trays as well as remove and rename trays to suit your project workflow. For example, perhaps you want to create a scrapbook page (see Chapter 16, "Making Digital Scrapbooks") that consists of several images. You should create a tray for the scrapbook page. If you have a collection of images that you want to print or send to an online photo printing service, create a tray for the images you want to use. Figure 3-26 displays the My Tray.

Figure 3-26
The Tray palette.

Adding Images to a Tray

Now that you're viewing an empty tray, you'll want to put images in it for your project. All you have to do is select the images you want and drag them to the appropriate tray. Follow these steps:

1. From the Navigation palette, select the folder containing the images you want. You may want images from several folders. That's fine; just start with the first folder of your images.

2. From the Organizer palette, select the image thumbnails you want to add. You can add the images individually or select multiple images.

3. Drag the image thumbnails to the new tray (see Figure 3-27). When you release the mouse button, the images appear in the new tray. They also remain in the original tray.

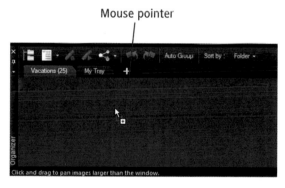

Mouse pointer

Figure 3-27
Adding images to a tray.

Figure 3-28 shows a tray with a number of images in it.

Figure 3-28
Easily add images to a tray.

If you added an image you don't want in the tray, you can easily remove it. Click the image you don't want and then press the Delete key. Removing an image from the tray does not remove the image from its folder or from your computer's hard drive.

Creating Additional Trays

 Because you're likely to have several projects going at once, you can add additional trays. All you have to do is click the Add Tray button on the Tray toolbar. The Add Tray dialog box appears. Enter a name for the new tray and click the OK button. A new empty tray appears along with the original ones and any others you created (see Figure 3-29). You can create an unlimited number of trays. Click the tray names to move between trays.

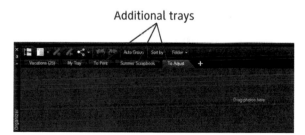

Additional trays

Figure 3-29
Create multiple trays.

Rename Tray

To rename any tray, click the tray name you want to change and then click the More Options button. From the Rename Tray dialog box, enter a new name and click OK.

Removing a Tray

If you've finished with a tray, you can easily delete it. You cannot delete the original default tray or the My Tray, but you can delete any additional trays you created. Deleting a tray deletes the tray and the image thumbnail shortcuts, but it does not delete the original images from your computer.

Just follow these easy steps to delete a tray:

1. Select the tray that you want to remove.

 2. From the Tray toolbar, click the More Options button.

3. Click Remove Tray. If the tray had no images, the tray immediately disappears. If the tray had any images, a confirmation box appears. Click Yes to remove the tray.

Working in Batches

A WONDERFUL TIME-SAVING feature included with PaintShop Pro is batch processing. Batch processing automates steps for you. There are two batch commands included with PaintShop Pro. One command works with saving images, and the other command works with renaming images.

The first command, which is actually named Batch Process, is great if you have a group of pictures you want to copy to another location or save as a different file format. The second batch process is the Batch Rename command, which assigns a different filename to a group of images. Let's look at the Batch Rename command first.

Renaming Images in Groups

Most digital cameras name their images by assigning a number to each image taken. Unfortunately, that's not very intuitive to the photographic contents. Suppose that you have a large batch of vacation photos that your camera named IMG_101, IMG_102, IMG_103, and so forth, but you'd rather they be named in a more descriptive manner, such as Arizona Trip 1, Arizona Trip 2, and Arizona Trip 3. Renaming these images one at a time can be tedious, especially if you have lots of them.

View the files in Figure 3-30. It's a list of 58 photographs taken by several family members during a recent vacation to Florida. I can use the PaintShop Pro Batch Rename command to rename them all at once so they are easier to identify. The following steps walk you through using the Batch Rename command.

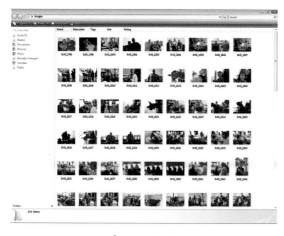

Figure 3-30
Rename any number of files at one time by
using the Batch Rename command.

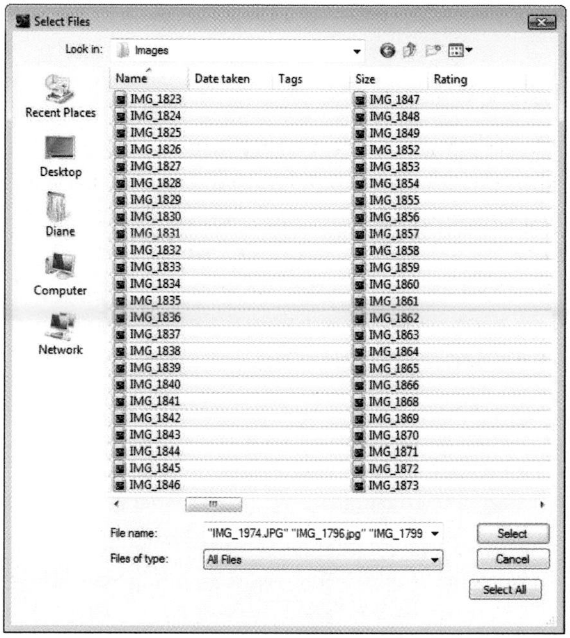

1. Click File ❯ Batch Rename. You see the Batch Rename dialog box.

2. Click the Browse button, which opens the Select Files dialog box, and navigate to the folder containing the files you want to rename.

3. Click the files you want to rename. You can use Shift-click to select a contiguous list of files or Ctrl-click to select noncontiguous files. Optionally, use the Select All button to select all images in the open folder (see Figure 3-31).

4. Click Select, and as you see in Figure 3-32, in the Files to Rename box, PaintShop Pro displays the files you selected.

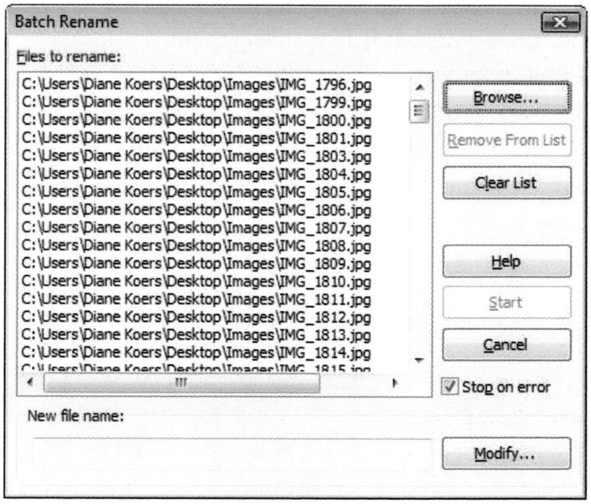

Select Additional Files

If you have files in other folders that you want to include, click the Browse button again and select those files. The newly selected files are added to the Files to Rename list.

Figure 3-31
Select the files you want to rename.

Figure 3-32
Selected images.

5. Now you need to specify the naming convention that you want PaintShop Pro to use. Click the Modify button, which opens the Modify Filename Format dialog box. You have a number of naming options available, including adding the date to the filename, retaining the original filename as well as the new filename, and adding the current time to the new filename.

6. In many cases, you'll want the Custom text and the Sequential options. In the Rename Options area, click Custom Text, and then click the Add button.

7. In the Custom Text text box, enter the name you want for the new images. For our example, I'm naming the images 2011 Florida - . In the next step, I'll have PaintShop Pro add a sequential number after the hyphen.

8. Add Sequence to the Included list, and in the resulting Starting Sequence text box, enter a number that you want the images to begin with. In my example, I'm using 01 as the beginning sequence number. Figure 3-33 shows the dialog box after making my selections.

9. Click OK, which closes the Modify Filename Format dialog box and redisplays the Batch Rename dialog box.

10. Click the Start button. PaintShop Pro executes the Batch Rename command. Figure 3-34 shows the list of files after PaintShop Pro renamed them.

Filename preview   Custom Text text box

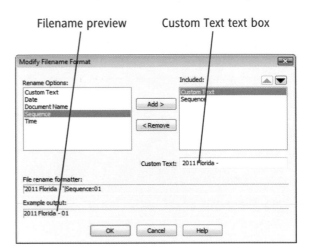

Figure 3-33
Specify a name and sequence for your images.

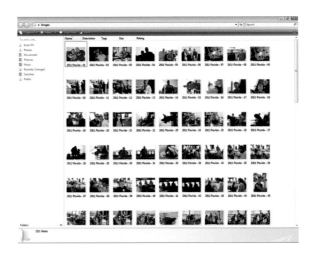

Figure 3-34
After renaming, you can more easily identify your images.

Using the Batch Process Command

The Batch Process command works similarly to the Batch Rename command in that it executes a single command to multiple images. Using the Batch Process command, you perform any of four functions. All Batch Process features are related to saving files.

Like the Batch Rename command, you access the Batch Process command through the File menu. When you select Batch Process, you see the dialog box shown in Figure 3-35.

You can convert your group of files to a new format. Because most digital cameras automatically save your image in JPEG format, which uses compression, you might want to change the photos from a JPEG format to a TIFF format or even a PSPIMAGE format to prevent accidentally resaving the images in JPEG again, which can cause quality loss. When you convert images to a new format, the Batch Process command leaves the originals alone, and it creates duplicate images with the new format.

You can copy your group of files to a new location. Suppose that you want to practice adjusting color on a group of vacation photos. By copying them to another location, you can work on the duplicates, leaving the originals intact. You could copy your images using the Windows Explorer, but using the Batch Process is easier, faster, and allows you to copy images from multiple folders in one step. Besides, this book is about PaintShop Pro, not Windows Explorer.

The next two options, Overwrite and Use Script, are related to scripts. *Scripts* are simple programs you create and save to perform automated tasks in PaintShop Pro. To use the Overwrite option, you must also specify a script in the Script text box.

When executed, the command runs the script and resaves the image in its original location, overwriting the original file. The Use Script command doesn't automatically save the image; it only runs the script. If you use the Use Script option, you should make sure the script contains a command to save the image. If the script doesn't contain a Save command, you're wasting your time running this option because PaintShop Pro runs the script on the image and then tosses away the entire process. Unfortunately, writing PaintShop Pro scripts is beyond the scope of this book.

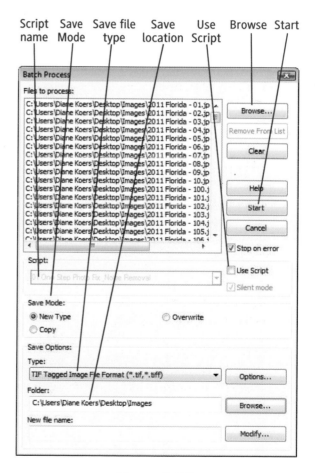

Figure 3-35
Select the images you want to modify and the options you want to use.

Depending on the options you select, some areas of the dialog box may be unavailable. Let's look at each area:

- ▶ **Files to Process**: Click the Browse button to locate and select the images you want to modify. If you add images in error, click the Clear button.

- ▶ **Stop on Error**: It's a good idea to have this box checked so that if you accidentally select a file that PaintShop Pro cannot open and process, it stops and displays an error message notifying you of the problem.

- ▶ **Save Mode**: This is where you select the function that you want Batch Process to run.

- ▶ **Script**: If you are using Overwrite mode or Use Script mode, you can select the script you want PaintShop Pro to run when processing the files. If you select Silent mode, no Script dialog box options appear, and the script runs as recorded. Scripts are not covered in this book, but you'll find an abundance of information on the web if you search for "PaintShop Pro scripts."

- ▶ **Type**: If you select the New Type mode, use the Type drop-down list to select the file type you want the images to take. If you do not select the New Type mode, this list is unavailable.

- ▶ **Folder**: Specify the folder where you want the Batch Process command to place the processed images. This option becomes available if you select New Type or Copy mode. If you don't specify a folder, PaintShop Pro places the processed images in their original folder. You should select a different folder if you select Copy mode; otherwise, the command copies the image on top of itself.

- ▶ **New File Name**: This works just like the Batch Rename command. You need to specify the naming convention you want PaintShop Pro to use for the new images by clicking the Modify button, which opens the Modify Filename Format dialog box. You saw the Modify Filename Format box earlier in Figure 3-33. If you leave the New File Name box blank, PaintShop Pro uses the original filename.

When you have selected all your options, click the Start button to begin the batch process. PaintShop Pro displays a Batch Process window similar to Figure 3-36. The Batch Process window displays each filename and its status, and the Job Progress bar indicates the conversion progress. Click the Abort button to stop the process, or click the OK button when the process is complete.

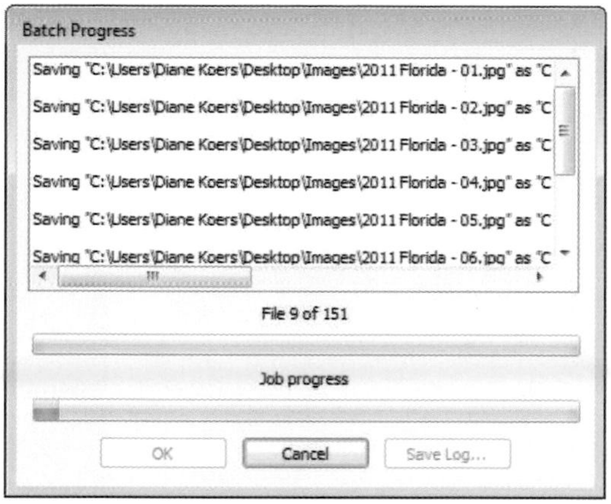

Figure 3-36
Processing images in a batch.

Other File Types

When converting files to some formats, you may see other dialog boxes providing different options.

Making Backups

PREPARE YOURSELF. I'm going to nag at you here. Okay, this section doesn't really have anything to do with PaintShop Pro. It's more of a personal plea. Back up your images. I repeat: back up your images. You know the silly (but popular) little saying, "Stuff happens." (That's not exactly how it goes, but you get the idea.) Well, it's true. Things happen. Now, I don't mean to sound pessimistic, but computers do fail, files do get deleted or corrupted, and disasters (such as fire or theft) can occur.

Well, you can always get another computer and reload your programs. But even millions of dollars can't buy back all the images you have stored on your computer. That's why backing up your images on a regular basis is important. Then, if disaster strikes, you can restore your images.

Whether you copy your images using Windows Explorer to an external drive, a CD, or a DVD, or you use a special backup program, don't procrastinate. Do it!

PaintShop Pro doesn't have a specific function for backing up your images, but you can use the Batch Process window. Before you use it, create a folder on your backup drive, CD, or DVD. Then, in the Batch Process window, choose Copy for the Save Mode. Point the folder location to the newly created folder on the flash, CD, or DVD drive.

Making Selections

PICTURE YOURSELF STANDING IN THE ICE CREAM STORE. So many different flavors are available, and your mouth waters at each one. But before you can begin to eat, you have to decide which kind you want. Perhaps you'll have a combination of several flavors.

We have to make many choices in our lives. Some choices are relatively simple ones, such as which ice cream flavor we want, which pair of shoes to buy, which bank we will use, or where we will go on vacation. Other choices are more complex, such as deciding on our profession or whether to get a family pet. But in all cases, before an action can occur, we have to select one or more of the choices.

To make changes to a portion of an image—whether the image is one you've created, a photograph, or another type of artwork—you need to tell PaintShop Pro what you want to change before you can specify how you want to change it. This is called *making a selection*. You can then make your change to the isolated selected area without affecting the rest of the image. You also need to select an area if you want to copy or cut it to the Windows Clipboard for use in other programs or images. PaintShop Pro includes a variety of different selection tools.

Working with Selection Tools

PAINTSHOP PRO INCLUDES three selection tools: the Selection tool (for shapes), the Freehand Selection tool, and the Magic Wand. These three tools have one purpose: to define the part of the image you want to work on. How they determine that area is what makes each of them unique.

If you open the image using the File ❯ Open command, the image appears in the Edit workspace. If you see the image you want in the Organizer palette, click the image and click the Edit tab. When the Edit workspace is active, the Tools toolbar seen in Figure 4-1 appears. Let's begin by taking a look at what each selection tool does differently from the other. All three selection tools occupy the space of the third icon on the Tools toolbar:

- ▶ **Selection tool**: Use this tool to define a common geometric shape.

- ▶ **Freehand Selection tool**: Use this tool to define an irregular shape selection.

- ▶ **Magic Wand**: Use this tool to define a selection based on color options.

Figure 4-1
The Tools toolbar.

Making a Shape Selection

The Selection tool is the fastest and easiest to use of the three selection tools. It selects a portion of your image in any one of 15 different shapes, including circles, rectangles, triangles, stars, and arrows.

Chapter 4

Throughout the rest of this book, we'll put selecting items into real use. For now, you can practice making selections by opening any existing image file.

 Click the Selection tool or, as a shortcut, just press the letter S. When the Selection tool is activated, the mouse pointer turns into a cross with a dotted box beside it. The Tool Options palette provides a number of different options for the Selection tool. In each of the following sections, we take an independent look at each option.

After you select your options from the Tool Options palette, you click and drag the mouse across the portion of your image window you want to select. As you draw, a solid line appears around the selected area, but as you release the mouse, the border of the drawn area is identified by a *marquee* of "marching ants"—moving black-and-white dashed lines. The area within the marquee is your selected area. Figure 4-2 illustrates a rectangular shape selection around the toucan's beak.

Remember that simply selecting an area does nothing to your image. It only tells PaintShop Pro that this is where you intend to take some action.

Hide Marquee

If, when working with a selected area, you find that the marquee is in the way, you can temporarily hide the "marching ants." Click the Selections menu and choose Hide Marquee.

Selection marquee   Mouse pointer

Figure 4-2
Using the Selection tool.

CHOOSING A SELECTION TYPE

After you select the standard Selection tool, one of the options on the Tool Options palette, seen in Figure 4-3, is the Selection type.

Selection type

Figure 4-3
The Selection tool's Tool Options palette.

As I mentioned earlier, there are 15 different shapes, which PaintShop Pro calls *types*, that you can choose from to make your selection. Click the Selection Type drop-down arrow to choose from the available selection shapes.

You can make your selection from any of the following shape types:

- ► Rectangle
- ► Square
- ► Rounded Rectangle
- ► Rounded Square
- ► Ellipse
- ► Circle
- ► Triangle
- ► Pentagon
- ► Hexagon
- ► Octagon
- ► Star 1
- ► Star 2
- ► Arrow 1
- ► Arrow 2
- ► Arrow 3

DISCOVERING FEATHERING

Feathering is a process that expands your selection and softens the edges of your selection, which in turn produces a gradual transition. The higher the Feather value, the softer the selection edges. You won't notice its effect on a blank canvas, but on an actual image, you can easily see the difference.

If you feather a selected object too much, it may appear to have a glow or to be furry. Typically, just a few pixels of feathering are sufficient, but the image size really determines the effect.

On a larger image, a 3-pixel feather has less of an effect than the same feather setting would have on a much smaller image. In contrast, a higher feathering setting might make the image edges lose tiny detail, such as what appears in hair, providing a softening effect. Just remember that this smoothing effect isn't always a good thing. It really depends on what you are selecting.

If you know before you make your selection that you want to add feathering, enter a value in the Feather box on the Tool Options palette, and the feathering will be applied to the selection as it is drawn. The value you enter is the distance from the selection (in pixels). Value ranges are from 0, which is no feathering, to 200, which is probably way more feathering than you'll ever need! In Figure 4-4, you see how the feathering affects the selection.

Figure 4-4
Using some feathering, a little feathering, and lots of feathering.

If you decide after you make your selection that you should add some feathering, choose Selections ➤ Modify ➤ Feather (or press Ctrl+H), which displays the Feather Selection dialog box shown in Figure 4-5. Enter the number of pixels in values from 0 to 200 that you want to feather the selection by, and then click the OK button.

Rounded Corners

If you have a rectangular selection, adding feathering may slightly round the selection corners.

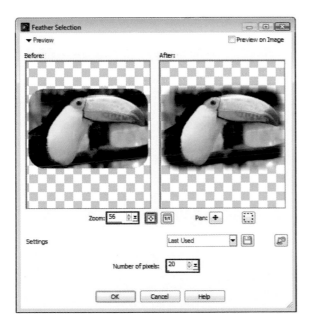

Figure 4-5
The Feather Selection dialog box.

SMOOTHING EDGES WITH ANTI-ALIAS

Anti-alias is certainly a mouthful of a word! It's a graphics term that digital artists use to refer to mathematical calculations and pixels on a screen. When an image is aliased, it has a somewhat jagged edge. Therefore, using anti-alias smoothes the edges of slanted lines and curves by filling in the pixels, giving a smoother appearance.

Actually, you see the anti-alias feature not only when you select portions of an image but when you are using some of the tools, such as the Text or Preset Shapes tool. Most tools that use anti-alias have a check box on the Tool Options palette to activate the anti-alias.

Look at the two circles in Figure 4-6. The image you see is zoomed in to show the effect of using anti-alias. The circle on the left with the hard jagged edge is drawn without the anti-alias feature, whereas the circle on the right with smoother blending of the edges is drawn with the anti-alias feature.

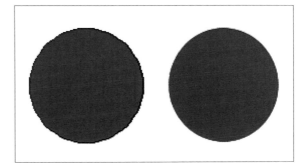

Figure 4-6
Using anti-alias.

Selecting a Mode

If you already have an area selected, the Mode options let you specify what you want to do when you make another selection. Three different options are available:

- ▶ **Replace**: Choose this option to deselect the existing selected area and select only a new area.

- ▶ **Add**: Choose this option to append the newly selected area to the existing selected area.

- ▶ **Remove**: Choose this option to eliminate areas from your selection. This is useful if you overselect the area and do not want to start over.

For more information, see the section later in this chapter titled "Adding To or Subtracting From a Selection."

Making a Custom Selection

Use the Custom Selection button if you want to make a selection of a specific size by entering the selection position in pixels for the left, top, right, and bottom positions. The Custom Selection dialog box seen in Figure 4-7 appears, where you enter the number of pixels for the outside edges of the selection you want. The Custom Selection selects only rectangular areas.

In Figure 4-7, you see the Custom Selection dialog box.

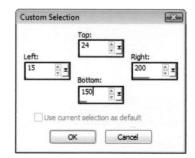

Figure 4-7
Indicating a specific selection area.

Note

Another Tool Options palette section, Create Selection From, has three options that apply when adding to an existing selection and when working with layers. See Chapter 8, "Developing Layers," for more information.

Drawing a Freehand Selection

Selecting with the Freehand Selection tool gives you a great amount of freedom in drawing the area you want to select. Use this tool to select irregularly shaped areas of an image. Using your mouse with the Freehand Selection tool might feel a little clumsy at first, but keep practicing; it gets easier. The Freehand Selection tool also works quite well when using a drawing tablet.

Zoom In First

Selecting with the Freehand Selection tool is much easier if you are zoomed in on the area that you want to select.

Similar to the Selection tool, with the Freehand Selection tool, the Tool Options palette provides a number of different options:

▶ **Selection Type**: Edge Seeker finds the edges between two areas with subtle color or light changes between them. Smart Edge lets you click along the edges of irregularly shaped areas with two areas of highly contrasting color or light. Use Point to Point to draw a straight border between selected points, which provides a selection with straight edges. With the Freehand Selection tool, you click and drag when you want to make a selection quickly.

▶ **Mode**: If you already have an area selected, Mode specifies whether you want to replace, add, or remove from the existing selection.

▶ **Feather**: Just like with the Selection tool, feathering expands your selection and softens the edges of your selection. The higher the Feather value, the softer the selection edges.

▶ **Range**: Range, which is available only when using the Edge Seeker selection type, allows you to specify the distance in pixels (0 to 15). The distance indicates from the point you click to where PaintShop Pro should search for an edge.

▶ **Smoothing**: Specifies the amount of smoothing for sharp edges or jagged lines for the selection border. Smoothing has a range of 0 to 40.

▶ **Anti-Alias**: Using anti-alias smoothes the edges of slanted lines and curves by filling in the pixels, giving a smoother appearance.

▶ **Use All Layers**: If this check box is marked, the tool searches for an edge in all layers of the area you select. If the check box is cleared, the tool searches for edges only in the current layer. This option is only available when the image has multiple layers and when you are using the Edge Seeker or Smart Edge selection types.

When you select the Freehand Selection tool, the mouse pointer turns into a cross with a lasso beside it. Click and hold the mouse button, and draw around the area you want to select. When using the Freehand Selection tool, it's best to make many small strokes. Using the cross as the guide, as you draw, a line appears. Double-click the mouse when you are finished, and the marquee will appear around the selected area. Figure 4-8 shows how I used the Freehand Selection tool with the Smart Edge option to select only the baby rabbit's face.

Figure 4-8
Selecting areas with the Freehand Selection tool.

Waving the Magic Wand

The third selection tool, the Magic Wand, works differently from the other two. The Selection and Freehand Selection tools select an area of the image, regardless of content, but the Magic Wand works by selecting pixels of equal or similar colors or brightness.

Through the Tool Options palette shown in Figure 4-9, you control which types of pixels you want the Magic Wand to select.

Figure 4-9
The Magic Wand Tool Options palette.

▶ **Mode**: If you already have an area selected, Mode specifies whether you want to replace, add, or remove from the existing selection.

▶ **Match mode**: The Match mode determines how the Magic Wand makes the selection. If you select None, the Magic Wand chooses all pixels. If you select RGB Value, the Magic Wand selects pixels based on the amount of color they contain. You'll learn about the color wheel and RGB in Chapter 7, "Understanding Color." If you choose Color, the Magic Wand selects pixels of the same color you select.

With Brightness, the Magic Wand selects pixels based on the amount of white they contain. Perceptual selects pixels based on shading and lightness. Traditional is similar to RGB mode, but it picks pixels that not only match the red, green, and blue values but base the selection on the lightness variations. All Opaque chooses only areas containing pixels. No transparent areas are selected. Finally, Opacity selects pixels based on their opacity.

▶ **Tolerance**: This controls how closely the selected pixels must match the initial pixel you click. With a range from 0 to 200, at higher settings, the Magic Wand tool selects a wider range of pixels.

▶ **Use All Layers**: With this box unchecked, the Magic Wand searches for matching pixels in the current layer only, but if checked, it searches in all layers.

▶ **Contiguous**: Mark this check box to select only matching pixels that connect to your original pixel. Unchecked, this option selects any image pixel meeting the other criteria you've set.

▶ **Feather**: Just like with other selection tools, feathering expands your selection and softens its edges. The higher the Feather value, the softer the selection edges.

▶ **Anti-Alias**: Using Anti-Alias smoothes the edges of slanted lines and curves by filling in the pixels, giving a smoother appearance. If you choose to use Anti-Alias, you can then select whether you want to use Anti-Alias from the inside or the outside of the selection marquee.

When you click the Magic Wand tool, the mouse pointer turns into a black cross with a magic wand beside it. Click the mouse on an edge of the image you want to select, which makes the marquee appear around the area according to the options you selected. In Figure 4-10, I used the Magic Wand tool to select the boy's yellow shirt.

Figure 4-10
Just like magic, PaintShop Pro selects all areas displaying similar pixels.

Modifying Selections

UNLESS YOU HAVE A PERFECT steady hand, your selection may not be exactly as you anticipated. Fortunately, PaintShop Pro provides the ability to modify your existing selection or simply deselect the selected area and begin anew.

Inverting a Selection

Sometimes the easiest way to select a complicated part of an image is to select the part of the image that you don't want and then invert the selection. For example, if you have a picture of a tree silhouetted against a blue sky, use the Magic Wand tool to select the sky and then invert the selection to select the tree.

Select the areas that you don't want. The marquee appears around the selected area. In Figure 4-11, I want to apply a different background.

It's easiest to use the Freehand Selection tool and select the boy's face and then select the Invert option. The image shows the areas around the face with the selection marquee.

Figure 4-11
Inverting the selection area.

By inverting the selection in this image, I was able to easily change the background, as you can see in Figure 4-12. There are several methods to change a background, but I used the Flood Fill tool, which you'll discover in Chapter 10, "Discovering Drawing Tools."

Figure 4-12
Making a change to the inverted selection area.

Deselecting

If you've selected an area in error, or when you've completed whatever you wanted to do to a selection, you need to remove the marquee of selection marks. Removing a selection does nothing to your image; it only removes the selection marks. To remove selection marks, choose Selections > Select None. The marquee disappears, and the area is no longer selected.

Expanding or Contracting a Selection Area

Did you make a complex selection only to find that you made it too tight or forgot to feather it? You can expand your selection with the Selections menu. You can expand the area that just stretches the selection without any feathering, or you can feather the area that both expands and feathers (softens the edges).

Make a selection and then choose Selections > Modify, which displays the Modify submenu. Click Expand or Feather and, in the resulting dialog box, enter the number of pixels you want to expand or contract the selection. The selection area expands or contracts by the amount you specify. In Figure 4-13, you see the Expand Selection box, where you can see in the Before pane that the area around the red pepper is too small. By expanding the selection 25 pixels, you see a much larger selection, showing some of the image's yellow background in the After pane.

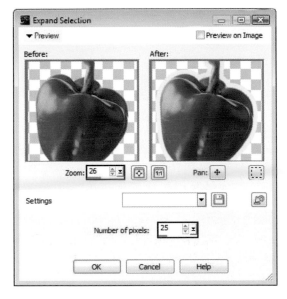

Figure 4-13
Expanding the selection area.

Adding To or Subtracting From a Selection

For whatever reason—whether you have multiple objects to select, your hand wasn't quite steady enough when you made the initial selection, or you've just changed your mind—you might need to modify a selection. Thankfully, you don't need to deselect and start over. Instead, you can add to or subtract from your initial selection. I mentioned this earlier in the chapter, but let's take a look at an example.

First, using any of the selection tools, select the first area you want. Then if you want to add to your selection, change the selection tool if desired, but no matter which tool you use, change Mode on the Tool Options palette to Add. Then select the second area you want to include. Both the original and the second area are marked with a marquee. You can continue to add as many areas to the selection as you need.

If you need to remove an area from the selection, use the preceding process, but change Mode on the Tool Options palette to Remove. Each time you select an area, PaintShop Pro removes it from the selection.

In Figure 4-14, on the top image, you see the area at the top of the red pepper where the mouse slipped and too much area was selected. In this example, I need to change Mode to Remove and, using a selection tool (in this case the Freehand tool), draw around the area I want to remove. In the picture on the bottom, you see where the overselection was removed.

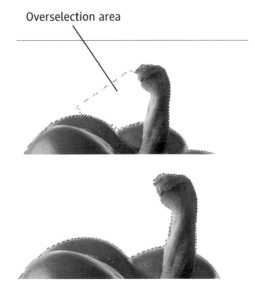

Figure 4-14
Removing from the selection area.

Selection Shortcut Keys

Optionally, hold down the Shift key to add to your selection area, or hold down the Ctrl key to remove from your selection area.

Using a Selection

AFTER YOU SELECT AN AREA, you can delete the selection by pressing the Delete key (which displays a transparent area where the selection was located), move the selection by dragging it to another area of the image, or add an adjustment or effect to the selected area.

To illustrate using a selection, I'll use an image of a rose and add a Gaussian Blur to the part of the rose. To begin, I'll use the Freehand Selection tool to select the portion of the rose I want to blur.

Once I have the selection, I want to apply a Gaussian Blur to the selected area. I click Adjust > Blur > Gaussian Blur. The Gaussian Blur command makes the image look as though it were taken with a camera using a special filter. You'll learn much more about adjusting images and applying filter effects in Chapter 9, "Adding Effects, Filters, and Deformations."

Like many other filters, Gaussian Blur displays the dialog box shown in Figure 4-15 for you to select options. If you do not see your image in the dialog box, click the Preview button to display the before and after images.

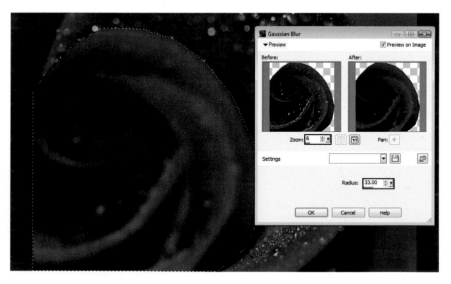

Figure 4-15
The Gaussian Blur dialog box.

For the results I want, I set the Radius at 33.00, giving a nice blurred effect to the selected portion of the rose. After making the selections and clicking OK, deselect the background by pressing Ctrl+D or choosing Select None from the Selections menu. In Figure 4-16, the image on the top is the original, but notice how, in the image on the bottom, part of the rose is still sharply in focus, while a portion of it is dramatically softened.

I added quite a bit of blur here to emphasize the concept. You may not want as much blur in your images.

Figure 4-16
Before and after pictures from using a selection.

5

Making Quick Fixes

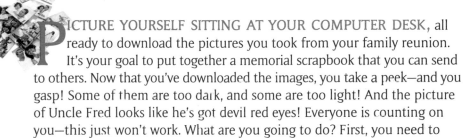**P**ICTURE YOURSELF SITTING AT YOUR COMPUTER DESK, all
ready to download the pictures you took from your family reunion.
It's your goal to put together a memorial scrapbook that you can send
to others. Now that you've downloaded the images, you take a peek—and you
gasp! Some of them are too dark, and some are too light! And the picture
of Uncle Fred looks like he's got devil red eyes! Everyone is counting on
you—this just won't work. What are you going to do? First, you need to
take a deep breath, and then you're going to let PaintShop Pro go to work
for you.

Using PaintShop Pro isn't going to make you a better photographer. That
only comes with knowledge, time, talent, a good camera, and lots of practice.
In most cases, however, PaintShop Pro can help you make your photographs
look like they should.

Previously, photographic technicians and specialists, called *retouchers*,
worked directly on film negatives and other media with brush and color.
It was a time-consuming and expensive process, but an important area of
photography. Most published photographs and other media images were
retouched in some manner. Today, virtually all the images you see in
advertising and magazines have been retouched and manipulated digitally.
There is a difference between photo correction and photo enhancement.
If you need to make the image look like it should, say, for example, to
remove digital noise or adjust the color, that's a *correction*. If you want to
actually modify the contents of the photograph, that's *photo enhancement*.

PaintShop Pro provides you with the tools you need to retouch images in resourceful and creative ways. You can remove or disguise blemishes, touch up dust spots, repair scratches, and perform many tasks that were once available only through the realm of the film retoucher.

Each of these tools offers basic settings, but you should know that these aren't the only tools to work with your images. PaintShop Pro includes many in-depth tools that allow you to get to the heart of your images and make the most minute changes you can imagine. However, most people find the automatic tools work quite to their satisfaction.

Playing It Safe

IN THIS CHAPTER AND THE NEXT, you'll discover lots of ways to correct and edit your images. Hopefully, after you apply some of these techniques, you'll have images you're quite happy with. But if not, let's take a look at some of the things you can do after you totally goof up an image:

▶ The most important step is to *never work* on an original image. Either make a copy by choosing Window ❯ Duplicate and perform your work on the copy, or make sure the PaintShop Pro Auto-Preserve feature is activated. When that feature is activated, when you first save any changes over an original image, PaintShop Pro places a copy of the original untouched image in a folder called Corel Auto-Preserve, which it locates in a folder just below the one containing the current image. If you duplicate the image and

work on the copy, it also helps you to compare the before and after effects by displaying both the original and the duplicated images side by side. Choose Window ❯ Tile Vertically (see Figure 5-1).

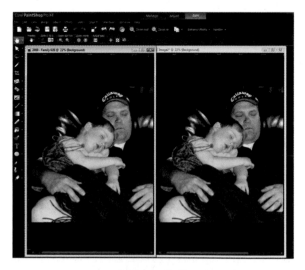

Figure 5-1
Compare images side by side.

Control Auto-Preserve

Although activated by default, you can control the Auto-Preserve feature by choosing File > Preferences > General Programs Preferences. Click the Auto-Preserve section to see the on/off option.

▶ Use the Undo function. From the Edit menu, choose Undo (or press Ctrl+Z). Each time you choose Edit > Undo, PaintShop Pro backtracks your actions one step. By default, you can undo up to the last 250 actions you took.

Undo Settings

You can change the number of Undo actions by choosing File > Preferences > General Program Preferences. From the Undo section, enter a number in the Limit Undo/Redo box, and click OK.

▶ Use the History palette. In the Edit workspace, choose View > Palettes > History or press the F3 button, which displays the History palette. The History palette lists all your actions (up to the limit you specify for Undo/Redo in your PaintShop Pro preferences). Your actions are listed with the most recent action on top. You can click any action to revert to the selected step.

One Step Photo Fix

PAINTSHOP PRO HAS MANY TOOLS you can use to help fix your photos. You can manually adjust the color balance, contrast, clarity, and saturation; smooth the edges; and sharpen the edges on each image. While you can open, close, and use each of these tools independently, PaintShop Pro also includes a One Step Photo Fix command that can automatically apply these features for you. It's an automatic feature, so you don't get to select any options, but most of the time it does a good job getting the most out of the photo without having to select and use each tool manually.

Adjusts the Entire Image

Different from using individual controls, which allow you to select and adjust a specific area, One Step Photo Fix adjusts the entire image.

With the image open and on your screen in the Edit workspace, you can access One Step Photo Fix from the toolbar or from the menu. From the toolbar, click the Enhance Photo button, which drops down a menu of options; then select One Step Photo Fix. PaintShop Pro immediately applies image adjustments.

Use the Menu

If you prefer to use the menu, you can select One Step Photo Fix from the Adjust menu.

Figure 5-2 illustrates an image both before and after using One Step Photo Fix.

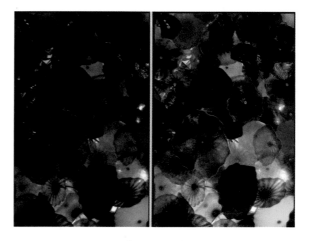

Figure 5-2
The image on the left is before using One Step Photo Fix, while the image on the right is after using One Step Photo Fix.

Smart Photo Fix

IN THE PREVIOUS SECTION, you discovered One Step Photo Fix, in which PaintShop Pro just took charge and fixed what it thought needed fixing. While that's fine for some images, for others you want a little bit more control. Smart Photo Fix is the tool you want to use in the latter case. While similar to One Step Photo Fix in the types of modifications it can do, Smart Photo Fix gives you the independent controls for brightness and other settings.

Choose Adjust ❯ Smart Photo Fix, which displays the Smart Photo Fix dialog box seen in Figure 5-3.

From the Smart Photo Fix dialog box, you can experiment with the various sliders to adjust Brightness, Saturation, and Focus settings until you give the image the look you want. In Chapter 6, "Manually Editing Images," you learn more about these individual image adjustments.

Like the One Step Photo Fix, all controls in the Smart Photo Fix commands work on the entire image, even if you've made a selection. Adjust the controls until you are satisfied with the After image, and then click the OK button.

Advanced Options

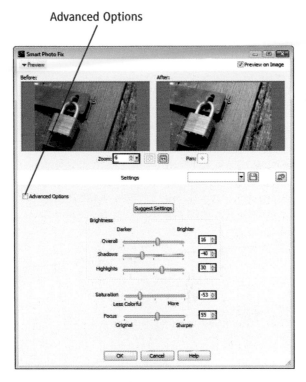

Figure 5-3
Adjust the individual settings in one dialog box.

Identifying the Enhancement Tools

WHEN YOU HAVE AN IMAGE OPEN in the Edit workspace, you see that the Tools toolbar, as shown in Figure 5-4, displays icons representing the more than 50 drawing tools available in PaintShop Pro. You'll need these tools to create and edit images, whether you create the images from scratch or edit a photograph or other artwork. Notice that some tools have an arrow next to them, which indicates that several similar tools are grouped together. For this chapter, we're only interested in a particular group of tools, called the Editing tools. You use the tools by selecting them, setting the desired options, and then making the desired correction.

Figure 5-4
The photograph editing tools.

 ▶ **Crop tool**: Eliminate unwanted or extra image areas.

▶ **Straighten tool**: Straighten a crooked image.

▶ **Perspective Correction tool**: Manage the perspective angle of buildings or other objects that appear to be leaning. (See Chapter 6.)

▶ **Red Eye tool**: Remove the red-eye often found in people or pet photographs.

▶ **Makeover tool**: Remove blemishes, whiten teeth, whiten eyes, apply a suntan, or make areas thinner.

▶ **Clone brush**: Copy pixels from one area of an image to another image area in the same or a different image.

▶ **Scratch Remover tool**: Remove scratches and other unwanted linear elements, including wrinkles!

▶ **Object Remover tool**: Cover unwanted areas in a photograph with a neighboring texture in the same photo.

Grouped Tools

PaintShop Pro groups some tools in flyouts. You can access all tools in a flyout by clicking the flyout arrow beside the tool.

Making Minor Retouches

RETOUCHING TOOLS ARE MOST commonly used for subtle alterations to an image, such as removing blemishes and other unwanted items. In Chapter 6, you discover some of the more detailed enhancement tools, sometimes called *enhancement brushes*, which you use in retouching. These tools, including Blur, Sharpen, and Smudge, bring out or change the focal point of the image, while other brushes change exposure limits through the saturation or hue in your image. These brushes take time and practice to master, but they are definitely worth the effort. For now though, let's take a look at some of the easiest fixes.

Fixing Red-Eye

We've all seen it. You snap a picture of friends, loved ones, or even your animals only to find that their eyes have taken on an eerie red glow. *Red-eye* is a basic fact of human biology because the pupils expand and contract in response to light exposure. In bright light, the pupils are small; in low light, they can become very big. When a camera flash erupts, the light travels through the dilated pupil and reflects light off the blood vessels behind the retina inside the eye. The camera picks it up as a distracting red spot.

Fortunately, red-eye is pretty easy to remove. PaintShop Pro provides two different methods to remove red-eye. The following steps show you how to use the fastest and easiest method:

1. With the image open in the Edit workspace, zoom in to the area with the red-eye.

Zooming

To zoom in to an area, click the Zoom In button, press the + key on the numeric keypad, or roll the mouse scroll button forward. To zoom out, click the Zoom Out button, press the – key on the numeric keypad, or roll the mouse scroll button backward.

2. From the Tools toolbar, click the Red Eye tool. The mouse pointer takes the appearance of a circle with an eye on it.

3. From the Tool Options palette, adjust the size of the mouse pointer so it's approximately twice the size as the redness you want to remove (see Figure 5-5).

Mouse pointer

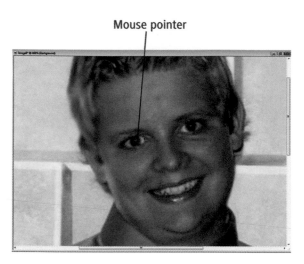

Figure 5-5
Adjust the mouse pointer to the red-eye size.

4. Click the mouse over the red-eye area. As
   you see in Figure 5-6, with just a click of the
   mouse, PaintShop Pro fills in the red area
   with gray pixels, which blend in with the
   surrounding corneal area.

Figure 5-6
Quickly and easily remove red-eye.

PaintShop Pro also includes a much more
powerful red-eye removal method, which even
lets you change the eye color. The following steps
guide you with the Red Eye Removal command:

1. From the Edit workspace, click the Adjust
   menu and select Red Eye Removal, which
   displays the Red Eye Removal dialog box you
   see in Figure 5-7.

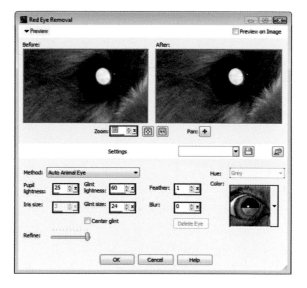

Figure 5-7
Use this dialog box to remove red-eye from
human or animal photos.

2. In the Before pane, center the subject's
   red-eye. If needed, use the Pan and Zoom
   controls to locate the desired area. Zoom in
   or out as necessary so the red-eye is large
   enough to work with.

About Red-Eye

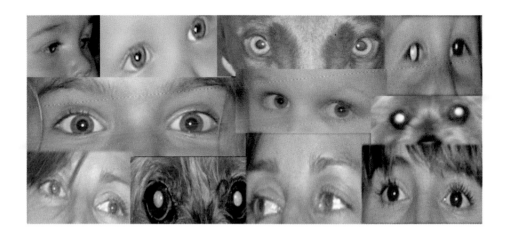

The term *red-eye* is particularly appropriate for people. The lighter the eye color, the more pronounced the effect can be. The red-eye effect can have a different appearance with animals. Many animals have a reflective layer in the back of their eyes that enhances their night vision. Studies have shown that the color of the reflective layer varies to some extent with the animal's coat color. For example, a black dog will have a green layer, producing a vivid green-eye effect. No matter what the color, the red-eye effect still makes the person or animal look possessed by a demon.

The best thing you can do is to prevent red-eye from happening when you take the photo. Here are a couple of tips:

> ▶ Move the flash away from the lens altogether.

> ▶ Use the red-eye reduction feature on your camera, which fires a few quick bursts of light that cause the pupil to react before the real camera flash goes off.

> ▶ Turn on a light or move the subject to a brighter area. The pupils become smaller, and the red-eye reaction is reduced.

> ▶ Have the subject look away from the lens, either above the camera or to the side opposite the flash, to reduce the reflection.

3. From the Method drop-down list, select whether you are working with a human eye or an animal eye. Try the Auto selections first, but if the pupil is partially hidden, you can manually select the correction area with the Freehand Pupil Outline or the Point-to-Point Pupil Outline options.

4. Click the Hue drop-down list, and select an eye hue. If you are working with animal eyes or the Freehand Pupil Outline and Point-to-Point Pupil Outline methods, this option will not be available.

5. Click the Color drop-down list and select an eye color or, in the case of an animal eye, an eye style. The animal choices include one cat eye option and two dog eye options.

6. Click anywhere inside the red area of the eye to select the eye automatically. You can also click and drag from the center of the eye to the outside edge of the red area. A circle appears around the selected area, and a control box for making adjustments encloses the circle. The Preview window displays the corrected eye.

   For the Auto Animal Eye method, drag the center rotation handle to rotate the selection. You can also reshape the eye from a circle to an ellipse by dragging its side handles.

Move Selection

To move the selection, drag it to a new location; to remove a selection, click the Delete Eye button.

7. In many cases, you won't need to do anything else, but, if necessary, the Red Eye Removal dialog box contains a number of additional adjustments tools:

   - Adjust the value for Pupil Lightness so that the corrected eye matches your perception of the natural color. Increasing the number makes the pupil lighter.

   - Change the Iris Size. Increasing the iris size decreases the pupil size. (Animal eyes don't have an iris.)

   - Adjust the lightness of the glint. A glint makes the eye look natural and lively. Lower values darken the glint; higher values lighten it.

   - Adjust the Glint Size. Larger values make the glint larger.

   - If desired, center the glint in the eye by checking the Center Glint check box.

   - Use the Feather setting to adjust how much feathering surrounds the corrected eye. Smaller values make the edges more defined; larger values blend the edges to the surrounding image areas.

   - If the photo is rather grainy, you can increase the Blur to blend the eye with surrounding pixels.

Avoid Overlap

If the eyelid covers part of the eye, you can use the Refine option to reduce the amount of correction and minimize its overlap with the surrounding skin area.

8. Repeat this process for the other eye if needed, and then click OK.

Figure 5-8 illustrates how the Red Eye Removal tool removed the red-eye effect from the dog's eyes.

Figure 5-8
Removing red-eye makes the eyes look natural.

Giving a Makeover

We've all seen magazines with photographs of models. You probably notice that their skin is smooth and silky looking, their eyes are clear, and their teeth are whiter than white. And they never have a pimple or unsightly mole anywhere. In reality, the models are like everyone else in that they get an occasional pimple or scratch at the most inopportune time. The magazine retouchers spend quite a bit of time making the models in the photographs appear flawless.

PaintShop Pro includes a variety of makeover tools with which you, too, can remove blemishes, whiten teeth and eyes, and even give the subject an instant suntan. You can even help the subject quickly lose extra pounds! Boy, Aunt Margaret is going to love you!

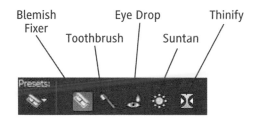 From the Tools toolbar, select the Makeover tool, and then, from the Tool Options palette seen in Figure 5-9, select the makeover tool you need.

Figure 5-9
The Makeover Tool Options palette.

REMOVING BLEMISHES

Removing blemishes, scars, wrinkles, moles, and the like is only a mouse click away. For example, take a look at the little girl in Figure 5-10. In the image on the left, on the girl's chin you see two unsightly blemishes. In the image on the right, there is no sign of the blemishes.

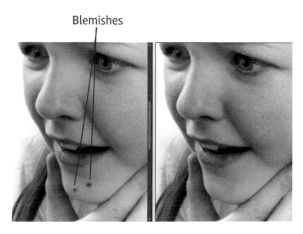

Figure 5-10
The image, before and after fixing the blemish.

To remove blemishes, follow these easy steps:

1. Zoom in on the blemish so you can see it well.

2. From the Tools toolbar, select the Makeover tool.

3. Select the Blemish Remover from the Tool Options palette. The mouse pointer turns into a small circle with crosshairs in it.

4. Choose a size that allows the small inner circle to enclose the blemish. The outer circle is for the material used to cover the blemish.

5. Choose a strength value between 1 and 100. A higher value applies more of the material outside the circle to the blemish area inside the circle.

6. Click the blemish. PaintShop Pro blends the pixels to cover the blemish area.

WHITENING TEETH

Everywhere you turn today, you see ads toting methods to whiten your teeth. You could go to your dentist and pay lots of money to professionally whiten them or use one of the do-it-yourself methods ranging from toothpaste to whitening strips. Or, you could just use PaintShop Pro and make teeth look their whitest in your photographs. I know, it's not the same as having them *really* whitened, but it's cheaper. The following steps show you how to whiten teeth in a photo.

Color Images Only

The Toothbrush function only works on color images, not grayscale.

1. Zoom in on the teeth so you can clearly see them.

2. Optionally, use the Freehand Selection tool and select the teeth area. This restricts the whitening to only the selected area.

3. From the Tools toolbar, click the Makeover tool.

4. Choose Toothbrush from the Tool Options palette.

5. Choose a strength control with values ranging from 1 to 100. You may have to try a setting and, if you aren't happy with the results, try a lower setting. If the setting is too high, you get a bright white, but sometimes the effect doesn't look like natural teeth.

6. Click the teeth. If the teeth are separated or partially obscured, you may need to apply this tool to each tooth individually.

Use Undo

If you aren't happy with the results, click the Undo button or press Ctrl+Z.

Look at the images in Figure 5-11. On the top, you see the image before whitening, and on the bottom, you see the image after teeth whitening.

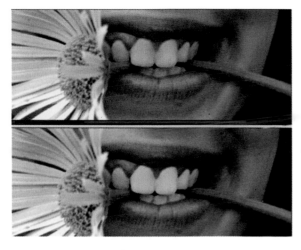

Figure 5-11
A brighter smile is only a mouse click away.

Brightening the Eyes

Your photograph subject may have eyes that look a little discolored. They may be pink or blood-shot, or they may be dull and gray. Babies' eyes often appear gray in photos. Whether the reason is not enough sleep or just a natural color tendency, you can brighten and whiten them using the Makeover tool in Eye Drop mode.

The Eye Drop function works pretty well, but you should know it won't completely clear up badly bloodshot eyes. Follow these steps for brighter and whiter eyes:

1. Zoom in on the eye so you can clearly see it.

2. Use the Freehand Selection tool with the Smart Edge option and select the eye. While this step is optional, doing so restricts the whitening to only the selected area (see Figure 5-12).

Selection area

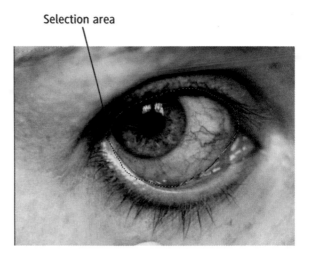

Figure 5-12
Select the eye area before applying drops.

3. From the Tools toolbar, click the Makeover tool.

4. Choose Eye Drop from the Tool Options palette.

5. Choose a strength. Values range from 1 to 100, with higher values whitening more of the eye area.

6. Click the whites of the eye. Repeat if necessary.

Don't Overwhiten

Don't try to remove *all* the red from the eye. It isn't natural and makes the person's eyes look unreal.

See Figure 5-13 for a before (top image) and an after (bottom image) example.

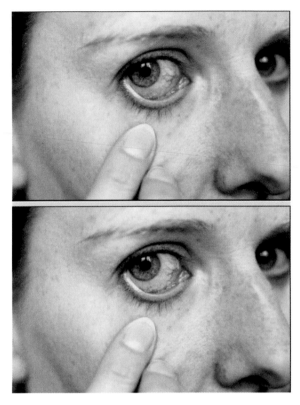

Figure 5-13
Clear up gray or bloodshot eyes with the
PaintShop Pro Eye Drop tool.

ADDING AN INSTANT TAN

Usually to get a good tan, you do one of two things: spend lots of time in the sun on the beach, or take numerous trips to your local tanning salon. If you can't do either of those, you could buy a bottle of the spray-on tanning stuff that usually gives you stripes afterward because you didn't get it on smoothly enough.

PaintShop Pro has the equivalent of the spray-on tan, but it won't leave you with stripes. One of the Makeover tool options can give your subject that "I just returned from a nice vacation" look. The following steps show you how to give an instant suntan:

1. Select the Makeover tool from the Tools toolbar.

2. From the Tool Options palette, select the Suntan mode icon.

3. Select a value from the Size control. Make the brush big enough that you can easily paint the skin area you want, but not so big that it brushes outside of the skin area. You may need to adjust the size periodically as you paint the tan.

4. Select a value from 1 to 100 from the Strength box. The Strength box controls how dark the tan is. A higher value produces a darker tan.

5. Drag the mouse cursor over the skin area. As you paint across the skin, the area turns darker.

Don't Tan the Hair

Avoid painting the hair and teeth. You may need to adjust your brush size as you get close to other areas.

Figure 5-14 illustrates a woman before and after giving her an instant suntan.

Figure 5-14
Add a little bit of tan or a lot of tan by adjusting the suntan strength.

Losing Pounds with Thinify

Without a doubt, PaintShop Pro is absolutely the best weight loss program in the world. With a click of the mouse, your subject can lose 10, 20, or 30 pounds or more! I sure wish it were this easy in real life!

The Makeover tool in Thinify mode compresses pixels along the horizontal sides of an area, making the subject area appear thinner. If you want to compress pixels vertically instead of horizontally, first rotate the image by choosing Image ❯ Rotate Right. After you apply the thinning effect, you can rotate the image back to its original state. Follow these steps:

1. On the Tools toolbar, choose the Makeover tool.

2. On the Tool Options palette, choose the Thinify mode.

3. Select a Strength control value from 1 to 100. The higher the value, the more pixels PaintShop Pro compresses.

4. Click the center of the photo subject. The pixels compress, and the subject appears thinner (see Figure 5-15).

Figure 5-15
Thinify: The fastest and easiest weight loss program ever.

When you apply the Thinify command, PaintShop Pro compresses the pixels on either side of the point you click. If you need more effect, either repeat step 4 or choose Edit ❯ Undo and reapply with a stronger strength. You should be aware, though, that too much Thinify can cause image distortion either in the background or the subject. It can also cause blurring on the edges of the image.

Avoid Blurring

To avoid blurring, before applying the Thinify command, increase the image canvas by choosing Image ❯ Canvas Size and add another inch or two to each side of the photograph. After resizing, apply the Thinify function, and then crop away the extra canvas around the photograph.

Smoothing Skin

Without enduring a painful chemical peel, you can have smoother looking skin in just a few brief steps. The PaintShop Pro skin smoothing feature removes small blemishes and wrinkles and smoothes the skin. Without affecting eyes or lips, skin smoothing softens skin tone pixels so they don't appear as deep. You can control the amount of smoothing you want to apply.

The skin smoothing feature is not one of the makeover tools you find on the toolbar. Instead, it's under the Adjust menu. Simply follow these steps:

1. Choose Adjust ❯ Skin Smoothing. The Skin Smoothing dialog box that you see in Figure 5-16 appears.

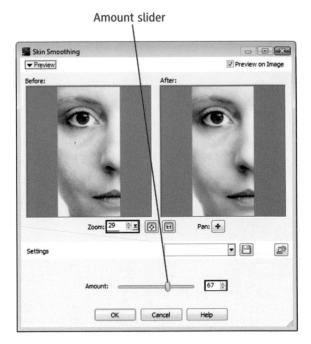

Figure 5-16
The Skin Smoothing dialog box.

Select Areas First

If other areas of the image are similar in color to skin tones, before you choose the Skin Smoothing command, you may want to select the area you want to modify.

2. Slide the Amount slider until you see the correction you want in the After preview picture. Be patient. This step can take several seconds to appear. Move the slider to the right to apply more smoothing, or move it to the left to decrease the smoothing amount.

3. Click the OK button. PaintShop Pro applies the smoothing to the image. Figure 5-17 shows a before and after picture.

Mix and Match Makeover Tools

The Skin Smoothing command cannot hide large blemishes or smooth deep wrinkles. To accomplish that, you'll need to use the Skin Smoother in addition to other makeover commands.

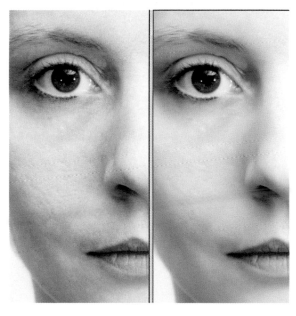

Figure 5-17
Before and after applying skin smoothing.

Removing Wrinkles and Scratches

Many of us have boxes full of old photos that we will "someday" put into beautiful albums. Unfortunately, since the images are not generally protected, they are inclined to get dust, scratches, tears, or creases. When you scan those images digitally, they pick up the same blemishes that are on the original. Fortunately, PaintShop Pro includes several tools to remove some of these marks from the digital image.

You can use the Scratch Remover tool to remove wrinkles, scratches, cracks, and other defects from your images, but you should know that this tool works best if the image background is relatively smooth. The Scratch Remover tool can be used only on background layers and only with images that are 16 million colors or more, or grayscale.

In this example, I'll begin with a picture of a woman and child with a large crease across the image. Follow these steps:

Create a Selection

To limit the correction to a specific area, first make a selection. This works well when you need to be careful not to remove important details near the scratch.

1. Zoom in to the area you want to work with. When working with the retouching tools, it's important to get in close to the damaged area. When you've finished retouching an area, zoom back out to view the overall image changes.

2. Select the Scratch Remover tool. Like the Clone brush, it's the eighth icon down on the toolbar and shares space with the Clone brush. The Scratch Remover mouse pointer icon looks like a trowel, the kind used to fill in cracks before you paint.

3. On the Tool Options palette, set the following options:

   - **Width**: When you choose the Scratch Remover tool and drag it along the scratch or crease, the length is determined as you drag, but you need to set the width, which is measured in pixels. Choose a width that is about 3 or 4 pixels wider than the scratch. If the width is considerably larger than the scratch, you lose image detail.

- **Selection boxes**: You can use two different shapes with the Scratch Remover tool. Select the flat-end option to correct scratches that are perpendicular to object edges in the image or are in an open area. Select the pointed-end option to correct scratches at an angle. The pointed end setting gets into small spaces and tight corners more easily than the blunt-ended version.

4. Center the mouse pointer just outside one end of the scratch; then click and drag the bounding box over the scratch. When the rectangle properly encloses the scratch, release the mouse button, and the scratch is removed (see Figure 5-18).

Enclose the area

Figure 5-18
For large scratches or wrinkles, work on small sections at a time.

Increase or Decrease Box Size

Press the arrow keys to move the starting point of the bounding box by 1 pixel. Press the Page Up or Page Down key to increase or decrease the width of the box by 1 pixel.

For the best results, follow these tips:

▶ Before using the tool, select the area that contains the scratch or wrinkle. If there is an abrupt change in color, you are often better off making multiple shorter selections than one long one.

▶ Choose the smallest possible width that completely encompasses the defect inside the inner borderlines, without touching the scratch or cut at any point. If your selection touches the scratch, you'll get unattractive smearing.

▶ For scratches or wrinkles over several different backgrounds, try removing the scratch a section at a time.

▶ Work in the direction of the scratch or wrinkle.

▶ You'll get a smoother repair if you stop and make a new selection when the angle of the scratch changes.

See Figure 5-19 to see the image both before and after removing the crease mark.

Figure 5-19
Removing the crease is the first of several changes to the image.

Changing Colors

Did you ever wonder what your favorite green dress would look like in blue? Or how about that hot car you've been eyeing—should you go with black or red or gray? The Color Changer tool in PaintShop Pro makes it easy to change the colors in your pictures, usually with just a single click. It's like magic in a mouse!

For Best Results

Although you can use the Color Changer tool on any photograph element, it works best on items such as carpet, clothing, and painted objects.

The Color Changer tool transforms the color of a photograph object but retains the original color shading and brightness. The following steps show you how:

1. Optionally, if you want to confine the color replacement to a specific area, select the area before applying the Color Changer, especially if there are similar colors elsewhere in the photograph. In Figure 5-20, I used the Freehand Selection tool to loosely surround the white sweater because I want to change the color only in the woman's sweater.

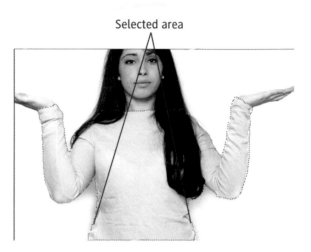

Figure 5-20
Select the area you want to change.

2. Select the Color Changer tool. It's the twelfth tool down the Tools toolbar and shares a space with the Flood Fill tool.

3. From the Tool Options palette, select a Tolerance setting. With values from 1 to 200, the higher the Tolerance control, the more liberally PaintShop Pro applies the new color. At lower settings, the color is applied only to areas most closely matching the spot you click when applying the color.

4. Choose an Edge Softness setting ranging from 1 to 200. A higher Edge Softness setting creates a subtle blend of the new color along the edges of the selection.

5. From the Materials palette, select the new color foreground you want.

6. Click the area you want to change.

Instantly, the Lady in White becomes the Lady in Pink, Blue, or Yellow (see Figure 5-21).

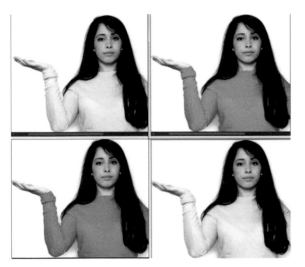

Figure 5-21
Change colors with a click of the mouse.

So far, you've seen quite a few ways to make your subjects look better. By combining the use of the different PaintShop Pro tools, you can give away a free makeover whenever you want to.

Deleting Unwanted Objects

Power lines, twigs, trash, people, and other unwanted objects often appear in an otherwise great photograph. Fortunately, PaintShop Pro provides several tools you can use to remove these items. One is the Clone brush, which you discover in the next section. Another is the Object Remover, but the best tool isn't really a tool on the toolbar; it's a process. It's called the Smart Carver, and you're going to love it! During the process, Smart Carver removes objects by making the photo wider, shorter, or longer without distorting the content.

Figure 5-22 shows you some people running down the beach, but I want to remove the man in the image. I'm going to use the Smart Carver to accomplish the task.

Figure 5-22
Remove unwanted objects in a photograph.

Begin by following these steps:

1. Choose Image ❯ Smart Carver. A Getting Started window appears.

2. Click Close. The Smart Carver dialog box opens.

3. Use the Zoom and Pan buttons to locate the image area you want to remove.

4. Click the Remove button.

5. Paint over the area you want to remove. Cover all the edges, but don't cover extra areas. Adjust the brush size as needed. In Figure 5-23, I've zoomed in to the man I want to remove and painted him with the Remove brush.

6. If you want to protect a specific image area from being removed or changed during the process, click the green Preserve brush and paint the area you want to save.

Preserve brush   Remove brush   Smart Carving directional tools

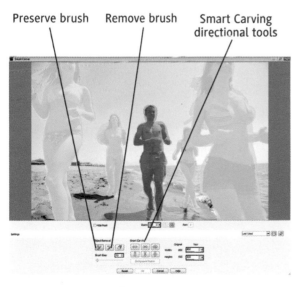

Figure 5-23
Remove unwanted objects in a photograph.

Use the Eraser

If you need to delete some or all of the Remove or Preserve brushstrokes, click the Eraser button and apply it to the brushstrokes you want to erase.

7. Apply the choices by choosing one of the Smart Carving directional tools. Pause your mouse over each directional tool to see an explanation. In my example, since the man is taller than he is wide, I need to contract the pixels horizontally to eliminate him. I'm going to use Auto-Contract to let PaintShop Pro make the decision as to how much to contract.

Reset

If you're not happy with the result, click the Reset button.

8. When you're finished, click OK. Figure 5-24 shows the photograph without the man.

Figure 5-24
So easy to use!

Using the Clone Brush

PaintShop Pro includes a tool called the Clone brush that provides a unique way to edit your images by using other parts of an image as a paint source. The Clone brush creates a brush that automatically matches the color and texture of the area you select. Using the Clone brush, you can remove unwanted items or add additional items.

Here's how the Clone brush works: you choose a source location somewhere in the picture. The source location can be part of the same image layer, another layer in the image, or an area from another image. When you paint with the Clone brush, you paste copies of pixels from the source location wherever you click. This tool is similar to the Object Remover tool in that it lets you identify the area to remove and then choose a background for covering that area.

In this first example, you see a peaceful pond with a beautiful pink flower. I'd like this image to have many of the pink flowers. I'll use the Clone brush to duplicate the flowers onto other areas of the photograph.

If necessary, you should zoom in so you can easily see the area you want to work with. In this example, I'm going to zoom to 200%.

Now select the Clone brush. The Clone brush is the eighth icon down from the top of the Tools toolbar. Since it shares this space with the Scratch Remover and Object Remover, you may need to pick it from the list. Just click the drop-down arrow on the right side of the tool and select Clone brush. A shortcut to selecting the Clone brush is to press the letter C.

Choose any Clone brush options. A number of selections are available on the Clone Brush Tool Options palette:

▶ **Shape**: Choose from square or rounded edges when painting.

▶ **Size**: Select the brush pixel size from 1 to 500.

▶ **Hardness**: Pick how sharp you want the edges of the tool to be. Settings are from 0 to 100, with 100 giving you the sharpest, hardest edge, and lower values giving softer, fading edges.

▶ **Step**: Select a value from 1 to 200 that determines the distance placed between applications of paint during a paint stroke. Using a lower number gives a smoother, more continuous appearance.

▶ **Density**: Sets the paint coverage. From values of 1 to 100, you'll usually want a higher number for more complete coverage. Using a lower number results in spotty paint coverage.

▶ **Thickness**: Works with the brush shape setting and controls how wide the brush is. With values of 1 to 100, a round brush and a setting of 100 provides a perfect circle, while a lower value with a round brush sets the brush to an oval. As you decrease the thickness, the brush becomes narrower.

▶ **Rotation**: Determines the rotation of the brush. Measured in degrees, select from 0 to 359.

▶ **Opacity**: Establishes how well the paint covers the image surface. At 100% opacity, the paint covers everything. Choose opacity numbers less than 100% if you want some of the underlying pixels of the original area to show through. At 1% opacity, the paint is almost transparent.

▶ **Blend mode**: Select from options that determine how painted pixels are blended with pixels on underlying layers.

▶ **Stroke**: Specify whether you want the paint to build up as you apply multiple strokes over the same area. If checked, the paint maintains a continuous color, and repainting an area has no effect. If not checked, each brushstroke over the same area applies more paint until the paint coverage reaches 100% opacity.

▶ **Aligned mode**: Check this box to have the Clone brush paint from the point of the source area relative to the first point you clicked on the target area each time you stop and start painting again. If the option is not selected, every stroke you paint repeats the source data.

▶ **Use all layers**: Use this when working with multiple layers. If checked, the Clone brush gathers information from all the layers merged together, but if unchecked, the Clone brush uses only the information on the current layer.

Work on Layers

Create a new raster layer (Layer > New Raster Layer; then click OK) on which to paint the cloned image. That way you can easily move the cloned area around if desired. Chapter 8, "Developing Layers," shows you all about layers.

You can use the default settings on most of the Clone brush options, but you'll definitely want to set the size, which determines the diameter of the paintbrush. If you make the brush too small, the cloning won't look natural, and it will take a long time to completely paint the desired element. If it's too large, you won't be able to get an accurate, natural-looking brushstroke. Start with a size that looks like it will allow you to paint in realistic-looking pieces. For the picture I'm using, the flowers are pretty small, so I set the size to 70 pixels. You'll want to change the size, depending on the area you are working in. For this example, I also clicked the Aligned mode option.

On the original image, right-click the beginning of the area you want to replicate; in this example, it's the flower on the lotus petal. A small circle appears where you clicked. Begin painting where you want the duplicated area. As you paint with the mouse, the image appears (see Figure 5-25).

Right-click here   Paint here

Now you see a pond of many lovely pink flowers in Figure 5-26. I also cloned the blue duck in the image so he won't be lonely!

Figure 5-25
Use the Clone brush to duplicate areas of an image.

Figure 5-26
The image after cloning.

Discovering the Object Extractor

IN THIS CHAPTER, YOU'VE ALREADY seen several ways you can copy one part of an image to another, including using the selection tools or the Clone brush. The selection tools work great if the object has clean distinct edges, and the Clone brush works great if you don't need a precise object. However, what about if you want to copy an image of an animal such as a giraffe or dog or a close-up of a girl with fluffy hair? Those tools just don't work as well on objects with "fluff."

PaintShop Pro X4 has a feature called the Object Extractor. Using the Object Extractor tool, you

can isolate objects containing fuzzy elements such as hair or fur and then duplicate the object to another image or another background. Using the Object Extractor is part of a process that includes the following:

▶ Outlining the edges of the image area you want to extract

▶ Adding a special fill inside the extract area

▶ Previewing the results and modifying if needed

▶ Viewing the cutout area

▶ Putting the cutout area into another image

You accomplish these tasks in the Edit workspace. Follow these steps:

1. Display the image you want to extract from.

2. Choose Image > Object Extractor. The Object Extractor dialog seen in Figure 5-27 appears, with the green Brush tool activated.

Figure 5-27
The Object Extractor dialog box.

3. Adjust the brush size by moving the Brush size slider. You want the brush large enough to cover the edge of your extract object. You can also specify an exact size for the brush (or eraser) by entering a value in the Brush size box.

4. In the Preview window, draw a line along the edges of the image area that you want to cut out. Make sure that your selection slightly overlaps the surrounding background and completely surrounds the extract area, including any fine fur or hairs (see Figure 5-28). If you need to modify the selection area, choose the Eraser tool, and drag over the area of the selection marquee that you want to delete.

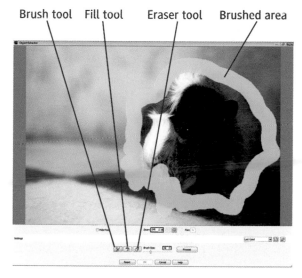

Brush tool   Fill tool   Eraser tool   Brushed area

Figure 5-28
Paint over the edges of the extraction object.

5. Click the Fill tool and click inside the area you want to extract. A red overlay covers the image area that you clicked. (Figure 5-29). If the selection outline is not closed, the fill covers the entire image. If that happens, click the Eraser tool to clear the fill, and then complete the selection outline with the Brush tool.

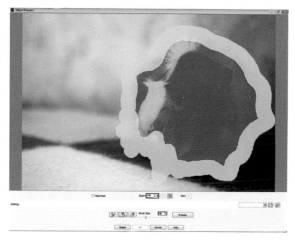

Figure 5-29
Click the area you want to preserve.

Reset Button

Click the Reset button to clear both the fill and the selection outline.

6. Click Process to preview the result. You see the area you painted, and the rest of the image becomes a transparency. You can click the Hide Mask option to see the remaining image detail, as seen in Figure 5-30. And if you need to edit your selection area, uncheck the Hide Mask, and then click Edit Mask to return to the previous view, where you can touch up the cutout and click Process again.

Hide mask

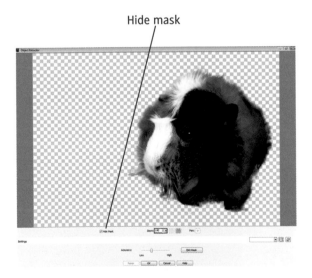

Figure 5-30
After Object Extractor processing.

Extract More Detail

If the object has an intricate or complex outline, you can refine the edge detail. Move the Accuracy slider to a higher value. The Accuracy slider is available only after you click Process.

7. Click OK and you return to the Edit workspace. Notice that the background layer becomes a regular raster layer. See Chapter 8 for more information about layers.

In Figure 5-31, you see where I added a solid gray layer beneath the guinea pig. When zoomed in, you can see the fine lines of the pig's fur.

Figure 5-31
View fine line detail after using the Object Extractor tool.

Manipulating Images

TILT YOUR HEAD TO ONE SIDE and stare at your television. Obviously, that perspective makes the onscreen images look a little lopsided and hard to follow. Straighten your head, and you can see the image much more clearly.

Next, picture your favorite tree in a forest among dozens of other trees. You want to focus exclusively on that specific tree, but it's not easy to tell your eyes what you want to exclude. With a photograph and PaintShop Pro, you can straighten images that came out crooked; crop away unwanted areas, allowing you to focus on a specific image area; and rotate an image.

Cropping

Use the Crop tool to permanently remove unwanted portions of an image. Cropping an image can create stronger compositions and change the image focus. Cropping also reduces the image file size and the computer memory needed to edit the image.

Cropping is one of the first steps in correcting a photograph, because any subsequent color changes you make can be affected by objects you may not even want in the photo. Many features, such as the One Step Photo Fix or Color Balance, use the entire image to make the feature changes. By eliminating superfluous areas of color, cropping can make color corrections more accurate.

If you do want to crop your photo, first decide what the subject should be and remove anything that distracts from the subject. You don't have to crop all your images; in fact, many images would lose their composition if extra space around a subject were cropped off. Remember the Rule of Thirds, and avoid placing a photo with the subject in the dead center.

The Rule of Thirds

The Rule of Thirds helps produce nicely balanced, easy-on-the-eye photographs by imagining your image divided into thirds both horizontally and vertically. You place important elements of your composition where these lines intersect, such as a third of the way up or a third of the way in from the left.

If you are planning on printing the image, don't crop it too small. Depending on the quality of the original photograph, your image may lose some resolution if you try to make it larger for printing. If you used a good resolution digital camera when taking the image, this would be a good time where all those extra pixels produced by the camera would come in quite handy, because the remaining cropped image would still be large enough to print at a reasonable size. See Chapter 14, "Printing and Distributing Images," for more information regarding size, resolution, and pixels.

The Crop tool is one of the easiest PaintShop Pro tools to use. You can crop your image to any size you want, or you can have PaintShop Pro restrain the crop so you can use one of many standard sizes, such as 4 × 6 or 5 × 7. You can access the Crop tool by clicking the fifth tool on the Tools toolbar, or you can press the letter R to activate it.

SETTING CROPPING TOOL OPTIONS

Before you actually crop the image, you should become familiar with cropping options. Each time you select a tool from the Tools toolbar, the Tool Options palette displays options specific to the selected tool. Click the Crop tool, and PaintShop Pro displays the Crop tool options, as seen in Figure 5-32.

The following list explains some of the tools on the Crop Tool Options palette:

▶ **Presets**: Select from standard print sizes. See "Cropping to a Specific Size" later in this chapter.

▶ **Width**: Enter a specific width for cropping, based on units.

▶ **Height**: Enter a specific height for cropping, based on units.

▶ **Specify Print Size**: Change the resolution of the crop area to a value that will result in a specific printable size. There are no more or no fewer pixels in the crop rectangle, but by changing only the resolution of the image, the default print size will be different than if this check box is not selected.

▶ **Maintain Aspect Ratio**: Constrain the crop area to keep its current proportions. If you're using a Preset size, this box is unavailable.

▶ **Units**: Specify the unit of measurement, in centimeters, inches, or pixels. If the Specify Print Size option is checked, you can only select from centimeters or inches.

▶ **Resolution**: Display the image resolution, based on the crop selection size and your unit of measurement.

▶ **Snap Crop Rectangle To**: Use Current Selection, the default, to snap the crop rectangle around the area you draw with your mouse. Use Layer Opaque to select all opaque (solid) areas in the current layer, and Merged Opaque to select all solid areas in all layers.

Figure 5-32
Pause your mouse over each tool option to see its name.

CROPPING TO YOUR SELECTION SIZE

If you want to exactly control the crop of your image, you can specify the crop size either in measurements or by drawing a boundary selection box. Select the Crop tool from the Tools toolbar. Notice how the mouse pointer changes to a plus sign with the crop tool attached.

Ignoring the predefined crop area supplied by PaintShop Pro, click and drag around the area of the photo you want to *keep*. As soon as you click in the image, the entire original image becomes shaded, the predefined crop area disappears, and the selected area you are drawing around brightens up so you can get a better idea of what your image will look like after cropping. See Figure 5-33, where I want to crop closer to the family.

Crop selection mini toolbar   Crop selection handles

Figure 5-33
Cropping permanently removes the image area outside the crop selection box.

Notice the small toolbar under the crop selection box. It's a special Crop toolbar and contains buttons for Apply, Crop to New Image, Clear, Display Grid, Rotate Crop Rectangle, and a list of selection sizes.

One of the tools on the Crop toolbar includes the Rotate Crop Rectangle which, when clicked, rotates the cropping selection from vertical to horizontal or from horizontal to vertical. Another tool is Crop as New Image, which allows you to automatically save the cropped area to a new file, thereby leaving the original uncropped.

Separate Multiple Images Quickly

The Crop As New Image option is great for when you scan multiple photographs onto a single image and then want to quickly separate them.

You can also make the following choices about your current crop selection:

▶ If you didn't select exactly the right size or location, you can adjust the cropping selection by clicking and dragging the crop selection handles located on the sides or corners until the cropping selection is the size you want. As you position your mouse pointer over the selection box handles, the mouse pointer turns into either a two- or four-headed arrow depending on which selection box handle you choose.

▶ If you want to move the selection box, place the mouse pointer inside the rectangle to move the entire rectangle around. If you are having difficulty getting the selection box exactly the size and location you want, you can start over by clicking the Clear button on the Crop mini toolbar.

▶ If you want to rotate the crop selection box, drag the square rotation handle located in the middle of the crop selection box until you find the rotation you want.

When you're satisfied with your selection area, click the Apply button, which is the check mark on the Crop selection mini toolbar. Optionally, you can double-click inside the selection area to accept the crop.

Undo the Crop

If you change your mind after you've cropped the image, click the Undo button on the Standard toolbar or, from the Edit menu, choose Undo Crop. Optionally, press Ctrl+Z to undo your last action.

Figure 5-34 illustrates the image after cropping. The family appears much closer than in the original photograph.

Figure 5-34
Focus on your subject by cropping to it.

Tool Options Palette Oddity

After cropping an image, you may notice that the Width and Height values in the Crop tool options are set to 1 if you are measuring in pixels and .100 if you are measuring in inches. No one seems to be sure why the values change, but this is not a reflection of the cropped image size. To see the image size dimensions after cropping, click Image ❯ Image Information and look at the Dimensions field.

CROPPING TO A PRESET SIZE

In the previous section, you discovered how to crop an image to any size you want, but to help you keep the image perspective and use a common print size, PaintShop Pro includes ten preset image sizes from which you can choose.

Follow these steps to crop your image to a preset size:

1. Select the Crop tool.

2. Click the Presets button. A list of available preset sizes such as those you see in Figure 5-35 appears. Preset sizes are measured in centimeters or inches.

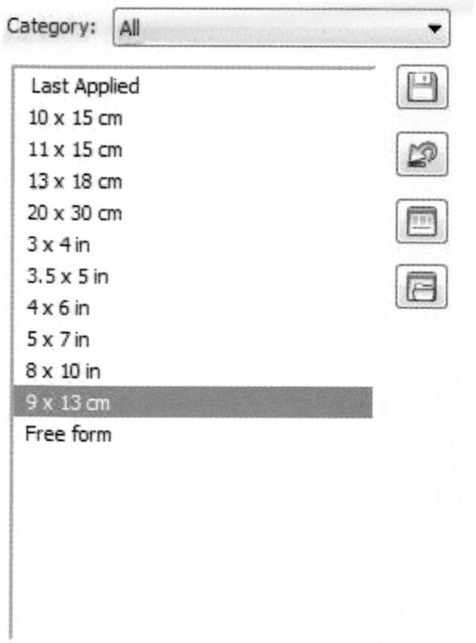

Category: | All

Last Applied
10 x 15 cm
11 x 15 cm
13 x 18 cm
20 x 30 cm
3 x 4 in
3.5 x 5 in
4 x 6 in
5 x 7 in
8 x 10 in
9 x 13 cm
Free form

Figure 5-35
Choose from standard image sizes.

Choose by Measurement Type

Click the Category arrow on the Presets button to segregate the options by measurement type.

3. Select the finished size from the Presets button. A crop selection box of the selected size appears in the upper-left corner of the image.

4. With the mouse pointer inside the crop selection box, click and drag the box until it is positioned over the image area you want to keep.

5. Click the Apply button.

CROPPING TO A SPECIFIC SIZE

If none of the preset sizes are what you want, you can specify your own exact dimensions by setting a measurement in the Width and Height boxes on the Tool Options palette. You can set the crop size up to 3 decimal points precise, either in inches or centimeters. If, for example, I needed the image size 7.819 wide and 6.167 tall, after choosing the Crop tool, I would enter those settings in the Width and Height boxes.

Be aware, however, that images cropped to odd sizes probably won't fit into standard picture frames.

Straightening

Sometimes a photo may not be as straight as you intended, and there's nothing quite as distracting as a photo that's slightly crooked. This commonly occurs in action shots where the camera wasn't quite level with the horizon. If an image is crooked, the best thing to do is retake the photograph or rescan the image. Often, though, those are not options. In that case, or if the image is only slightly crooked, PaintShop Pro includes a toolbar tool that helps align crooked photos and scanned images. Like the rotate feature, if the picture is seriously crooked, you may see some image distortion. The Straighten tool works best when the image has a strong vertical or horizontal feature such as that of a building or a horizon.

Straightening line

Figure 5-36
Drag the straightening line along the image section you want to straighten.

On the Tools toolbar, click the Straighten tool. The Straighten tool is the sixth tool on the toolbar, along with the Perspective Correction tool. After you select the Straighten tool, PaintShop Pro places a straight line through the middle of the image.

Look at Figure 5-36, which shows a beautiful lighthouse that definitely needs straightening. Drag the straightening line to the area on which you want to align. In this example, I want to straighten to the grass, so I need to drag the straighten line down to the grass line. Click and drag one of the bar end handles to align it with the part of the image that you want to use as the guide for straightening.

On the Tool Options palette, besides the typical presets, Apply and Reset tools, choose from these options as seen in Figure 5-37:

Apply

Figure 5-37
Straightening options.

▶ **Mode**: Auto, Make Vertical, or Make Horizontal: PaintShop Pro automatically straightens the image based on the position of the straightening bar, rotates the image to make the straightening bar vertical, or rotates the image to make the straightening bar horizontal, respectively. Usually, you will use the Auto mode.

▶ **Crop Image**: Use this option to have PaintShop Pro crop the edges of the image to make it rectangular after straightening. If you do not select this image, PaintShop Pro attempts to fill the blank rotated area with a solid background color.

▶ **Rotate All Layers**: Mark this check box to have PaintShop Pro straighten all layers in the image.

▶ **Angle**: Instead of visually aligning to the straightening bar, use this box to enter a specific angle for the straightening bar.

Like many other PaintShop Pro tools, you click the Apply button to apply the straighten feature. Figure 5-38 illustrates the image before and after straightening. Notice the automatic cropping that took place after straightening. By the way, I also used the Scratch Remover tool to eliminate the unsightly power lines.

Figure 5-38
View the image before and after straightening.

Rotating

You can rotate an image by 90 degrees to change its orientation to horizontal (landscape) or vertical (portrait). Some of today's cameras contain sensors that automatically rotate your photos to the correct orientation. If not… well, PaintShop Pro has a tool designed just for rotating images. You'll also find this feature handy if you accidentally held the camera upside down!

You saw in Chapter 3, "Becoming More Organized," that you can rotate images in the Organizer palette by clicking the image you want to rotate and then click either the Rotate Left or the Rotate Right button. Each time you click the rotate buttons, the image rotates 90 degrees. While in the Edit workspace, you can also click Image ❯ Rotate Right or Image ❯ Rotate Left.

If you want to more specifically manage the degree of rotation, you use the PaintShop Pro Free Rotate command. To begin, in the Edit workspace, open the image you want to rotate.

Choose Image ❯ Free Rotate (or press Ctrl+R), which displays the Free Rotate dialog box seen in Figure 5-39.

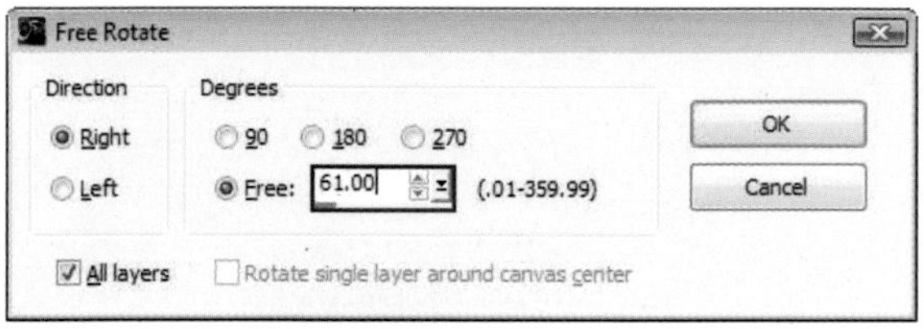

Figure 5-39
Select the degree of rotation.

Choose a direction to rotate and the amount you want to rotate the image. Rotation values range from .01 to 359.99 degrees. If you are working with an image that has layers (see Chapter 8), you can choose whether you want to rotate only the current layer or all layers. Click OK when finished.

Using the Learning Center

THROUGHOUT THIS CHAPTER, you learned many ways to edit your images. In Chapter 6, you'll discover even more detailed ways to fine-tune your photographs. However, PaintShop Pro includes another way to help you through the process. When you opened PaintShop Pro, the Learning Center appeared on the left side of the screen. In Chapter 1, "Getting Acquainted," I had you close it, but let's display it again and see what it can do for us. Choose View > Palettes > Learning Center or press the F10 key.

The Learning Center displays steps and information designed to help you complete common tasks you might want to perform using the PaintShop Pro tools. Figure 5-40 illustrates the Learning Center home page.

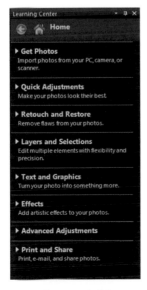

Figure 5-40
Quickly complete tasks using the Learning Center.

The following steps show you how to make selections from the Learning Center:

1. From the home page, click a task, and topics related to the selected task appear. For an example, I'll click the Retouch and Restore button. Topics related to retouching and restoring appear as shown in Figure 5-41.

Back button   Home button

Figure 5-41
A topic list appears.

111

2. Click a topic. I'll click the Makeover Topic button. The Makeover button appears selected on the Tools toolbar and, in the Learning Center, procedures and helpful information related to the topic appear (see Figure 5-42).

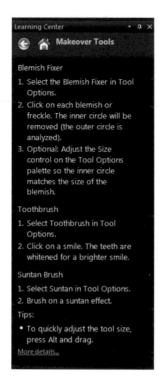

Figure 5-42
Instructions are provided for the task you selected.

3. Follow the instructions provided in the Learning Center.

The steps you see in the Learning Center vary depending on the task you select. Some tasks display a dialog box. Additionally, if you click a tool from the toolbar, instructions for the selected tool appear in the Learning Center. In Figure 5-43, you see instructions for using the Straighten tool.

Helpful Buttons

If you choose an option by mistake, click the Back button. To return to the Learning Center home page, click the Home button.

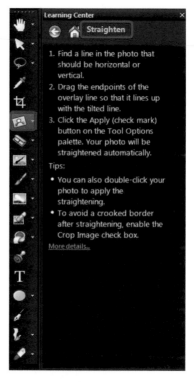

Figure 5-43
Let the Learning Center help you with a variety of tasks.

Manually

Editing Images

PICTURE YOURSELF A GOURMET CHEF. You have a reputation to protect, and you use only the finest ingredients measured to the precise detail. It's the same way with correcting photographic issues. You want the detail to be clear and precise. Even if the pictures don't start that way, you can correct many image problems. In Chapter 5, "Making Quick Fixes," you discovered the many quick fixes included with PaintShop Pro. In this chapter, you'll discover more detailed methods to correct image defects, correct distortion, and rectify lighting issues. Many photos need multiple corrections, so you should look at each image as a project.

If you can identify the parts of your photo that need improvement, PaintShop Pro can provide ways to make these improvements, from balancing your color or contrast to making specific, detailed adjustments, such as working with channel mixers, thresholds, and histogram modifications.

Using PaintShop Pro Dialog Boxes

BEFORE YOU ACTUALLY BEGIN adjusting your photos, let's take a brief look at how the photo adjustment dialog boxes work. Figure 6-1 shows the Digital Noise Removal dialog box. (You'll discover Digital Camera Noise Removal later in this chapter.) For now, let's review the controls that many PaintShop Pro dialog boxes have in common:

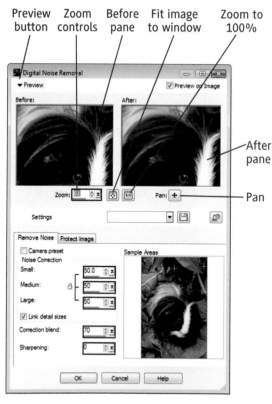

Figure 6-1

The top half of the dialog box offers common controls, while the bottom half contains controls specific to the adjustment you are making.

▶ **Preview**: Click this arrow to hide or redisplay both the Before and the After panes.

▶ **Preview on Image**: When checked, lets you see the current changes as you make them on the image (under the dialog box) without accepting the changes until you click OK.

▶ **Before pane**: Displays your image before you make any changes with the dialog box.

▶ **After pane**: Displays the effects of your changes on your image.

▶ **Zoom controls**: Zoom in or out on your image. When you zoom, both the Before pane and the After pane zoom.

▶ **Fit Image to Window button**: Quickly zooms out on the image so you can see the entire image in both the Before and After panes.

▶ **Zoom to 100% button**: Quickly zooms in on the image.

▶ **Pan button**: Click and hold this button to display another window containing a small version of your image, with the zoomed area indicated by a rectangle. Drag the rectangle to a different part of the image you want to preview. The Pan button only works if you cannot see the entire image in the Before and After panes.

▶ **Settings**: Choose from a variety of preset control options.

▶ **Save Settings**: Click this to save your customized settings for future use.

▶ **Reset to Defaults**: Click this button to reset the control options to the factory default settings determined by PaintShop Pro.

Randomize Button

Some dialog boxes contain a Randomize button. Each time you click the Randomize button, it "rolls the die" and randomly changes all the settings pertaining to the feature you are working with. It's a fun feature, but it's generally not very practical.

Photo Improvement Steps

KEEP IN MIND THAT AS YOU TRY to improve the color balance, brightness/contrast, and other attributes of photographs, none of the methods can add detail or color that isn't there. All techniques work well with photographs that have, say, all the colors somewhere, but with too much of one hue or another. You can remove the extra color, leaving a well-balanced picture behind. Or you can beef up the other colors, so they are in balance once again. PaintShop Pro can do that by changing some pixels that are relatively close to the color you want to increase to that exact color.

But remember that removing one color, or changing some colors to another color, doesn't add color to your image; either way, you're taking color out. So, if you have a photograph that is hopelessly and overpoweringly green, you're out of luck. When you remove all the green, there may be no color left behind. Or you can add magenta until your subject's face turns purple, and all you'll end up with is a darker photo.

You must start with a reasonable image; color correction is better suited for fine-tuning than major overhaul.

You'll find that most photographic improvements fall into a couple of general categories, with some photos requiring multiple improvements:

▶ Adjust color, contrast, and saturation

▶ Fix color aberrations

▶ Remove noise and scratches

▶ Clarify and sharpen images

▶ Make depth adjustments

▶ Correct flash problems

▶ Adjust lens distortions

Many of these improvements can be made in either the Adjust workspace or the Edit workspace. For the purpose of giving a better explanation of each process, we'll make the adjustments in the Edit workspace.

In many situations, you can make the improvements you want to only a portion of your image. You need to select the portion you want to modify before you choose the enhancement.

Adjusting Color

When you use the One Step Photo Fix, it modifies a number of different components, including color, saturation, contrast, and clarity. But what if your image doesn't need adjustment in all those areas? In that case, you can implement each correction independently of the others.

You can often improve a photo dramatically by adjusting the colors. Different types of lighting and cameras and the processing that occurs inside the camera can cause incorrect coloring in photos. Also, scanned images may have unnatural color casts. Fortunately, PaintShop Pro has several adjustments you can make to change the color climate in your image.

Apply to Entire Image or Selection

If you only want to adjust color on a portion of an image, select the area you want to change prior to implementing the adjustment.

ADJUSTING COLOR TEMPERATURE

Photos taken indoors, especially with nonfluorescent lighting, tend to look more orange, while photos taken in bright sunlight tend to have a bluish tint to them. To create natural-looking colors and remove any stray or odd color cast commonly found in digital images, try the Color Balance command. Just follow these easy steps:

1. From the Edit workspace, choose Adjust ❯ Color Balance, which opens the Color Balance dialog box.

2. To allow PaintShop Pro to make small automatic color corrections, leave the Smart White Balance check box selected. If you don't want PaintShop Pro to make these automatic corrections, remove the check mark.

3. Drag the Temperature slider to the left for cooler temperature lighting, such as with sunlight or fluorescent bulbs, which adds a bluer cast to the image. Or drag it to the right for warmer temperature lighting, which mimics more indoor lighting and provides a warmer orange tint.

Advanced Options

If you want to further fine-tune the temperature, click the Advanced Options check box and make your selections from the additional options that appear.

4. Click the OK button. Figure 6-2 illustrates an image before and after changing the temperature. Notice that the image on the right has a richer, warmer, more natural coloring.

Figure 6-2
An image before and after making color balance adjustments.

Optional Method

You can also change the color balance in the Adjust workspace.

CHANGING COLOR CAST

Another way to make color corrections is by changing the overall color cast in an image. You can individually adjust the amount of red, green, and blue in your image. Choose Adjust ➤ Color ➤ Red/Green/Blue. You see the Red/Green/Blue dialog box shown in Figure 6-3. Notice that the original image has a distinctive bluish cast to it.

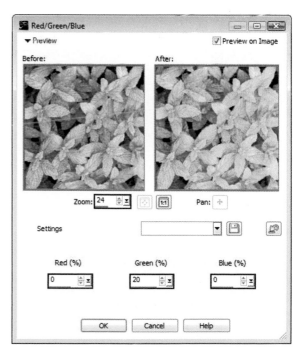

Figure 6-3
The Red/Green/Blue dialog box.

In the Red, Green, and Blue color controls, drag the slider or use the up/down arrow to change the percentage for each color you want to modify. These let you adjust the proportions of a particular color, from –100% to 100%. You can either add one color or subtract its two component colors. Here are a few particulars you may want to recognize:

▶ A value of 0% preserves the original value.

▶ Using a positive value adds more of the selected color.

▶ Using a negative value removes some of the selected color.

▶ Reducing the amount of blue adds a yellow cast to the image, reducing the amount of green adds a magenta cast to the image, and reducing the amount of red adds a cyan cast to the image.

When you finish making your adjustments, click the OK button to accept your changes. In Figure 6-4, you see an image before and after changing the RGB color values. In this example, I increased the green value and slightly decreased the blue value.

Figure 6-4
An image before and after making red, green, and blue adjustments.

Restoring Faded Images

Sometimes images, especially older ones, can become faded and lose their color and contrast. The PaintShop Pro Fade Correction option can bring back life to these older photographs. Choose Adjust ❯ Color ❯ Fade Correction. The Fade Correction dialog box appears, as shown in Figure 6-5.

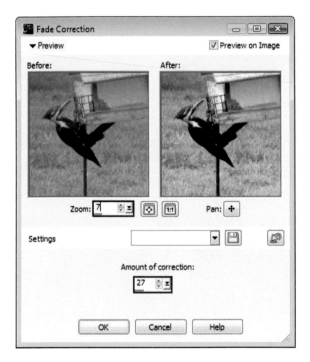

Figure 6-5
The Fade Correction dialog box.

If you have a specific area on which you want to focus the color change, make sure you see the area in the Before pane. Adjust the correction amount by typing a value, dragging the slider, or clicking the spinner arrows until you reach the value you want. For the best results, don't use more correction than you actually need.

Too much correction causes the highlight and shadow areas to lose their detail and blend together. Click the OK button when you are finished. Figure 6-6 shows a photograph before and after applying fade correction.

Figure 6-6
An image before and after making fade correction adjustments.

Using Contrast Enhancement

The Auto Contrast offers an instant contrast boost for those photos that may have too much darkness in them, perhaps from not enough flash or an incorrect light perspective. *Contrast* is defined as the measure in a picture of the tonal scale between black and white or the distribution of lightness values.

Typically, images with fewer tones have higher contrast. In most images, objects in the distance can be lower in contrast than the foreground objects, but all foreground objects should display the same contrast you'd expect from objects lit by the same illumination source.

When choosing a subject for a high-contrast image, make sure the most important part of the subject matter has one of the lightest tones in an image. If most of the tones in an image are too similar to each other, the image has a low contrast and appears flat or dull. If the tones are spread widely across the scale, the image's contrast is high.

As the contrast is boosted, the dark tones and most mid-tone areas will become black, while the lightest tones will remain white. If your key subject matter is too dark, it will turn black along with the other mid- and deep-tones and not be visible in your finished image.

You'll find PaintShop Pro's brightness and contrast enhancement feature useful for improving the tone distribution of your image. The following steps show you how to use the Brightness/Contrast controls:

1. From the Edit workspace, choose Adjust > Brightness and Contrast > Brightness/Contrast or press Shift+B, which displays the dialog box you see in Figure 6-7.

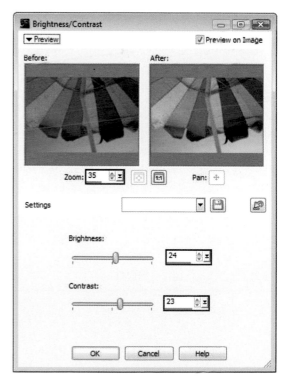

Figure 6-7
Use the Pan button to view different sections of your image.

121

2. In the Before pane, center an important part of the image. If needed, use the Pan button to locate the desired area. Zoom in or out as necessary.

3. Set the strength of the brightness or the contrast until the After pane displays the image correction you want. Brightness values range from −255 to +255, and Contrast values range from −100 to +100.

4. Click OK.

In Figure 6-8, the image on the left is before using Brightness/Contrast enhancement, and the image on the right is after adjusting the brightness and contrast.

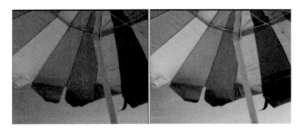

Figure 6-8
An image before and after adjusting the brightness and contrast.

Optional Method

You can also manage the brightness and contrast in the Adjust workspace.

Using Fill Light/Clarity

New to PaintShop Pro X4 is the Fill Light/Clarity option. When your image has dark shadows hiding much of your detail, try using the Fill Light feature. Fill Light works by opening and brightening dark shadows, thereby revealing more image detail. One advantage of Fill Light is that during the process of brightening shadows, Fill Light doesn't touch the image black point.

Clarity adjusts the image contrast, similar to Sharpening, but it does it by brightening the mid-shadows without touching the highlights. It doesn't touch the darkest shadows either. Clarity specifically finds the larger edges and adds contrast to them.

You adjust the Fill Light by following these steps:

1. Choose Adjust ❯ Brightness and Contrast ❯ Fill Light/Clarity, which displays the Fill Light/Clarity dialog box seen in Figure 6-9.

2. Slide the Fill Light slider to the right until your image appears the way you want it. Values range from 0 to 127, and the higher the setting, the lighter the shadows become.

3. Slide the Clarity slider to the right or left. Values range from −127 to 127. Positive values enhance the contrast, and negative values blur and soften the edges.

4. Click OK when you are finished.

I recommend you use Fill Light/Clarity with care. Overdoing it can ruin your shadows and contrast.

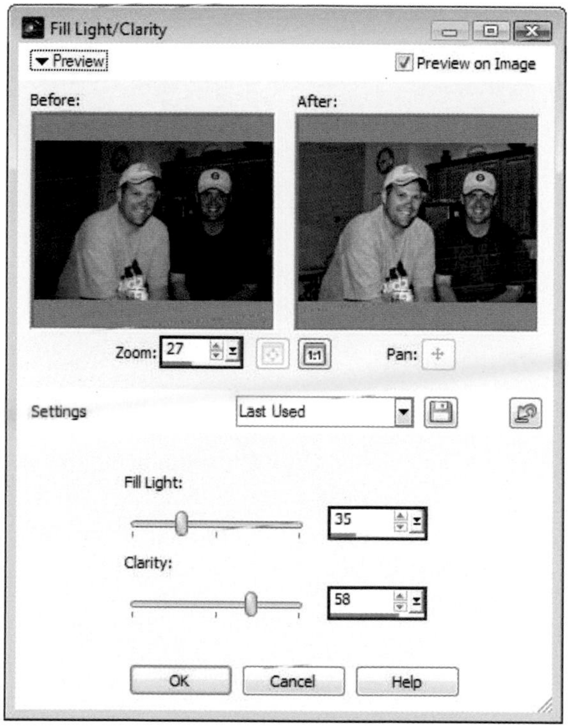

Figure 6-9
An image before and after adjusting Fill Light/Clarity.

Working with Hue and Saturation

One of the more common problems faced by photographers is photos with colors that are dull and appear washed out, or both; yet, when you took the image, you saw the image in vibrant beautiful color. The reason this happens is quite simple. The human eye dynamically allows you to see a greater range of colors than your camera. Cameras only record a fixed amount of red, green, and blue. Often these dull, drab images can be corrected by adjusting the saturation. Typically you'll want to adjust the hue and saturation after you have adjusted the brightness and contrast of your image.

Just what is hue and saturation? *Hue* is the expression of color values within a picture, and *saturation* is the intensity illustrating how much of the hue is composed of the pure color, and how much is diluted by a neutral color such as black or white. Saturation is more of a measure of how different a color is from a neutral gray of the same brightness.

An image with good color saturation can display subtle color changes distinctly so that the human eye perceives them as being different from one another. If similar colors blend together or if colors appear dark, they are oversaturated. Colors that appear washed out are undersaturated. If a color image is completely desaturated, it appears to be a grayscale image. Increasing the hue and saturation values can give your image brighter, more vibrant color.

PaintShop Pro includes a Hue and Saturation command that is useful for improving the image by automatically adapting to the color content of each image. This feature is most effective when used across an entire photo, without selections, because then the entire range of colors is available for analysis.

The following steps show you how to adjust the image hue and saturation:

1. Choose Adjust ❯ Hue and Saturation ❯ Hue/Saturation/Lightness, which displays the dialog box you see in Figure 6-10.

Optional Keyboard Method

Optionally, press Shift+H to open the Hue/Saturation/Lightness dialog box.

123

Figure 6-10
Shift your image colors through this dialog box.

4. If desired, select a preset from the Settings drop-down menu, or make your selections manually:

- Adjust the Hue slider left to right, which also changes the rotation on the color wheel. A positive value indicates a clockwise rotation and increased hue, and a negative value indicates a counter-clockwise rotation and decreased hue. Hue values range from −180 to +180.

- Drag the Saturation slider up or down. Saturation values range from −100 to +100, with a negative value decreasing the saturation.

- Drag the Lightness slider up or down. Lightness values range from −100 to +100, with a positive value increasing the lightness.

5. Click OK to accept the changes and close the Hue/Saturation/Lightness dialog box.

Figure 6-11 shows the result of choosing the preset option Aged Color Shift. This option gives a completely different appearance to the original image.

2. In the Before pane, center an important part of the image. If needed, use the Pan button to locate the desired area. Zoom in or out as necessary.

3. From the Edit drop-down list, choose Master if you want to change all the colors at once, or choose an individual color if you want to edit a specific color range.

Figure 6-11
An image before and after adjusting the Hue/Saturation/Lightness values.

Removing Noise

I'm one of those people who don't like a lot of noise. When I'm driving, I rarely listen to the radio or play CDs, as I prefer the silence of my thoughts and the ability to absorb the beauty around me. Similarly, I don't like the distraction of having the television going when I'm trying to read or write. In photographic images, the same idea applies. Keep the noise and distraction away. Digital noise appears as tiny speckles that appear on the image and distract from the subject matter.

Figure 6-12
Digital camera noise.

Most digital images contain some noise, some more than others, and usually result from taking photos with the camera set at extreme high-speed levels, but with longer than normal exposure. Many high-end digital cameras offer noise reduction features, but you can remove most unwanted noise with PaintShop Pro. A noise reduction tool should remove objectionable noise but still retain a natural low level of noise.

DIGITAL CAMERA NOISE

There are several types of digital noise, and before you determine which PaintShop Pro feature you use, you need to determine the type of noise you want to eliminate. If the image noise is relatively constant throughout the image, similar to sensor noise or film grain, the Digital Camera Noise Removal (DCNR) is the tool best suited for you. Generally, the DCNR does not remove impulse noise, JPEG artifacts, or moiré patterns.

Figure 6-12 illustrates camera noise. I've circled the area in question to make it easier for you to see.

Overall, the DCNR feature works like this. The filter automatically scrutinizes the image to determine uniform areas in shadow, midtone, and highlight regions. Each pixel is examined and compared to what is expected for a noise-free image having that particular color and lightness. This is done for every scale of image noise, taking image texture into account. By a complicated mathematical calculation, a resulting pixel is computed as a combination of the original image along with different proportions of luminance (the amount of light that passes through a particular area) and chrominance (the quality of light that causes the sensation of color) smoothed at different scales. During this process, edges in the image are smoothed to preserve the edge information. The result is an image in which each pixel has its own unique combination of luminance and chrominance.

To launch the DCNR filter, from the Edit workspace, click the Adjust menu and choose Digital Noise Removal. You'll see a Digital Noise Remover dialog box like the one shown in Figure 6-13.

Figure 6-13
Like many other PaintShop Pro dialog boxes,
the DCNR filter provides a range of settings to
control the quality of the result.

PaintShop Pro places two sampling markers on
the image, but you can move the sampling
markers to other areas of the image. Position the
mouse in the middle of the sampling marker.
Your mouse turns into a four-headed arrow.
Drag the box to the area you want to sample.

The DCNR filter works best with at least three
noise samples in the image. Place one in the
shadow areas, one in the midtone areas, and one
in the highlight area. In other words, select a
sampling from a dark area, a light area, and an
area in between. Another trick in DCNR sampling is that, if the image contains large distinct
regions of different hues, such as red, green,
blue, or yellow, it may be helpful to place a
sample in each hue region even though these
regions may have similar brightness values.

If you want to create more sampling areas, in
the Before pane, drag the cursor over the areas
you want to correct, which creates a correction
box in the Before pane and places the additional
crosshair in the Sample Areas window. You can
have a maximum of ten sampling regions,
although three or four are typically sufficient.

Sampling Areas to Avoid

**Avoid sampling pure black and pure
white areas of the image, as these areas
may result in underestimated noise. Also,
avoid sampling image edges, as this can
result in excessive smoothing.**

You need to select sampling areas, which are
indicated by small boxes in the Before pane.
(If you don't see a Before and After pane, click
Preview.) In each sampling area, PaintShop Pro
makes a separate analysis of the noise, determining whether it finds small-scale, medium-scale,
or large-scale noise. We'll learn more about noise
scale a little later in this section.

Now you need to select the setting for the sampling areas. There are three levels of noise details: Small, Medium, and Large. Each visual noise level equates to audio noise levels of "fairly quiet," "busy noise," and "rambunctiously loud" or, as they would be known around my house, "the dog snoring," "the television on," and "the kids fighting over a crayon" type noise.

Each of the Small, Medium, and Large detail sliders in the Noise Correction group controls how much noise is removed at each of the scales. You can control each noise level independently or keep them linked. Most of the time, keeping the levels linked produces the best result. The higher the setting of each slider, the more noise of that scale is removed, but higher settings can also destroy image detail.

Next is the Correction blend setting. During the correction process, the DCNR creates a "de-noised" image, which is then blended with the original image. The Correction blend setting determines how much of the corrected image and the original image you want to blend. Values range from 0%, which is no noise reduction, to 100%, which is full noise reduction; the default is 70%. If you were to blend at 100%, your image would have no natural noise in it, resulting in an overly smoothed image.

The last correction setting on the Remove Noise tab is the Sharpening setting. Just like it sounds, this setting controls the percentage of sharpening you want to add back to the image after the noise reduction. The control does not function like a conventional sharpening filter so, typically, this control is best left at around 10. We'll discuss sharpening in more detail later in this chapter.

If you have specific areas of the image that you want to protect from noise correction, click the Protect Image tab and, while holding down the Ctrl key, click the mouse over the region you want to protect.

Click OK to accept your DCNR settings.

Optional Method

You can also repair the digital noise in the Adjust workspace.

IMPULSE NOISE

Sometimes, image noise occurs in specific parts of the image rather than over the entire image. This is known as *impulse noise*, and examples of impulse noise might be stuck sensor pixels, hot pixels visible at long exposures, or specks of dust on a print or slide. To remove impulse noise, you might want to look at one of PaintShop Pro's many other noise removal features. Here are just a few of the noise removal features available under the Adjust > Add/Remove Noise menu:

▶ **Despeckle:** The Despeckle command can remove subtle graininess from an image. It works by examining the brightness of each pixel in comparison to surrounding pixels.

▶ **Edge Preserving Smooth:** Use the Edge Preserving Smooth command to remove noise in an image without losing edge details. This command finds details such as object edges and preserves them, while smoothing the areas between the edges.

When selecting Edge Preserving Smooth options, it's best to choose the smallest amount of smoothing that removes the specks, while retaining image detail. The Edge Preserving Smooth command is also helpful to minimize film grain. See Figure 6-14 for a look at the Edge Preserving Smooth dialog box.

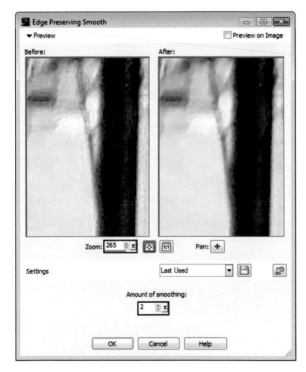

Figure 6-14
Edge Preserving Smooth changes are best viewed under a high zoom ratio.

▶ **Median Filter**: The Median Filter command is similar to the Despeckle command in that it subtly removes areas of noise in the image. The difference between the Despeckle command and the Median Filter command is that, instead of comparing neighboring pixel brightness, Median Filter calculates an average value of the nearby pixels and applies the result to the area in question.

▶ **Texture Preserving Smooth**: Use the Texture Preserving Smooth command to remove noise or specks in an image while preserving texture details. This command examines an image's pixels to determine if they display textured or smooth areas. Few noise adjustments are made in textured areas, and smooth areas are adjusted to remove noise. For example, if you are looking at a prairie scene, noise may be excessive for a face or sky, which we know to be smooth in real life, but we expect the grassy areas to have some texture or noise. The Texture Preserving Smooth command can remove the noise from the sky but leave it present in the grassy area.

DUST SPOT NOISE

Many images pick up dust spots that need touching up. The spots could come from dust on a scanner bed, the camera lens, or any number of places. The bottom line is that you will want to clean those up.

PaintShop Pro includes a wonderful noise filter, called the Salt and Pepper filter, which can remove black or white specks, such as those caused by dust. The Salt and Pepper filter works by comparing an area of pixels to the surrounding pixels and adjusting an area that is a speck to match those surrounding pixels.

You can remove the dust from a selected area of your image or from the entire image. To illustrate this, look at the old photo seen in Figure 6-15. As you can see, this photograph needs quite a few fixes, including dust spot removal.

Choose the Salt and Pepper filter by selecting Adjust > Add/Remove Noise > Salt and Pepper Filter. The Salt and Pepper Filter dialog box shown in Figure 6-16 appears. In the Before pane, I've put a box around some of the dust-spotted areas.

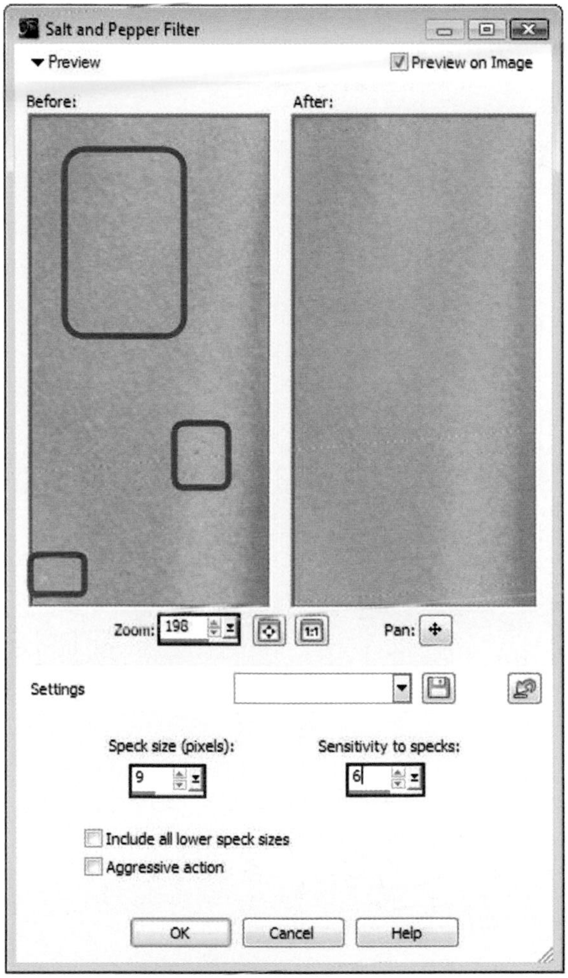

Figure 6-15
An old photograph that needs dust removal.

Figure 6-16
The Salt and Pepper dialog box.

The Salt and Pepper filter uses the following options:

- ▶ **Speck Size**: Establishes the minimum size in pixels of the largest speck that you want PaintShop Pro to remove. The value is always an odd number.

- ▶ **Sensitivity to Specks**: Determines how different an area must be from its surrounding pixels to be considered a speck.

- ▶ **Include All Lower Speck Sizes**: Check this box if you want PaintShop Pro to remove all lower speck sizes. Results are usually better if you mark this check box.

- ▶ **Aggressive Action**: Tells PaintShop Pro how hard to work in correcting the dust spots.

Select the settings you want to use and click OK to remove dust specks from your photograph.

Sharpening Your Images

High *acutance*, or sharpness, is a photography fundamental. Photography awards are won and lost because of sharpness. A problem arises with digital photography or scanning that can make edges appear blurred because of detail being lost during the digitization process.

Can you ever recover the lost detail? Not really, but through sharpening, you can make it appear as though you have. By increasing differences between neighboring pixels, PaintShop Pro enhances image edges, thereby making them appear sharper, whether they really are or not.

You can use sharpening commands to enhance detail in photos, but remember that none of the sharpening commands can add detail that was not saved in the original image. PaintShop Pro includes a number of different tools you can use to sharpen your images: High Pass Sharpen, Sharpen, Sharpen More, and Unsharp Mask. Each has a specific use, but most professionals prefer the High Pass Sharpen or the Unsharp Mask tool over the others.

Apply Sharpening Last

You should not apply sharpening effects until you are finished with other corrections, including color and tone. Sharpening should be the last effect you should apply. This general rule applies to all sharpening tools.

Sharpen and Sharpen More improve image clarity by increasing the contrast between adjacent pixels, where there are significant color contrasts, usually at the mid- and high-contrast image edges. Just like it sounds, the Sharpen More command sharpens with a stronger effect than the Sharpen command. PaintShop Pro automatically applies these commands to the image without input from you, but it also tends to tweak the wrong parts of a picture and make it look grainy, like an old 35mm photo. While the Sharpen commands may be faster and easier, you lose a great deal of control over the sharpening, so a lot of photographers don't use them anymore. Access the Sharpen and Sharpen More commands by clicking the Adjust menu and selecting Sharpness.

Unsharp Mask, like Sharpen and Sharpen More, works more on the mid- to high-contrast edges of an image, but you have much more control over the process. Despite what its name indicates, Unsharp Mask actually sharpens your image. The principle behind it is exaggerating the light-dark contrast between the two sides of an edge.

The process actually mimics a traditional film compositing technique by taking two or more copies of the image, manipulating them, and then merging them. One copy is translated into a negative image, while the others are slightly blurred. The images are then combined; the light areas of the blurred images cancel out the dark areas of the negative, but the blurring around the edges has nothing to cancel them out, which results in lighter and darker lines on either side of the edges. That, in turn, adds the appearance of sharpness.

You access the PaintShop Pro Unsharp Mask feature by selecting Adjust ❯ Sharpness ❯ Unsharp Mask. You'll then see a dialog box like the one in Figure 6 17.

There are three settings for the Unsharp Mask feature: Radius, Strength, and Clipping. Let's take a look at what each of these settings does.

▶ **Radius**: The Radius setting determines the number of pixels to adjust around each edge. The practical effect of this is to specify how large a region is darkened or lightened. As this number increases, so does the apparent sharpness of the image. Setting too high a number, though, can result in harsh edges with lighter pixels around all the edges, especially if you also increase the Strength setting. The range is from .01 to 100, but the default setting is only 2. Lower values sharpen only the

edge pixels, while higher values sharpen a wider band of pixels. The effect is much less noticeable in print than onscreen, because a small radius (for example, 1 pixel) represents a smaller area in a high-resolution printed image. Therefore, use lower values for onscreen images and higher values for high-resolution printed images.

The main thing to keep in mind is the original resolution of your image. Low-resolution images can't benefit from much more than one to three pixels' worth of edge sharpening, while higher-resolution images can accommodate values of 10 or more. You'll know right away if you have set your values too high because you will see thick, poster-like edges that aren't realistic, accompanied by a high degree of contrast.

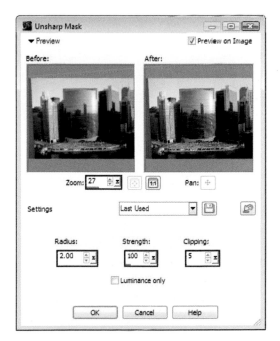

Figure 6-17
Use the Unsharp Mask dialog box to sharpen your image.

▶ **Strength**: The Strength setting refers to how much sharpening you are applying. In other words, it controls the contrast change along the edges in your photo, making dark colors darker and light colors lighter. The Strength range is from 1 to 500, with 100 being the default. As a general rule, 100% to 150% is the most useful range for this variable. Start with the default and see if you like the effect; if not, increase it gradually.

Use Strength Cautiously

Be careful about increasing Strength too much; you can end up with a noisy photo with harsh edges and too much contrast.

▶ **Clipping**: The Clipping setting determines how much contrast must exist between the pixels before the filter will be applied to an area. Low contrast equals a blurry, soft image, whereas high contrast tends to mean a sharp, hard image. A very low setting means that edges with relatively small contrast differences will be accentuated. High settings mean that the difference must be great before any additional sharpening is applied. The Clipping setting has a range of 0 to 100, with a default setting of 5. Normally, you'll need to change the Clipping only when the default value produces an image with excessive noise or some other undesirable effect. Try setting the Radius and Strength settings first; then experiment with Clipping to see if you like the results any better.

Also, remember that all three of these values work together. If you use a high Clipping value because your picture was taken in low light and suffers from some digital noise, you may want to increase the Strength to 150% to beef up the sharpening effect.

Obviously, the Unsharp Mask tool is extremely useful, but it also has a problem in that it can increase any noise present in the file. Particularly noisy photographs, therefore, can suffer when Unsharp Mask is applied. In that situation, you may want to use the High Pass Sharpen filter.

The High Pass Sharpen filter emphasizes color transitions between highlights and shadow colors. The High Pass Sharpen filter also preserves the contrast of edges and areas of high detail, while leaving the rest of the image a neutral gray. From the Edit workspace, choose the filter by selecting Adjust ❯ Sharpness ❯ High Pass Sharpen. The High Pass Sharpen dialog box seen in Figure 6-18 allows you to set a radius and strength, similar to the Unsharp Mask, but it also has an option for a Blend mode. You can also apply the High Pass Sharpen filter from the Adjust workspace.

Chapter 8, "Developing Layers," explains Blend modes when you work with layers. Although you don't actually create a new layer with the High Pass Sharpen filter, the effect is available with three different blend modes:

▶ **Hard Light**: Adds highlights and shadows

▶ **Soft Light**: Adds soft highlights or shadows

▶ **Overlay**: Adds a blend of both hard and soft light in that it retains the colors and patterns but still preserves the image shadows and highlights

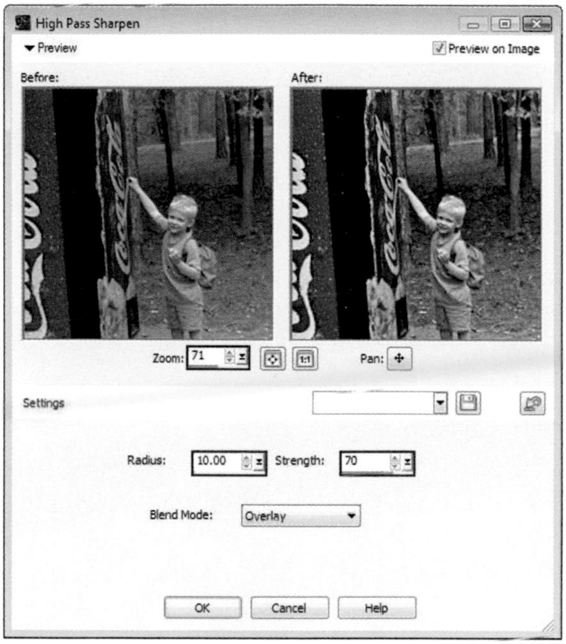

Figure 6-18
The High Pass Sharpen dialog box.

Adding Depth of Field

One mark of a professionally created photograph is depth of field. *Depth of field* is the amount of distance between the nearest and farthest objects that appear in a photograph. Photographers often provide their images with depth of field by using expensive lenses and special camera settings. If not, you can replicate the effect using the PaintShop Pro depth of field adjustment feature.

Depth of field can be quite subjective in that what is adequate depth of field for one image may be unacceptable for another. It is all a matter of personal preference when trying to determine the appropriate use of depth of field to enhance an effect in a photograph.

Depth of field does not abruptly change from sharp to unsharp, but it instead occurs as a gradual transition. In fact, everything immediately in front of or in back of the focusing distance begins to lose sharpness. Follow these steps to add PaintShop Pro's depth of field adjustment:

1. Open the image you want to modify and choose Adjust ❯ Depth of Field. The Depth of Field dialog box seen in Figure 6-19 appears.

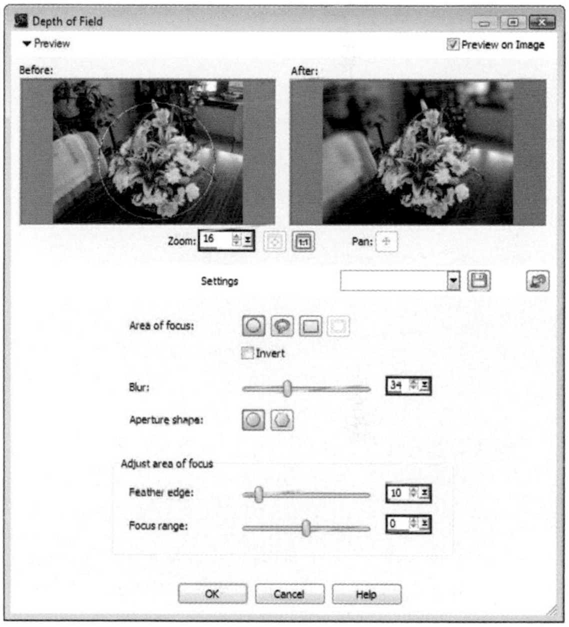

Figure 6-19
The Depth of Field dialog box.

Be Patient

Each time you change a setting in the Depth of Field dialog box, PaintShop Pro updates the After pane. The depth of field process is complex, and it may take a moment to display the After picture.

2. The first setting you use indicates the image area you want to focus on. The focus area is the area that stays sharp, and everything outside of the focus area gets blurred. There are three ways to select the focus area. You can draw a circle around the area, draw a rectangle around the area, or use the Freehand Selection tool. Select the tool you want to use.

No Preselection Allowed

If you designate a selection area before opening the Depth of Field dialog box, PaintShop Pro ignores the selection area. You must select the modification area from inside the Depth of Field dialog box.

3. Next, in the Before pane, click and drag the mouse until the area you want to keep sharpened is in the marquee. If you want to reverse your selection area, click the Invert check box.

4. Now you need to adjust the Blur slider. The higher you set the control, the more blur PaintShop Pro applies to the background (unselected area).

5. Choose either a circular or a hexagonal aperture shape. The aperture shape affects the blurred area.

6. Experiment with the Feather Edge settings. The Feather Edge control makes the transition between the edge of the selected area and the nonselected area gradual and smooth.

7. If necessary, increase or decrease the Focus Range control, which increases or decreases the size of your selection.

8. Click the OK button. Figure 6-20 illustrates a before and after picture.

Figure 6-20
An image before and after applying depth of field.

Adjusting Lightness Levels

Another way to adjust image brightness and contrast, as well as gamma, is with the Levels command with which you can improve the exposure of your photo. Adjusting the gamma changes the brightness values of middle gray tones. You can apply the adjustments directly to the image or to an adjustment layer.

Apply to Limited Area

Select an area prior to choosing the Levels command to limit the correction to a specific area.

Choose Adjust ➤ Brightness and Contrast ➤ Levels (see Figure 6-21).

You can adjust the red, green, and blue (called RGB) channels together or independently by selecting an option in the Channel drop-down list.

The black diamond indicates the image's brightness values; you can increase the contrast by dragging the black diamond to the right to darken the dark values. Drag the clear diamond to the left to lighten the lighter values. To change the value of medium gray, drag the gray Gamma diamond left or right.

Figure 6-22 illustrates the image before and after adjusting the levels.

Black diamond   Gamma diamond   Clear diamond

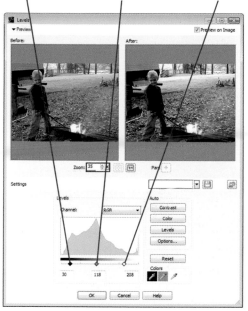

Figure 6-21
Change the individual channel brightness levels with this dialog box.

Figure 6-22
Correct exposure using the Levels adjustment.

Recalling Histograms

You've already discovered several PaintShop Pro tools to adjust color, contrast, and brightness, but one way to view the image tonal values is the Histogram tool, which provides a useful graphical representation of the Red, Green, Blue, Grayscale, Hue, Saturation, and Lightness values in your image. Casual users may not want to use the Histogram tool, but for image-editing professionals, the Histogram is a powerful tool for understanding and correcting images.

A histogram consists of a series of up to 256 different vertical lines in a graph, arranged horizontally with the black tones represented on the left side of the graph, the white tones at the right side, and the middle tones located (you guessed it) in the middle of the graph. The taller each of the lines is, the more tones are present at that brightness level. A typical histogram has one or more peaks, and the black-and-white tones often don't extend to the theoretical limits possible for the image (0 for pure black at the left side and 255 for pure white at the right side).

As a general example, if you are working with an overexposed photo, you might see most of the tones concentrated at the right side of the histogram, whereas an underexposed photograph might have most of the tones concentrated on the left side. With such an image, you could analyze the image weaknesses using the Histogram tool and then use the other PaintShop Pro adjustment tools to correct the problem.

PaintShop Pro includes a Histogram palette, which you can display or hide as needed by pressing the F7 key or selecting View > Palettes > Histogram.

Select a Specific Area First

Select an area to limit the Histogram tool to the selection area.

The histogram graph, like the one you see in Figure 6-23, represents how many pixels are at each value in the selected channel. The vertical axis is the number of pixels from zero to the highest number. The horizontal axis represents the 0 to 255 value for each channel. Use the check boxes to turn on or off the display of the various channels.

Here's how a histogram works:

- If a line spikes, there are lots of pixels in that value range.

- If a line is relatively flat and close to the horizontal axis, there aren't many pixels in that value range.

- If the graph is spread out, the image is probably pretty balanced and can be easily corrected if needed.

- If the lines are compressed into a narrow area, the image probably doesn't contain enough detail to be easily corrected.

- If the grayscale is mostly on the left, the image is probably too dark; if the grayscale is mostly on the right, the image is probably too light.

- If the grayscale lines aren't spread out much, you might want to increase the contrast.

Channel selections   Statistical information

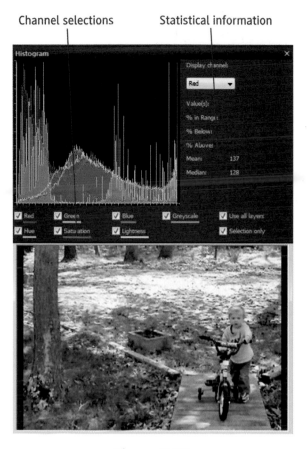

Figure 6-23
The curves of the histogram tell a story about
the photo's tonal values.

▶ **Value(s)**: Value shows the count or quantity (from 0 to 255) of the point over which the cursor is positioned in the graph.

▶ **% in Range**: This statistic displays the percent of image pixels that are the value of the selected point or range. The number in parentheses is the number of pixels that are the selected value. For example, if the Percentile reads 70, pixels are brighter than 70% of all the pixels in the image.

▶ **% Below**: This represents the percentage of image pixels that are below the value of the selected point or range.

▶ **% Above**: The percent of image pixels that are above the value of the selected point or range.

▶ **Mean**: This represents the average intensity value of all the pixels in the image. If the number is low, it will confirm that the image is rather dark; a high number means that the image is, on average, very bright.

▶ **Median**: The median is the middle number in the range of intensity values; half the individual values are higher than the median, while half are lower.

A couple of other available options on the Histogram palette include the Use All Layers box which, if checked, graphs all layers in the image, and the Selection Only box which, when marked, graphs only the active selection.

The numeric display at the right of the palette probably looks like a lot of mumbo jumbo at first glance, but as you become experienced using the Histogram palette, you'll find this information increasingly valuable. It displays statistical information regarding the various channels and the image pixels:

You can't actually change levels from the Histogram palette, but you view the results of the changes as you make them by using the other PaintShop Pro commands.

Repairing Distortion

Sometimes pictures can suffer from lens distortion issues, including *barrel distortion*, where the subject lines bow outward, making the subject appear spherical, or from *pincushion distortion*, where the subject lines bow inward and look pinched at their center. Although distortion is frequently found in cameras with inexpensive lenses such as disposables, you'll sometimes find it in digital camera images, too. Digital camera lenses must be wider than their film counterparts to capture the same area. As a result, pictures taken with digital cameras can suffer from lens distortion. Typically, you'll find that wide-angle lenses, especially when used at their extremes, can cause barrel distortion, and telephoto or zoom lenses, again when used at their extreme settings, can cause pincushion distortion.

Another type of lens distortion is called *fisheye*. Fisheyed images look like they have been pasted onto a sphere or blown up like a balloon. Lines that should be straight are curved, and edges look compressed. Unwanted fisheye distortion is rare.

In general, distortion is most noticeable when you have a straight edge near the side of the image frame. Take a look at the images in Figure 6-24. The image on the bottom shows no distortion, but the image on the top has quite a bit of barrel distortion. The street curb is curved, and the building almost looks full, like it could pop at any moment.

Figure 6-24
Barrel distortion causes the subject to bow outward.

Fortunately, PaintShop Pro includes correction tools to manage image distortion. For the lens corrections to work properly, the axis of the camera lens must coincide with the center of the image; therefore, you should apply any lens distortion corrections before you crop your image.

Follow these steps to remove lens distortion:

1. Turn on the grid for a point of reference (View > Grid).

2. Click the Adjust menu and, at the bottom menu, you'll see the three lens correction options: Barrel, Fisheye, and Pincushion Distortion Correction. Select the option you want to use. A dialog box, similar to the one seen in Figure 6-25, will open.

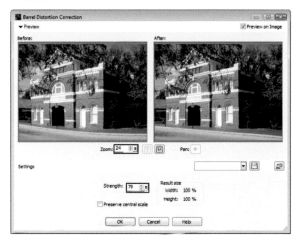

Figure 6-25
The image is resized as you adjust the strength.

3. Focus your attention on horizontal or vertical elements that are curved, and adjust the settings until the elements become straight. As you change the settings, the After pane displays the reformed image.

Preview on Image

Click the Preview on Image button to see the effect on the image against the grid.

4. Select whether you want PaintShop Pro to preserve the central scale of the image. This option determines whether the scale of the center of the picture remains the same or is adjusted. If you don't check the box, PaintShop Pro will not change the image size, but if the box is checked, PaintShop Pro adds or removes pixels to or from the image. The resulting size ratio is displayed in the Result size area.

5. Click OK. PaintShop Pro removes the distortion—in this example, barrel distortion.

Take a look at Figure 6-26, which displays an image before and after correcting a fisheye distortion. In this example, I selected the Preserve Central Scale option which then, along with correcting the distortion, removed pixels and cropped the image.

Figure 6-26
Correcting image distortion.

Changing Perspective

Sometimes, especially when you're taking photographs of tall objects, the images may appear to lean. This is called Perspective Distortion, and it usually occurs when you are holding the camera at an angle to the subject.

You can often correct this distortion by using the Perspective Correction tool. The concept behind the tool is that you will designate the object that should be straightened using the grid lines you see when you select the tool. The grid lines help you delineate the subject; when they're applied, the image is cropped, so the angle disappears. Be aware that because it does crop your image, you may lose some areas around the outside. Follow these steps to use the Perspective Correction tool:

1. From the Tools toolbar, click the Perspective Correction tool. It's the sixth tool down and shares a space with the Straighten tool. After you select the tool, a boundary box with handles appears.

2. On the Tool Options palette, if it's not already selected, click the Crop Image check box. After you apply the perspective, this option crops the image to a rectangular shape. It crops the areas outside the boundary box.

3. On the Tool Options palette, set the number of grid lines you want to display. In Figure 6-27, I chose 7 because I see 6 vertical areas in the building, and I threw in one more for good measure.

4. Drag each handle of the boundary box to a corner of the subject—in this example, the building.

5. Click the Apply button.

Boundary box   Boundary box handles

Figure 6-27
Setting the area for perspective correction.

Figure 6-28 illustrates our image before and after correcting the perspective. Notice the disappearance of much of the blue sky.

Figure 6-28
Changing perspective.

Restore Cropped Data

If the correction causes some image data to fall outside the image canvas, you can restore that data by increasing the size of the canvas. Choose Image > Canvas size.

Adjusting Lighting

One of the hardest things to get right in a photograph is the lighting. Too much light, too little light, or a combination of the two can ruin an otherwise perfect photo.

But PaintShop Pro can provide two lighting effects to repair an incorrectly lit image. Let's look at backlighting and fill flash, first to understand what each type of lighting does, and then to learn how PaintShop Pro can help.

When the sun is in front of the photographer, coming directly at the camera, you have what is referred to as *backlighting*; that means the light is behind the subject. Backlighting can produce some wonderful images, but learning how to backlight can be tricky. This type of lighting can be effective for pictures of people outdoors in bright sunlight because, in bright sunlight, the sun might hurt their eyes, causing them to squint. Backlighting helps to eliminate this problem.

Backlighting is just as it sounds: light that comes from behind your subject. This can make a beautiful photo, or it can turn a beautiful photo into a disaster. Backlighting is what turns a palm tree into a silhouette against the sunset. In this case, backlighting is a good thing that adds to the photograph.

But the same thing can happen if you want to take a photograph of a person who has a strong backlight behind him, such as the sun, sky, or bright lights. The camera reads the brightness behind the main subject and sets its internal meter to expose properly for the extra light. This underexposes your subject and usually turns it into a silhouette. You can avoid this by using a fill flash. A fill flash fills in the needed light, chasing away the shadows from your subject caused from the bright light behind.

BACKLIGHTING

Backlighting is also used to produce a silhouette effect. If a subject is translucent or semitranslucent, like flower petals, delicate leaves, or even jellyfish, backlighting can reveal the object's internal details and often make it glow with beautiful iridescence.

However, too much backlighting can cause a problem by washing out the entire image. A similar problem involves photos with too much flash on the subject. If your images appear too dark or washed out to see all the details, chances are your digital camera captured all the information you needed to lighten or darken areas in your photos, and it pulled out the details in the development process. PaintShop Pro includes a backlighting filter to help you darken the bright, overexposed areas of a photo.

Click the Adjust menu, and then select Backlighting. PaintShop Pro displays the Backlighting Filter dialog box that you see in Figure 6-29.

Figure 6-29
Experiment with the Strength setting until you get the best result for your image.

The Strength setting determines how much you want PaintShop Pro to darken the lighter areas, and the Saturation setting controls the overall dispersion of the photo's colors.

FILL FLASH

Another lighting problem occurs when photos taken in bright light have little detail in the shadow areas because the camera is attempting *not* to overexpose the brighter areas. If you have taken outdoor photos of people without a flash, chances are the subjects' faces were too dark or had harsh shadows under the eyes.

But you already know that on a bright day, if you place the subject so that his back is to the sun, it keeps him from squinting. The problem is that the existing daylight may not be enough to illuminate your subject properly. A brief burst of light from a flash, called *fill flash*, can add sparkle to the eyes and soften harsh shadows.

The PaintShop Pro fill flash filter lightens the darker, underexposed areas of a photo. If your photo background is too dark, or you feel there's too much difference between the photo light and dark areas, this filter is a good choice to correct that problem. In people pictures, this usually means dark eye sockets and unattractive shadows under the nose and lips. The fill flash filter lightens these shadows to create more attractive portraits (see Figure 6-30).

Figure 6-30
The fill flash allows you to see more detail
in the men's faces.

Figure 6-31
See more detail in your image after using the
fill flash filter.

Fill flash is not limited to people pictures. Take a look at Figure 6-31. Here you see some beautiful flowers, but the leaves are very dark. After adding the fill flash filter, you can see more detail in the leaves.

To apply the fill flash filter, click the Adjust menu and choose Fill Flash. PaintShop Pro displays the Fill Flash Filter dialog box where, similar to the Backlighting Filter dialog box, you select the strength of the light you want to apply.

Working with Black, White, and Grayscale

When it comes to converting color images to black-and-white images, you have several choices. The method you select depends both on the look you want for your image and the image itself. Some photographs lend themselves better to one way over another.

Let's try three different methods using the two different images you see here:

Figure 6-32
Images converted to grayscale have a tendency to look a little flat.

The first method is to use PaintShop Pro's grayscale conversion feature. When you convert an image to grayscale, PaintShop Pro changes the color depth to 8 bit and uses a palette that contains white, black, and 254 shades of gray. The Greyscale function is under the Image menu and offers no options; it simply converts the photo by replacing each pixel in the image with a gray that matches its Lightness value.

Figure 6-32 illustrates our two images after using the Image, Greyscale command.

The second method involves simply removing the color saturation by using the Hue/Saturation/Lightness tool in the original image. Click the Adjust menu, select Hue and Saturation, and then select Hue/Saturation/Lightness. Set Saturation to −100, which removes all color from the image. Then click OK.

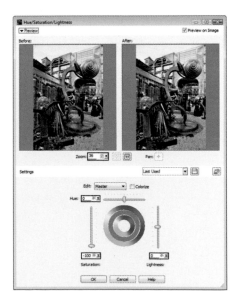

Using this method produces the images as you see them in Figure 6-33.

Figure 6-33
Using this method can bring out some details but leave other areas looking a little dull.

The third method takes a little more work on your part, but it can produce some interesting results. It uses the Channel Mixer command, which you access by clicking Adjust ❯ Color ❯ Channel Mixer.

First, you need to change the image to monochrome, which looks like a grayscale but has a color depth of 16 million colors. To do this, if it's not already selected, check the Monochrome check box. The Output Channel drop-down list displays Grey. When you adjust the color channels in the next step, you change the amount of each channel that is used to create the monochrome image.

Black and white is a personal preference, and everyone is different, so you need to experiment with the Gray Source channel settings until your image takes on the look you want. By adjusting these figures, you are reducing the amount of the color by a percentage. For example, if you are editing the Red channel and set the Red value to 50%, you reduce the amount of red in the image to 50% of its original amount. You'll probably also need to lighten or darken the color channel by setting a Constant value (see Figure 6-34).

Figure 6-34
Using the Channel Mixer produced a dramatic effect.

So, as you can see, in Figure 6-35 which illustrates the three different variations, each option produces different results. There's no right or wrong method when converting images to black and white. It depends on your taste and the image itself.

Figure 6-35
Choose the method most pleasing to you.

Working with RAW Files

MOST DIGITAL CAMERAS PROCESS and compress the pictures you take immediately after capturing the image. This can be helpful, because it keeps your file sizes low by using JPEG compression. It also automatically takes care of color correction, including white balance, tint, and exposure. However, many professional photographers prefer to have more control over how each image is processed. Many of the higher-end cameras in today's market can shoot in RAW mode. RAW mode does not compress the images and leaves them completely unprocessed, giving you more data to work with. For example, a RAW photo comprises up to 16,384 levels of brightness as compared to a processed JPG photo, which contains 256 brightness levels.

RAW image files are sometimes called *digital negatives*, because they fulfill the same role as negatives in film photography: that is, the negative is not directly usable as an image, but it has all the information needed to create an image. With the image still in a "negative" state, you couldn't easily print or edit it with a graphics editor like PaintShop Pro. Until now.

Early PaintShop Pro versions didn't include a RAW camera lab where you could process your images the way you want them. You had to have third-party software to manage the RAW photograph. But beginning with the previous version, PaintShop Photo Pro, a RAW image converter is included. Therefore, you have complete control over the image, which you can then leave as a read-only RAW file or export to an editable JPG, GIF, PNG, or other file type.

JPG and the other file types are widely used because they are small, and just about any program can read them because they are an industry standard format. They are small because they are created with a lossy compression, which, as the phrase implies, loses some data. Sometimes the loss can be noticeable.

But having your digital camera save in JPG format means that all the in-camera settings for color balance, color temperature, sharpening, and so forth are processed by the camera and embedded in the file.

RAW files are in a special format unique to each camera manufacturer. The files are compressed losslessly, so they lose no information in this compression. No sharpening or white balance is applied in the camera, which in turn, through PaintShop Pro, gives you more correction and adjustment flexibility without degrading the final image quality.

One of the few disadvantages of working with RAW files is that they are not compressed. They are bigger in size—often two to three times bigger than compressed images—and so require more storage space on your camera's memory card and computer hard drive. But to a professional photographer, the ability to control the finest details, such as the white-balance, tint, hue, and exposure adjustments, far outweighs the disadvantages.

Using the RAW Image Editor

RAW image files include a separate header file that stores information such as white balance, temperature, and saturation settings. You can adjust these settings in the Camera RAW Lab in PaintShop Pro. The Camera RAW Lab includes a number of processing settings for developing a RAW image file.

The easiest way to get a RAW image into the Camera RAW Lab is to select the image thumbnail from the Manage workspace and click the Edit tab. Because the image is a RAW file, the Camera RAW Lab dialog box seen in Figure 6-36 opens with the image automatically.

Figure 6-36
The Camera RAW Lab dialog box.

Supported RAW Formats

Different camera manufacturers use their own proprietary format. Often they also change the format from one camera model to the next, and PaintShop Pro works with most of them. If you want an updated list of supported camera models and their RAW file formats, go to www.corel.com and search the Corel Knowledge Base for RAW.

There are quite a few adjustment settings in the Camera RAW Lab dialog box:

▶ **Brightness**: The image lightness or darkness. Ranges from −3 to 3.

▶ **Saturation**: The dispersion of colors throughout the image. Ranges from −100 to 100.

▶ **Shadows**: The shading that appears around image areas. Ranges from 0 to 100.

▶ **Scenario**: A collection of lighting scenarios.

▶ **Temperature**: The color temperature of the White Balance setting. Ranges from 2000 to 15000.

▶ **Tint**: Overall tonal image tint. Ranges from −100 to 100.

▶ **Highlight recovery**: A collection of options that typically are used on images that are overexposed.

▶ **Threshold**: Reduces digital noise, which is color specs or graininess that appears on some images. Ranges from 0 to 100.

There is also a histogram that is dynamically updated as you make changes in the dialog box. See "Recalling Histograms" earlier in this chapter. Adjust any of the controls until the image takes the appearance you want.

To keep the selected image settings so that they will be applied to the RAW photo each time you open it, mark the Save Image Settings check box. PaintShop Pro saves the setting in the RAW file header. To start over, click the Reset button.

When you have the image the way you want it, do one of the following:

▶ Click the Edit button to accept the modifications and further edit the image in the Edit workspace. Remember that you must then save the image in another format.

▶ Click the Apply button to accept the settings and return to the Organizer.

▶ Click the Cancel button to disregard any adjustments.

Copy Processing

If you're working with multiple RAW photos and they all have similar processing needs, you can copy the editing instructions from one RAW photo to many RAW photos. See "Applying Editing to Multiple Photos" in Chapter 3, "Becoming More Organized." You cannot apply captured edits of a RAW file to a regular image format file; conversely, you cannot apply captured edits of a regular image format file to a RAW file.

Converting RAW Photos

A RAW file image format is read-only, meaning you cannot directly edit a RAW image in the Adjust or the Edit workspace. If you make edits in the Camera RAW Lab and you want to keep those edits, you must convert the RAW image to another format such as JPG. Then you can make further edits or even print the image in the Adjust or Edit workspaces. When converting a RAW image, PaintShop Pro leaves the original RAW image and creates a copy in the new format.

The following steps show you how to convert a RAW file to another file type:

1. From the Manage workspace, select one or more RAW files you want to convert. Make sure you finish using the Camera RAW Lab before you convert the file. You cannot change an image from a finished format such as JPG or TIF back into a RAW file.

2. Right-click the thumbnail in the Organizer palette, and from the shortcut menu, choose Convert RAW. The Batch Process dialog box seen in Figure 6-37 appears prompting you for an image format.

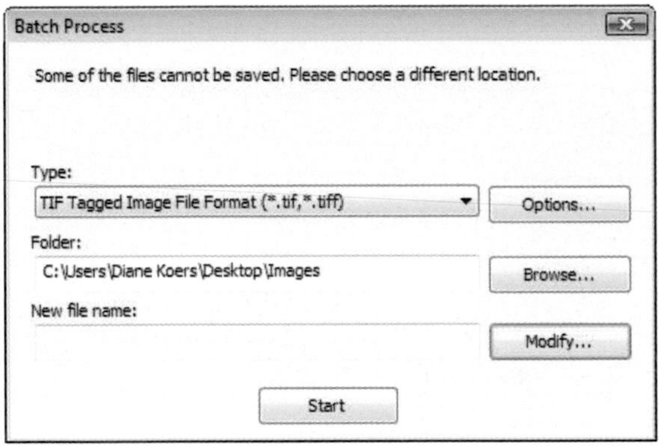

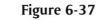

Figure 6-37
Converting a RAW image to another format.

3. Select an image format. The default choice is JPG, but click the drop-down arrow, and you can choose from many different formats.

4. Select a folder for the new image. Either type a file location in the Folder text box, or click the Browse button and select a location.

5. If you want the image to have a new filename, enter the new name in the New File Name box. Changing the filename is optional.

6. Click Start. The conversion process begins. Be patient; sometimes this process can take several minutes. See Figure 6-38.

7. Click OK to close the Batch Process dialog box.

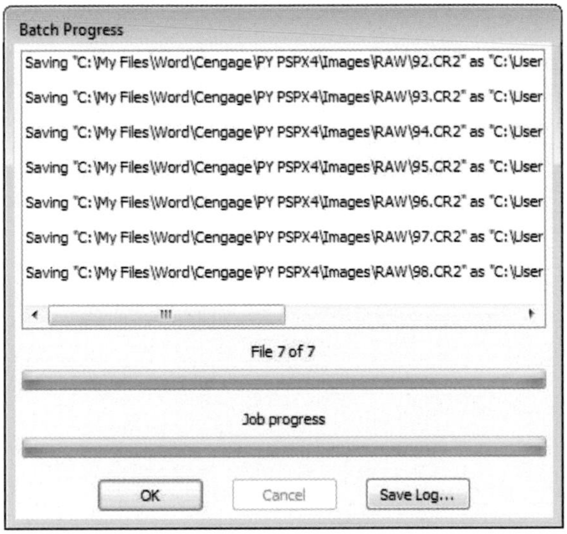

Figure 6-38
The Batch Process dialog box after the conversion.

Using Photo Blend

NEW TO PAINTSHOP PRO X4 is a feature called Photo Blend. With Photo Blend, you can combine photos of the same scene to remove, swap, or add details in the final image. For example, remove cars and people from a scene, swap in the best smiles from a series of group photos, or include multiple poses of the same person in one image. Unlike most PaintShop Pro photo enhancements that are accomplished in the Edit workspace, you access the Photo Blend feature from the Manage workspace.

The following steps show you how to use the Photo Blend feature:

1. From the Organizer palette in the Manage workspace, select two or more photos you want to blend.

2. Choose File > Photo Blend. A Getting Started window may appear; if so, click the Close button. Step 1 of the Photo Blend wizard appears, with a panel on the left with Step 1 options (see Figure 6-39).

3. Click the Align button.

Figure 6-39
Step 1 of the Photo Blend Process.

4. From the image tray along the bottom of the screen, click the thumbnail of the image that you want to change the least, and click the Lock button. Locking the image preserves more of the background. The selected image appears in the Custom editing area, which is the large preview portion of the window.

5. Now you need to tell PaintShop Pro which areas of this particular image you want to keep. Click the Brush In button, and then click and drag your mouse over the areas you want to preserve. The area appears in green. You don't have to be exact, but if you want to zoom in for better control, use the zoom controls that appear.

Change Brush Size

Drag the brush size slider to the right for a larger brush size, or drag it to the left for a smaller brush size.

6. Click the Brush Out button, and then click and drag your mouse over the areas you want to eliminate. The area you paint over appears in red. In Figure 6-40, I want to get rid of the go-kart and the dog in the background and keep the image of the boy.

7. Click the next thumbnail from the tray and repeat steps 5 and 6. Do this for each image you want to blend. See Figure 6-41. In this example, I only want to get rid of the boy.

Remove this area   Keep this area

Figure 6-40
Select the areas you want to keep and get rid of.

Figure 6-41
Mark each image in the merge.

8. Click Process. PaintShop Pro runs the Photo Blend and shows you the resulting image and Step 2 of the Photo Merge process (see Figure 6-42). If the resulting image isn't quite what you wanted, click the Back button. After you click the Back button, you can adjust the areas you want to keep or eliminate.

Figure 6-43
Adjust the image as needed.

Figure 6-42
After processing the Photo Merge.

9. In Step 2 of the Photo Merge, as you see in Figure 6-43, you can use any of the tools on the left to fine-tune your image color, contrast, and other features.

10. When you are finished, click the Save and Close button. The Save As dialog box appears. From there you can navigate to the folder you want to save the image in; give the file a name, and choose a file type. The default file type is PSPIMAGE.

Understanding Color

PICTURE YOURSELF STANDING ON A VERANDA looking out over the gentle ocean waves. It's a gorgeous day with blue skies. The emerald green palm trees are gently stirring with the breeze, and the warm azure water is beckoning you.

Now picture the same scene, but where the skies look green, the trees look brown, and the water appears gray. It's not the same feeling at all, is it? Skies are supposed to be blue, not green. When images aren't the color you expect them, the feeling behind the image changes dramatically. Likewise, sometimes our photographs don't come out in the same color we viewed with our eyes.

The visual world, as we see it, is populated by colored objects. Typically, we see the world as having a rich tapestry of colors or colored forms—fields, mountains, oceans, hairstyles, clothing, fruit, plants, animals, buildings, and so on. Colors are important in both identifying objects (locating them in space) and in re-identifying them. So much of our perception of physical things involves our identifying objects by their appearance. Colors are typically so essential to an object's appearance that any account of visual perception must contain some account of colors. A theory of color is doubly important because visual perception is one of the most important elements of perception and our acquisition of knowledge of the physical world and our environment, including our own bodies.

This chapter provides an in-depth look at the color theories that are useful when working with PaintShop Pro. You'll learn more about the most frequently used color models and the differences between the way color is viewed in the real world and how it is captured by a film or digital camera, displayed on your monitor, and produced from your printer.

This chapter is intensive and may cover more about color than you want to know, but because a big chunk of a photograph relates to color, it's good to know how and why it works as it does. As you progress through this book, you will work with photographs, editing them into the way you think they should look.

Describing Color

STUDIES SHOW THAT PEOPLE respond to color. We all know that red means stop and green means go. Photographers know that color is a powerful tool that can grab the eye, lead attention to specific areas of an image, and, through some unknown process, generate feelings that run the emotional gamut from ardor to anger.

Conversely, bad color can ruin an image. It's a fact of life that a well-composed image that might look sensational in black and white can be utterly ruined simply by presenting it in color with inappropriate hues or saturation. Bad color can override every other aspect of a photograph, turning wheat into chaff. But what, exactly, is bad color?

The most interesting thing about color is that the concepts of "good" and "bad" can vary by the image, the photographer's intent, and the purpose of the finished photograph. The weird colors of a cross-processed image are bad if they show up in your vacation pictures, but they're wonderfully evocative in a fashion shoot. A photo that has a vivid red cast may look terrible as a straight portrait but interesting when part of a glamour shot taken by the glowing embers of a fireplace. A picture of a human with even the tiniest bit of a blue tinge looks ghastly, but it might add the desired degree of chill to a snowy winter scene.

Strictly speaking, you don't have to understand how color works to use it to make corrections or generate striking effects. It's entirely possible to use trial-and-error experimentation to arrive at the results you want. However, just as you don't need an electrical engineering degree to operate a toaster, it's good to know a little something about electricity before you go poking around inside with a fork.

Our lives are full of color, and generally we accept color as part of our lives in a casual and nonchalant manner. But color affects us deeply, on a physical level, an emotional and psychological level, and a spiritual level. Our individual identities are largely expressed by our own personal understandings or feelings toward color. We learn to manipulate it and master it even while most of us have no true understanding of what color is.

Our nervous system requires input and stimulation. With respect to visual input, we become bored in the absence of a variety of colors and shapes. Consequently, color addresses one of our basic neurological needs for stimulation.

If we question how we relate to color in our lives, we see that our personal color preferences affect our fashion, our art, and our interior and exterior environments. Color is cool. Color is hot. It can encourage us or adversely affect our health and well-being. Color portrays feelings in that it can be erotic and sensual, calming and passive, expressive and vital. Colors represent emotions and convey subliminal messages.

Take a look at the following color representations:

- **Red**: Red is a symbol of liveliness and power. Considered a warm color because of its relationship with fire and heat, red represents danger, anger, blast, fire, heat, liveliness, love, blood, and revolution.

- **Yellow**: Yellow shows brightness and represents the sun. It is a color of life and light, and it often represents wealth, happiness, freshness, brightness, fulfillment, richness, and spirituality.

- **Blue**: Blue shows silence and coolness. It is related to sky and water. In our perception of blue, we often feel distance. It also represents faith, truth, seriousness, silence, and stability.

- **Orange**: Orange typically indicates a symbol of knowledge. It also represents happiness and freshness. Orange also is known to make us hungry.

- **Green**: Green is nature's color, and nature gives us freshness. Green makes us feel relaxed. It represents liveliness, freshness, wealth, and clarity. You'll often see green in hospitals.

- **Purple**: Because purple is a mixture of red and blue, it represents qualities of both colors. It is associated with spirituality, mystery, aristocracy, and passion. It may also symbolize mourning, death, and nausea. Some say purple is the color of royalty.

- **Black**: Black comes from the absence of all colors, which indicates darkness. Darkness gives rise to ill-omened things, such as murder, theft, and robbery. The color black is often used to represent inauspicious events.

White: White is from light, which consists of all colors. It represents purity, clean nature, truthfulness, and brightness.

Colors of the sun and fire, such as red, yellow, and orange, express warmth and appear on the right side of the color wheel, while colors of snow and ice, such as blue, violet, and green, emit the feeling of being cold or cool and appear on the left side of the color wheel. Take a look at Figure 7-1, showing a photograph of a church in winter. The blue hue surrounding the snow outdoors feels cold and lonely, but the red roof welcomes you into the warmth of the church.

Figure 7-1
Blue makes us feel cold, and red makes us feel warm.

In reality, color is a scientific phenomenon, measurable and definable with rules and boundaries. Throughout this chapter, we'll look at some of those measurable rules and boundaries. But the way we experience color is personal. No color is seen the same way by any two people—especially people of different cultures.

Acknowledging Why Color Is Important

Color is considered a "soft science," but it plays a pivotal role in all our visual experiences. Notice that most of us wear white for coolness in the summer and black in the winter for warmth. Earlier, I mentioned some of the emotions put into play with color. Here is more research information about color:

▶ Studies show that color can improve readership by 40%, learning from 55% to 78%, and comprehension by 73%.

▶ Color influences brand identity in a variety of ways. Remember the green ketchup?

▶ Color increases participation. Studies of telephone directory ads show that ads in color are read up to 42% more often than the same ads in black and white.

▶ Color affects your appetite. If you're hungry, seeing blue may help ward off snacking, while seeing orange can make you even hungrier. Why? Because blue food is a rare occurrence in nature. There are no leafy blue vegetables, no blue meats, and aside from blueberries and a few blue-purple potatoes from remote spots on the globe, blue just doesn't exist in any significant quantity as a natural food color.

Consequently, we don't have an automatic appetite response to blue. Furthermore, our primal nature avoids foods that are poisonous. A million years ago, when our earliest ancestors were foraging for food, blue, purple, and black were "color warning signs" of potentially lethal food.

▶ Tests indicate that a black-and-white image may sustain interest for less than two-thirds of a second, whereas a colored image may hold a person's attention for two seconds or more. (A product has one-twentieth of a second to halt the customer's attention on a shelf or display.)

▶ People cannot process every object within view at one time. Therefore, color can be used as a tool to emphasize or deemphasize areas. For example, a large insurance company used color to highlight key information on its invoices. As a result, it began receiving customer payments an average of 14 days earlier.

▶ In another recent study of business professionals, from 76% to 92% of the participants believed the following statements: Color presents an image of impressive quality. Color can assist in attracting new customers. Customers remember presentations and documents better when color is used. Color makes them appear more successful. Color gives them a competitive edge. The use of color makes their business appear larger to clients.

As you see, color influences many aspects of our lives, whether or not we realize it when it happens.

Determining What Makes Up Color

What makes color work? As I mentioned earlier, you don't have to understand how color works to use it to make photograph corrections or add striking effects. It's entirely possible to use trial-and-error experimentation to arrive at the results you want. It's just a good idea to understand the basic concepts behind color.

Daylight, or white light, is made up of numerous waves or impulses, each having different dimensions or wavelengths. When separated, any single wavelength produces a specific color impression to the human eye. What we actually see as color is known as its *color effect*. We see color because of light. However, it's not the light waves that are colored. When light rays strike an object, the object absorbs certain waves and reflects others, and this is what determines the color effect.

For example, when we observe a blue ball, it appears blue because it reflects only blue light and absorbs all other light. The ball does not have color in itself. The light generates the color. What we see as color is the reflection of a specific wavelength of light rays off an object.

That's because human perception of color originates in our brains from the variation of the wavelengths of light that reach our eyes. We see color because the retina of the eye contains rod cells and three types of cone cells, which respond to a different wavelength of light. Different wavelengths reflect different light that we see and perceive as color. We typically see an object as a color, such as a blue sky, green grass, or a pink ribbon. But, in a sense, color is an optical illusion.

Color Characteristics

The human eye perceives color in terms of three characteristics—hue, saturation, and brightness (HSB), while computer monitors display colors by generating varying amounts of red, green, and blue (RGB) light. But color is really what we see as a result of three factors interacting: light, the object, and the observer.

When light rays hit an object, the object absorbs some light and reflects some light. All the colors we see reside in a continuous color spectrum (see Figure 7-2), but we can't directly sense each of those colors individually. Instead, each of the three kinds of cone cells in our eyes "sees" a different set of frequencies, which happens to correspond to what we call red, green, and blue (RGB). Our brains process this RGB information and translate it into a distinct color that we perceive.

Figure 7-2
Human eyes perceive thousands of colors in the spectrum.

White results when light waves are reflected from a surface. Everyone knows that to keep cooler in the summer, you wear white or light colors, which also keep the sun rays reflected, not absorbed. Just the opposite, however, is true when wearing darker colors or black in winter, because those colors absorb the light waves, converting them into heat.

Understanding the Color Wheel

To help you understand color concepts, we use a color wheel. A *color wheel* is the color spectrum bent into a circle that describes the relationship between colors. Traditional color wheels use three primary colors: red, yellow, and blue (the first or starting colors used to mix the wheel).

Primary colors are hues that are mixed to create all other colors. Between them are shown the *secondary colors*: orange, green, and purple (colors made by mixing the primary colors). The colors between the primary and secondary colors are called *tertiary colors*. They are named for their parent colors, listing the primary color first, as in yellow green.

There are many different types of color wheels, the simplest being a red, yellow, and blue one. Primary colors are basic and cannot be mixed from other elements.

The red, yellow, and blue color wheel is useful as a conceptual model for color because the relationships are easy to see. This system is easy to understand and has been used for years to teach color relationships. It does, however, fail to accurately depict color relationships and does not show the relationship between the additive and subtractive color theories. It also does not work well to mix all the colors of the spectrum. Figure 7-3 illustrates a simple red, yellow, and blue color wheel.

To get a secondary color of green, orange, or purple, you mix two primary colors. Notice that each secondary color on the color wheel is bounded by two primaries. These are the components that you need to mix to get a secondary color. For example, you mix primary red and primary yellow to get secondary orange, while you mix primary blue and primary yellow to get secondary green. Finally, you can mix primary red and primary blue to get purple (or violet). See Figure 7-4.

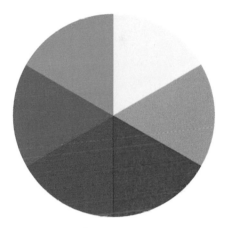

Figure 7-4
Primary and secondary colors.

When viewing the color wheel, look at the colors directly across from each other. These are called *complementary colors* or *color opposites*. Violet and yellow are complementary; blue and orange are complementary; and red and green are complementary. These colors contrast with each other in the most extreme way possible.

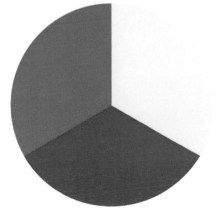

Figure 7-3
Primary colors.

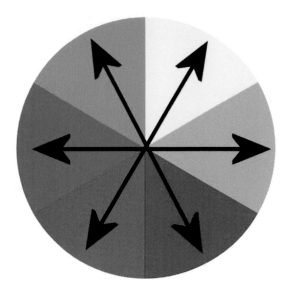

If you continue blending the colors along with different hue, saturation, and lightness settings, you end up with millions of different color variations. We'll take a look at hue, saturation, and lightness later in this chapter.

Next, we look at the tertiary, or intermediate, colors, which occur by mixing a secondary color with a primary color. In Figure 7-5, you see six intermediate colors: red-orange, red-violet, blue-violet, blue-green, yellow-green, and yellow-orange.

Defining Color Models

A *color model* is a system for specifying the components of color. There are a number of different generic and some specific color models. Artificial color systems, which include computer scanners, monitors, printers, and other peripherals, attempt to reproduce, or model, the colors that we see, using various sets of components of color. If the model is a good one, all the colors we are capable of detecting are defined by the parameters of the model. The colors within the definition of each model are termed its *color space.* Nearly all color spaces use three different models, such as colors like red, green, and blue or qualities such as hue, saturation, and brightness.

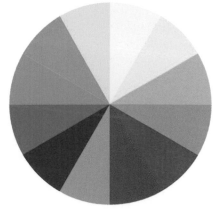

Figure 7-5
A simple color wheel showing primary, secondary, and intermediate colors.

The international standard for specifying color was defined in 1931 by the Commission Internationale L'Eclairage (CIE); it is a scientific color model that can be used to define all the colors that humans can see. However, computer color systems are based on one of three or four other color models, which are more practical because they are derived from the actual hardware systems used to reproduce those colors.

None of these systems can generate all the colors in the full range of human perception, but they are the models with which we must work. In PaintShop Pro, you use the RGB and HSL color models to select and manipulate color. If you are printing, you might use the CMYK color model.

Understanding RGB Color

RGB stands for red, green, and blue, the colors used by most monitors and video output devices. If you're old enough, you might remember when you had to adjust your TV color because the people's faces were too red or too green. You were working with RGB settings. All colors on the screen, whether on your television or computer screen, are a combination of red, blue, and green.

Traditional computer monitors produce color by aiming three electronic guns at sets of red, green, and blue phosphors (compounds that give off photons when struck by beams of electrons), coated on the screen of a display. LCD and LED monitors use sets of red, green, and blue pixels to represent each picture element of an image that is switched on or off, as required. If none of the colors is displayed, we see a black pixel. If all three glow in equal proportions, we see a neutral color—gray or white, depending on the intensity. We call this color model the *RGB model*.

The RGB color model is called an *additive model*, because the colors are added together. As you discovered when working with the color wheel, a huge selection of colors can be produced by varying the combinations of light. In addition to pure red, green, and blue, you can also produce cyan (green and blue together), magenta (red and blue), yellow (red and green), and all the colors in between.

No display device available today produces pure red, green, or blue light. Only lasers, which output at one single frequency of light, generate absolutely pure colors, and they aren't used for display devices. We see images through the glow of phosphors, LEDs, or LCD pixels, and their ability to generate absolutely pure colors is limited. Color representations on a display differ from brand to brand and even from one display to another within the same brand.

Moreover, the characteristics of a given display can change as the monitor ages and the color-producing elements wear out. Some phosphors—particularly blue ones—change in intensity as they age, at a different rate than other phosphors. So, identical signals rarely produce identical images on displays, regardless of how closely the devices are matched in type, age, and other factors.

In practice, most displays show far fewer colors than they are theoretically capable of showing. Actually, the number of different colors a display can show at one time is limited to the number of individual pixels or the screen resolution you set on your monitor. For example, at 1024 × 768 resolution, there are only 786,432 different pixels. Even if each one were a different color, you'd view, at most, only around three-quarters of a million colors at once.

Adjusting the amount of red, green, and blue in your image makes color corrections by changing the overall color cast. Reducing blue adds yellow, reducing green adds magenta, and reducing red adds cyan to the image. A value of 0% indicates the original value. If you want to add more of a color, use a positive number, but if you want to remove some of a color, use a negative number.

You can either increase the opposite color on the color wheel or reduce the amount of adjacent colors on the color wheel. For example, to color-correct an image containing too much yellow, either increase the amount of blue or decrease the amount of red and green.

APPRECIATING HSL COLOR

The Hue/Saturation/Lightness color model, also known as HSL, is a convenient way to manage color for some operations. In this model, individual colors are represented as they are in a rainbow, as a continuous spectrum, and arranged in a circle.

Hue is the color reflected from an object, such as red, yellow, or orange. *Saturation* represents the vividness of the color, which is actually from the amount of gray in the color, from 0 (entirely gray) to 255 (fully saturated color). *Lightness* represents the perceived amount or intensity of light in the color. Lightness ranges from 0, which is no light, or black, to 255, which is total lightness, or white.

PaintShop Pro provides a tool that adjusts these three elements individually. For example, if you want to adjust the saturation of a color without modifying its hue or brightness, HSB mode, from the Edit workspace, click the Adjust menu, select Hue and Saturation, and click Hue/Saturation/Lightness (see Figure 7-6). The color rings represent the colors in the image; the outer ring represents the original values, and the inner ring represents the adjusted values.

You should know that the Hue value is not on the typical hue scale of 0 to 255. Instead, the value is the number of degrees of rotation around the 360-color wheel from the pixel's original color. A positive value indicates a clockwise rotation, and a negative value indicates a counterclockwise rotation. For example, when the Hue value is at 180, blue becomes yellow and green becomes magenta.

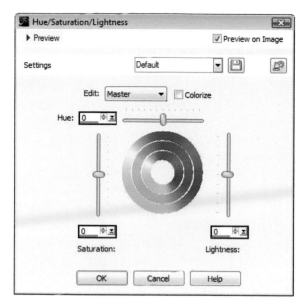

Figure 7-6
The Hue/Saturation/Lightness color model
starts with a color circle.

To adjust the values, drag the Hue, Saturation, or Lightness sliders. Hue values range from –180 to 180, and the Saturation and Lightness values range from –100 to 100. A value of 0 means no change.

By selecting an option from the Edit drop-down list, you can edit the master color ring, or you can choose a specific color range to adjust. Additionally, checking the Colorize box turns the image into a two-color image.

Because the HSL color model deals with a continuous range of colors that may vary in brightness or richness, human eyes perceive its color more naturally than they do other color models.

WORKING WITH CMYK COLOR

Another way of producing color is one that is put to work whenever we output our PaintShop Pro images as hard copies using a color printer. This kind of color also has a color model that represents a particular color gamut. The reason a different kind of color model is necessary is simple: When we represent colors in hard copy form, the light source we view by comes not from the image, as it does with a computer display. Instead, hard copies are viewed by light that strikes the paper or other material and then is filtered by the image on the paper; then it is reflected back to our eyes.

This light starts out with (more or less) equal quantities of red, green, and blue light and looks white to our eyes. The pigments that the light passes through before bouncing off the paper absorb part of this light, subtracting it from the spectrum. The components of light that remain reach our eyes and are interpreted as color. Because various parts of the illumination are subtracted from white to produce color, this color model is known as the subtractive system.

The three primary colors are cyan, magenta, and yellow, and the model is sometimes known as the CMY model. Usually, however, black is included in the mix, for reasons that will become clear shortly. When black is added, this color system becomes the CMYK model. (Black is represented by its terminal character, *K*, rather than *B* to avoid confusion with the additive primary blue.)

In CMYK output devices, such as color printers or printing presses, cyan, magenta, yellow, and, usually, black pigments (for detail) are used to represent a gamut of colors.

It's obvious why additive colors (RGB) won't work for hard copies: it is possible to produce red, green, and blue pigments, of course, and we can print red, green, and blue colors that way. (That's what is done for spot color.) However, there would be no way to produce any of the other colors with the additive primaries. Red pigment reflects only red light; green pigment reflects only green. When the two overlap, the red pigment absorbs the green, and the green absorbs the red, so no light is reflected, and we see black.

Cyan pigment, on the other hand, is supposed to absorb only red light. In theory, it reflects both blue and green, producing the blue-green shade we see as cyan. Yellow pigment absorbs only blue light, reflecting red and green, while magenta pigment absorbs only green, reflecting red and blue. When we overlap two of the subtractive primaries, some of at least one color still reflects. Magenta (red-blue) and yellow (red-green) together produce red, because the magenta pigment absorbs green, and the yellow pigment absorbs blue. Their common color, red, is the only one remaining. Of course, each of the subtractive primaries can be present in various intensities or percentages, from 0 to 100%. The remainder is represented by white, which reflects all colors in equal amounts.

You'll recall that RGB displays aren't perfect, because the colors aren't pure. So, too, it is impossible to design pigments that reflect absolutely pure colors. Equal amounts of cyan, magenta, and yellow pigment should produce black. More often, what you'll get is a muddy brown. When daily newspapers began their changeover to color printing in the 1970s, many of them used this three-color system, with mixed results.

However, better results can be obtained by adding black as a fourth color. Black can fill in areas that are supposed to be black and add detail to other areas of an image. While the fourth color does complicate the process a bit, the actual cost in applications like offset printing is minimal. Black ink is used to print text anyway, so there is no additional press run for black. Moreover, black ink is cheaper than critical process color inks, so it's possible to save money by using black instead of laying on three subtractive primaries extra thick. A typical image separated into its component colors for printing is shown in Figure 7-7.

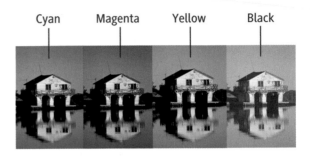

Figure 7-7
Full-color images are separated into cyan, magenta, yellow, and black components for printing.

The output systems you use to print hard copies of color images use the subtractive color system in one way or another. Some output devices, such as ink-jet printers, color laser systems, and thermal wax transfer printers, are unable to print varying percentages of each of the primary colors, so they must simulate other colors by *dithering*, which is the process of creating the illusion of new colors and shades by varying the pattern of dots. A few printers, such as a thermal dye sublimation printer, can vary the amount of pigment laid down over a broader range. These printers can print a full range of tones, up to the 16.8 million colors possible with 24-bit systems.

Viewing Common Color Problems

BAD COLOR CAN RUIN AN IMAGE. It's a fact of life that a well-composed image that might look sensational in black and white can be utterly ruined simply by presenting it in color with inappropriate hues or saturation.

Sometimes a horrid-looking image may have nothing more wrong with it than the balance of colors used to represent the image. Other times, the balance may be okay, but you'd like to make the colors look horrid to produce a desired special effect in your image.

Balancing Color

Color balance is the relationship between the three colors used to produce your image—most often red, green, and blue. You need to worry only about three different factors:

▶ **Amount of red, green, and blue**: If you have too much red, the image appears too red. If you have too much green, it looks too green. Extra blue makes an image look as if it just came out of the deep freeze. Other color casts are produced by too much of two of the primary colors when compared to the remaining hue. That is, too much red and green produce a yellowish cast; red and blue tilt things toward magenta; and blue and green create a cyan bias. Figure 7-8 shows an image with red and green color casts.

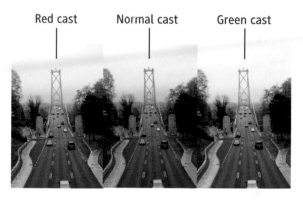

Red cast   Normal cast   Green cast

Figure 7-8
Too much of one color can corrupt the entire image.

▶ **Saturation**: How much of the hue is composed of the pure color itself, and how much is diluted by a neutral color, such as white or black? Figure 7-9 shows an image with low, normal, and high saturation.

Low saturation   Normal saturation   High saturation

Figure 7-9
An image with different saturation levels.

▶ **Brightness/contrast**: Brightness and contrast refer to the relative lightness/darkness of each color channel and the number of different tones available. If, say, there are only 12 different red tones in an image, ranging from very light to very dark, with only a few tones in between, then the red portion of the image can be said to have a high contrast. The brightness is determined by whether the available tones are clustered at the denser or lighter areas of the image. Many professionals use histograms to represent these relationships. A histogram is a graph that shows what proportion of an image falls into the brightness and contrast areas. Figure 7-10 shows an image with the contrast and brightness set low, normal, and high.

Figure 7-10
Change an image's contrast and brightness.

Splitting Color Channels

You've seen how images work with the three color models. Each type of color information is stored in *channels*, or planes, of colors. Both RGB and HSL use three channels: red, green, and blue or hue, saturation, and lightness. The CMYK model uses four channels: cyan, magenta, yellow, and black.

PaintShop Pro provides a feature, called Split Channels, whereby you can separate the image into RGB, HSL, or CMYK color channels. Although you cannot create or edit an image using the CMYK model, you can still split the image into the four channels.

Using the Split Channel command creates a new grayscale image for each color channel, leaving the original image unchanged. For example, you can split an image into separate RGB grayscale images named Red, Green, and Blue. Each grayscale image represents the percentage and location of a color (such as red) or, if splitting an HSL image, the characteristic (such as lightness) within the image. You access the Split Channel command through the Image menu in the Edit workspace. Figure 7-11 shows an image after being split into the RGB channels.

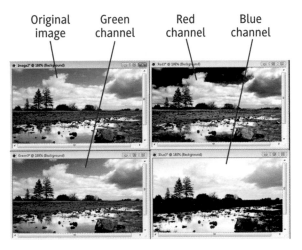

Figure 7-11
Splitting an image into separate color channels.

Working with Materials

COLOR AND STYLE ARE PROBABLY the most important elements when you're creating and working with graphics. Even minor changes to color settings can dramatically alter your image. Style takes into account special combinations such as gradients, patterns, and textures, including the appearance of brick, wood, leather, or sand. PaintShop Pro provides all these options on the Materials palette.

The Materials palette is hidden when you first open PaintShop Pro. Depending on several variables, it may automatically open when you select a painting tool such as the Paint Brush or Flood Fill tool. (See Chapter 10, "Discovering Drawing Tools.") You can manually turn it on from the Edit workspace by choosing View > Palettes > Materials or pressing the F6 key. And, like all other PaintShop Pro palettes, you can leave it docked or float it around on your screen.

The Materials palette has three different tabs that allow you to swap between three different methods of choosing materials.

We'll look at all three methods shortly:

Frame allows you to select a color by its hue and select the saturation and lightness from within the rectangle.

Rainbow allows you to directly choose a color.

Swatches provide you quick access to frequently used materials. The Swatches tab has additional options along the bottom of the Materials palette. The appearance of the Swatches tab changes as you use different materials.

Using the Materials Palette

Within every tool are two defined areas: foreground and background. For example, if you are creating a box with a perimeter around it, PaintShop Pro uses just the foreground color. If the box has a filled-in center, PaintShop Pro uses the background color.

The swatches at the bottom of all the tabs on the Materials palette represent the current foreground and background colors along with a pattern or texture. Together, the color, pattern, gradient, and texture are called the *properties*. The first box (the one to the left) is the Foreground and Stroke properties, whereas the box on the right is the Background and Fill properties (see Figure 7-12). There are also two smaller swatches, just to the left, that indicate the Foreground and Stroke color and the Background and Fill color.

Foreground and Stroke properties

Background and Fill properties

Figure 7-12
These swatches indicate the currently selected color and other properties.

You may not see the Materials palette with the swatches below it as in the previous figure. If you have other palettes docked under the Materials palettes, PaintShop Pro may move the swatches to the left of the Materials palette.

As I mentioned earlier, there are three different tabs appearing at the top of the Materials palette.

Each of these tabs displays your color options in a different mode. From the Frame mode, first you click a color from the rectangular area surrounding the outer area of the palette—blue for example—which changes the color swatch to blue. Then you drag the small circle in the center of the rectangle until the swatch meets the hue and lightness you want for your color (see Figure 7-13). Use the left mouse to select the color and drag the dot if you want to change the Background and Fill color, and use the right mouse button to work with the Foreground and Stroke color.

Frame tab

Drag this to change hue and lightness

Click a color from here first

Figure 7-13
Choosing a color from the Frame mode.

From the Rainbow mode (see Figure 7-14), as you move the mouse, which looks like an eyedropper, over the colors, you see a tip box that displays the RGB values of the color you are currently pointing to. When you find the color you want, click the left mouse button to make that color the Foreground and Stroke color, or click with the right mouse button to make that color the Background and Fill color.

Swatches provide you with quick access to frequently used materials. When using the Swatch mode, you simply click a box to select the color (see Figure 7-15). Click with the left mouse button to select the Foreground and Stroke color, and click with the right mouse button to select the Background and Fill color. The Swatches tab has additional options along the bottom of the Materials palette, where you can add and delete swatches as well as control what the swatches display.

Rainbow tab

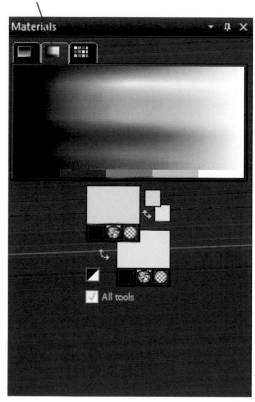

Figure 7-14
Choosing a color from Rainbow mode.

Additional options

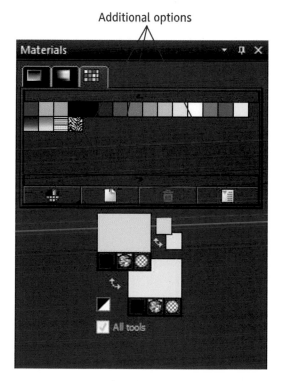

Figure 7-15
Choosing a color from Swatch mode.

Working with Other Materials

There's certainly more to life—and images—than color. The Materials Properties swatches on the Materials palette work with colors, patterns, gradients, textures, and transparency. The three buttons at the bottom of each Materials Properties swatch are what you'll use to set your material style.

Each of the swatches has three icons that run along the bottom of the swatch. As you point your mouse to each icon, a ToolTip tells you what each icon represents.

The first button, called the Color button, is where you determine if you want to use a solid color, a gradient, or a pattern. As you click the Color button, additional options appear, as you see in Figure 7-16. The second button, the Texture button, is an on/off toggle button where you turn the Texture feature on or off. The third button, called the Transparency button, is where you designate that you want nothing for the foreground or the background. The Transparency button is also an on/off toggle button.

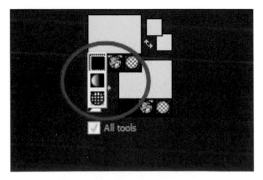

Figure 7-16
Selecting swatch properties.

▶ The solid circle represents solid colors.

▶ The vertical stripes represent gradients.

▶ The checkered circle represents patterns.

▶ The small dots represent textures.

▶ The circle with the line represents the international "No" symbol and means "transparent," or none of the other choices.

Quickly Display Recently Used Materials

Right-click a swatch to display a palette of recently used materials.

Selecting from the Material Properties Box

To finely tune the color, gradient, pattern, or texture, you use the Material Properties dialog box. From the Edit workspace, click on either Material Properties swatch to bring up the Material Properties dialog box for that swatch. After the dialog box is open, you can alter your choice to any of the three basic materials—color, gradient, or pattern—by clicking the appropriate tab.

Choosing Color Properties

The first Material Properties tab shown in Figure 7-17 represents the Color options. The Color dialog box consists of several elements:

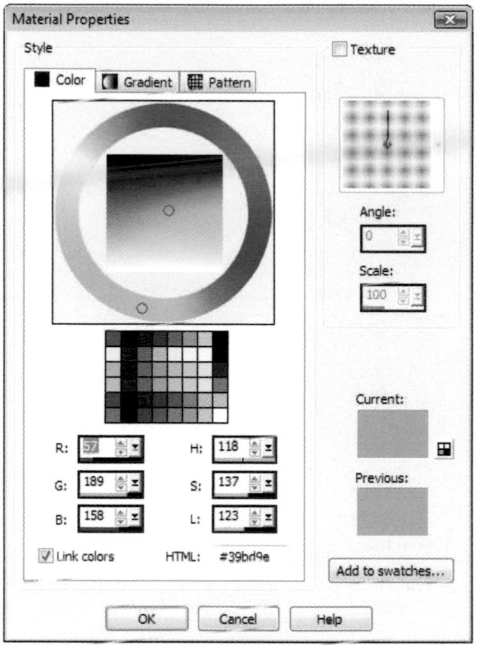

Figure 7-17
Selecting color options.

▶ **The color wheel**: The color wheel represents various hue values. Click on a color, or drag the little circle to select a color. Then you must select a saturation/lightness.

▶ **Saturation/Lightness box**: After you've selected a color, in the square middle box adjust the saturation and lightness by clicking the mouse or dragging the little circle until the sample box represents the color you want.

▶ **Basic Colors palette**: This palette represents 48 of the more common colors in a Materials palette, including many primary and secondary colors in several steps of lightness, plus grayscale.

▶ **RGB and HSL values**: Here you can see the RGB and HSL values of your selected color or enter and adjust the values of the color you want to be displayed. You can type the numeric values into the RGB or HSL fields or adjust the corresponding sliders.

No matter which tab you use, as you make choices on the Material Properties dialog box, on the lower-right side of the dialog box, you see the current and previous selection sample. If the material you pick is one you expect to use frequently, click the Add to Swatches button, give the swatch a name, and click OK. Then when you choose the Swatch mode, you'll also see the newly added material.

Generating Gradients

Gradients are created from the gradual blending of colors. PaintShop Pro includes multiple pre-designed gradients. Many more gradient designs are available free from the web—and if you're really creative, you can even design your own. The Gradient tab options allow you to choose one of four styles of gradient—linear, rectangular, sunburst, or radial. After opening the Materials Palette dialog box, follow these steps to select a gradient fill:

1. Click the Gradient tab, where you see the gradient options shown in Figure 7-18.

Gradient swatch arrow

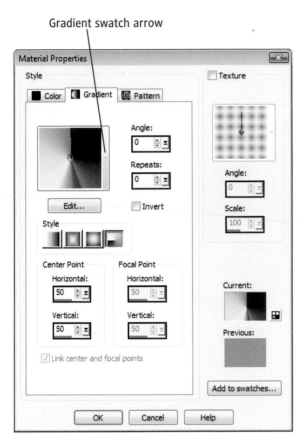

Figure 7-18
Selecting gradients.

2. Click the Gradient swatch arrow, which displays a gallery of gradients.

3. Select the gradient you want to use.

4. Optionally, adjust the angle of the texture. You can rotate the pattern up to 359 degrees.

5. Click a gradient style. You can have the gradient originate from the sides, from the inside, from the outside, or from a corner. Experiment a little. You'll find many different variations of the selected gradient.

Reverse Gradient

To reverse the gradient pattern, click the Invert check box.

PICKING PATTERNS

In addition to gradients, PaintShop Pro includes many different patterns to use in the foreground or background of images. You can also use any existing image, such as a drawing or a photograph, as a pattern.

Pattern Lines or Fill

If you want the line to have a pattern, use the Foreground and Stroke swatch; however, if you want the interior of a shape to have the pattern, click the Background and Fill swatch.

The Pattern tab allows you to choose any installed pattern, rotate it, and scale it from 10% to 250%. Any open image automatically appears as a possible pattern and can be saved in the Patterns folder in the PaintShop Pro folder and will load ever after.

Open the Material Properties dialog box and follow these steps:

1. Click the Pattern tab. The Pattern tab appears on top.

2. Click on the Current Pattern swatch arrow. A selection of patterns appears, similar to those shown in Figure 7-19. Notice that the currently open image also appears as a pattern choice.

Click here to select a pattern

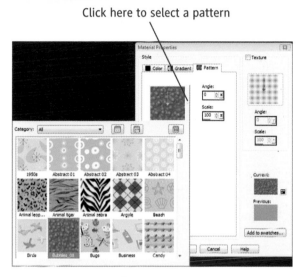

Figure 7-19
Picking a pattern.

3. Click on the pattern you would like to use. A sample appears in the Current box.

4. Optionally, adjust the angle of the pattern. You can rotate the pattern up to 359 degrees.

5. Optionally, adjust the scale of the pattern. If you are going to fill a small image with the pattern, you might want to make the pattern smaller and tighter.

Tinkering with Textures

Using texture effects gives an image a three-dimensional appearance, as though the image were created on a textured surface. Textures are transparent and simulate depth. After you open the Material Properties dialog box, follow these steps to select a texture:

Combine Textures

You can use textures with colors, patterns, or gradients.

1. From any of the three tabs (Color, Gradient, or Pattern), click the Texture check box. A check in the box indicates that the Texture feature is activated.

2. Click the texture swatch arrow. A gallery of textures appears, such as what you see in Figure 7-20. By default, PaintShop Pro divides the textures into three different categories: Art Media, Geometric, and Photo. You can filter the category you want to see by choosing an option from the Category drop-down list.

3. Click the texture you want to use. A sample appears in the Current box, combined with the current color.

4. Optionally, adjust the angle of the texture. You can rotate the pattern up to 359 degrees.

5. Optionally, adjust the scale of the texture. If you are going to fill a small image with the texture, you might want to make the texture smaller and tighter.

Texture check box   Texture swatch arrow

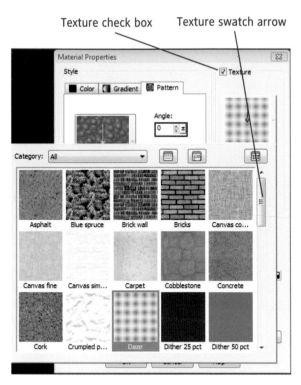

Figure 7-20
Choosing a texture.

Reversing Color Selections

PaintShop Pro provides an easy way to reverse your foreground and background properties or colors without your having to select them both again. Simply click the double arrow next to either the Foreground and Stroke Properties swatch or the Background and Fill Properties swatch. PaintShop Pro then reverses the two Material Properties swatches.

Reverse Colors with the Mouse Buttons

When painting or filling objects, you can temporarily reverse the foreground and background colors by using the right mouse button.

Locking Color Choices

Toward the bottom of the Materials palette is an All Tools check box. When the All Tools check box is unchecked, the colors and styles are unlocked. This means that each tool you use can have its own combinations of colors, patterns, gradients, and textures. When unlocked, if you switch tools (such as from the Paint Brush to the Flood Fill tool), the color and style selections change from the Paint Brush colors and styles to the same colors or styles in effect the last time you used the Flood Fill tool. If you lock the colors, the current settings are used for all tools.

All Tools

The All Tools check box is only available when certain tools are selected.

Reviewing Other Color-Related Features

THE PREVIOUS SECTION was about choosing color, gradients, patterns, textures, or transparency using the Materials palette. PaintShop Pro provides a couple of other color-related features you might find useful.

Using Materials When Creating a New Image

When you're creating a new image, you can select a solid color, gradient, pattern, texture, or transparency for the image background. Click the New Image button on the Standard toolbar, or choose File > New, which displays the New Image dialog box shown in Figure 7-21.

If you want the background of the new image as a transparency, click the Transparent check box. If you want the image background to have a color, gradient, pattern, and optionally a texture, click the Color box, which displays the Material Properties dialog box. From there, you can make your selections, as you learned in the previous sections.

Picking Color from an Image

Often you want to create something using a color in an image. When you're using the Materials palette, it can be difficult to find the same color with the same hue and lightness. Fortunately, PaintShop Pro includes a tool where you can pick up a color from any open image.

Transparent check box   Color selection box

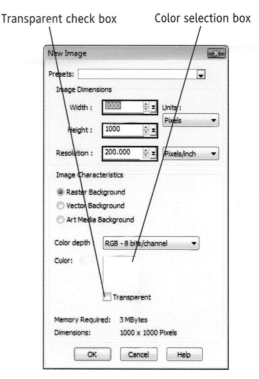

Figure 7-21
Selecting materials for a new image.

Select the Dropper tool, which is the fourth tool on the Tools toolbar. Using the Dropper tool, click anywhere on the image where you see the color you want. As you move your mouse over the various image areas, a ToolTip appears showing you the RGB values you are currently pointing to (see Figure 7-22).

Dropper tool

Figure 7-22
Picking colors from an open image.

When you see the color you want, click with the left mouse button to set that color for the Foreground and Stroke color, or click with the right mouse button to select that color for the Background and Fill color.

Counting Colors

When you create a new image, you have to select the maximum number of colors to be in that image. Want to know how many are actually in a particular image? With your image open in the Edit workspace, click Image > Count Image Colors. You see an information box such as the one in Figure 7-23, which states the total number of colors in the current image.

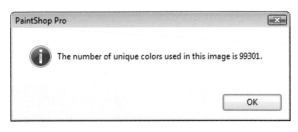

Figure 7-23
Let PaintShop Pro count the different colors.

Click OK to close the dialog box.

Creating a Negative Image

Just like a negative you get when you take your film to the drugstore for processing, you can create a negative of any image. Creating a negative image reverses all the color values in the image to their exact opposite.

With the image open in the Edit workspace on your screen, click Image > Negative Image. PaintShop Pro reverses all color values in the current image. In Figure 7-24, you see two exact copies of a photograph, with the second one as a negative.

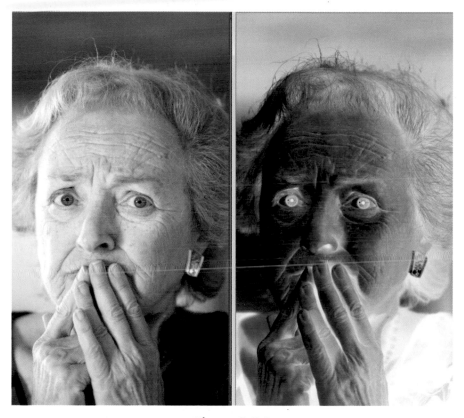

Figure 7-24
View an image as a negative.

Developing Layers

PICTURE YOURSELF OUTSIDE ON A BLUSTERY, rainy cold day. You're all bundled up. Closest to your skin you might have a t-shirt and a sweater over the shirt. Next, you don your jacket and a neck scarf, and then finally a raincoat to keep you dry. Now imagine that you live in the Midwest, where the weather changes rapidly. It stops raining, so you peel off the raincoat. The wind dies down, too, so you don't need the neck scarf, and later you don't even need the jacket.

Hikers, bikers, walkers, and even little children dress in layers. When dressing in layers, it's helpful to remember that each layer must perform a specific task. One layer is to keep you comfortable, another to keep you warm, and yet another to keep you dry. Each layer has its own purpose, and you can easily remove or shift the layers as necessary. So what does this have to do with a computer software program?

PaintShop Pro has layers also. Just like clothing layers, each PaintShop Pro layer can have its own use, and you can easily move around the layers or delete them if you don't want them. This chapter discusses layers and how you use them. It also considers blending and blend modes, which is how multiple layers interact with each other.

Here are a few examples of how you might use layers with your images:

▶ **Add text or other graphics such as picture tubes**: By placing these on their own layers, you can easily move them into a desired position. You'll work with picture tubes in Chapter 10, "Discovering Drawing Tools."

▶ **Make color and tone adjustments**: By adding adjustment layers, you can experiment with different color corrections without actually affecting the original image.

▶ **Create collages**: By placing photographs on their own individual layer, you can position each image where you want it in a collage.

▶ **Apply filters and effects**: Apply special effects to a duplicate layer of the original image, and blend the two.

▶ **Protect the original image**: Make a duplicate layer of the photograph and make any changes to the duplicate, thereby preserving the original from undesired changes.

Understanding Layers

LAYERS ARE ONE OF THE BEST features of PaintShop Pro. Once you start using them, you'll never want to be without them. Think of PaintShop Pro layering as putting each portion of your graphics image on a separate, thin sheet of paper, such as tracing paper. Layering makes it much easier to edit or move a particular portion of the image, because as you edit one portion of the image, you won't disturb the other portions. Then you can shuffle the order of the layers (sheets). If you are making composite images, you'll find layers particularly helpful.

All images have at least one layer. When you open a digital photograph or a scanned image in PaintShop Pro, the image is on the background layer. For most photographic enhancements, such as cropping, correcting colors, or retouching, you can work on this background layer without ever adding another layer. However, there are many ways to use layers with your photographic images to make changes easier and create interesting effects, especially when you intend to do more complex work, such as adding elements to the image, creating photo compositions, adding text and other effects, and so forth. Figure 8-1 illustrates two individual images (left and center) which, when combined through image layers, become the image on the right.

Figure 8-1
Blending two images to make a third image.

Discerning Layer Types

PaintShop Pro supports many different layer types. The layer type you use depends on your needs. Besides the original background layer that occurs with each image, PaintShop Pro layer types include background, raster, vector, art media, mask, and adjustment. For example, often when working with photographs, you'll use adjustment layers, which enable you to make easily changeable modifications to your photographs. PaintShop Pro supports up to 500 layers, but most likely, your computer memory won't fully support that many layers, each with its own settings. Most images use only a few layers. Let's look at the different layer types.

BACKGROUND LAYERS

Every image has at least one layer, appropriately called the *background layer*. This layer is the bottom layer in an image. Background layers are a type of raster layer in that they contain raster data, but background layers have some limitations to them that regular raster layers do not.

For example, you cannot change the background layer order in the stack because it's always on the bottom, and you cannot change a background layer blend mode or opacity. See "Using the Layers Palette," later in this chapter, for a description of blend mode and opacity. You can, however, change a background layer to a regular layer and then make any desired adjustments.

RASTER LAYERS

Raster layers, sometimes called *regular layers*, are layers with only raster data, which is the individual pixels you see in photographs. You can use raster layers for painting, retouching, effects, filters, and other commands, and you can, but generally don't, use raster layers for shapes or text.

VECTOR LAYERS

Vector layers are layers with only vector objects that are composed of geometric characteristics, such as lines, shapes, and text. When you edit vector objects, you edit these lines and curves, rather than editing individual pixels like you do on raster layers. Vector graphics maintain their clarity and detail when scaled to any size, making them easy to edit. Before you can add filters or effects to a vector layer, you must convert the vector layer to a raster layer.

ART MEDIA LAYERS

PaintShop Pro automatically creates art media layers when you begin using any of the Art Media tools, such as the oil brush, pastels, or crayons. *Art media layers* function similarly to vector layers because the objects on art media layers are easy to move around and manipulate.

ADJUSTMENT LAYERS

PaintShop Pro provides *adjustment layers* to make color and tonal corrections instead of changing the image directly. Adjustment layers are non-destructive, correction layers that modify an image color or tone but place the changes on individual layers instead of the original layer. You can place each correction type on its own layer to test various color corrections or to see how several corrections look when you combine them.

MASK LAYERS

A *mask layer* is basically an adjustment layer that modifies opacity, which then shows or hides portions of underlying layers. You use masks to create sophisticated effects. For example, you can mask all details around the main subject in a photograph or use a mask to create a picture frame that fades away at the center to reveal the subject. Mask layers cannot be the bottom layer in an image.

Using the Layers Palette

THE EASIEST AND FASTEST method to layer management is through the Layers palette, although you can also accomplish layer tasks through the Layers menu. Display the Layers palette in the Edit workspace by choosing View > Palettes > Layers or pressing the F8 key.

Located in the Palette Bin, the Layers palette shows you all the information about each layer in your image and provides a place to create, delete, rename, hide, group, and generally manage your image layers. Let's take a closer look at a Layers palette of an image with multiple layers (see Figure 8-2).

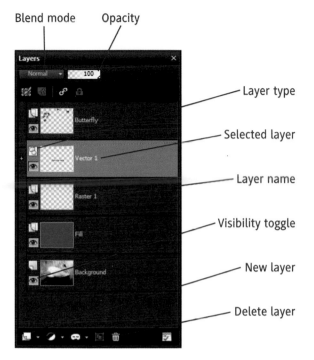

Blend mode   Opacity

Layer type

Selected layer

Layer name

Visibility toggle

New layer

Delete layer

Figure 8-2
Pause the mouse over the layer name to see a larger
thumbnail representation of the layer contents.

View the Layers Palette

**If you don't see the Layers palette, choose
View > Palettes > Layers or press the
F8 key.**

The following list describes the icons you see on
a layer:

> ▶ **New Layer**: Click this button to automat-
> ically create a new layer. A drop-down list
> of layer types appears.

> ▶ **Delete Layer**: Click this button to delete
> the selected layer. A confirmation box
> appears.

▶ **Opacity**: *Opacity* measures how much
an object blocks light transmission (the
opposite of transparency). When the
opacity is lower, the resulting image is
more transparent. Background layers do
not have opacity control.

▶ **Blend Mode**: This feature displays a
combination of pixels of the current layer
with the pixels of all the underlying layers;
however, it is for display only; at this point,
the layers are not actually combined.

▶ **Lock/Unlock**: This option lets you lock
transparent pixels in an image so that only
the nontransparent pixels can be edited.

▶ **Visibility Toggle**: The eye icon indicates
that the layer is visible. On occasion, you
might want to hide one or more layers so
that you can more easily view and edit
objects on the remaining layers. Click the
visibility icon to hide or display the
selected layer.

▶ **Layer Type**: Each layer icon represents a
different layer type. For example, a raster
layer icon has two small rectangles: one
clear and one solid.

▶ **Layer Name**: When you start adding lots
of layers, you want to give each layer a
unique name to identify quickly what it
holds.

Change the Layers Palette Size

**To change the Layers palette thumbnail
image size, choose File > Preferences >
General Program Preferences. From the
Palettes section, set any desired options
and then click OK.**

Creating Layers

PaintShop Pro provides several methods to add new layers. The three most common layer types (raster, vector, or adjustment) can be added by clicking the New Layer icon on the Layers palette and selecting a layer type from the resulting drop-down list. You can also add any layer type, including adjustment layers, through the Layers menu. When you add any new layer, PaintShop Pro names it sequentially, such as Raster 2 or Vector 3. Whether you choose to create a new raster or vector layer from the Layers palette icon or by choosing one from the Layers menu, a dialog box like the one seen in Figure 8-3 appears.

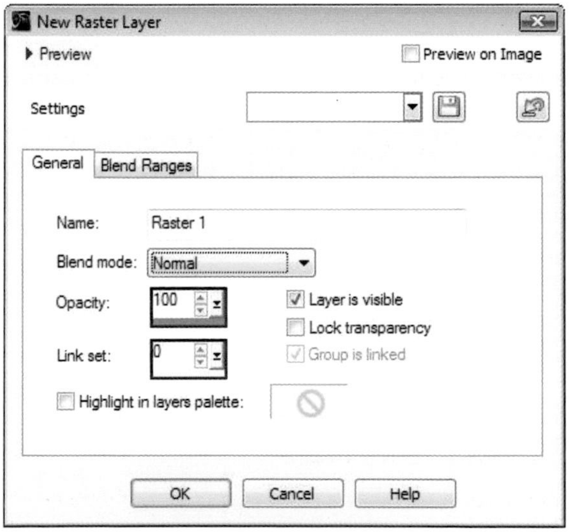

Figure 8-3
New Raster Layer dialog box.

From this dialog box, you can give your layer a name, select a blend mode and opacity, and group the layer with another layer. PaintShop Pro places new layers above the layer that was last selected. The new layer also becomes the active layer.

Adding Adjustment Layers

A slightly different dialog box appears if you add an adjustment layer. You'll learn more about adjustment layers later in this chapter.

PaintShop Pro creates some new layers automatically. For example, if the current layer is a raster layer and you create a shape, line, or text, PaintShop Pro automatically puts it on its own vector layer. You can then decide whether you want additional shapes or additional text on the same shape or text layer or another new one. Additionally, if you paste a selection from the current image or a different image, PaintShop Pro automatically places the selection on its own new layer unless you specify differently from options on the Edit menu.

Creating Solid Layers

If you create a new raster layer and you want it a solid color, select the Flood Fill tool from the Tools toolbar, choose a color, and then click anywhere in the layer. PaintShop Pro fills the layer with the selected color.

Changing Layer Opacity

In Chapter 2, "Working with PaintShop Pro Files," you read that opacity is the density of a brushstroke. You also read that a higher value applies a more solid color effect, and a lower value results in a more transparent effect. Layers also have an opacity setting that determines the density or sheerness of the current layer, which determines how much of a lower layer is allowed to show through.

You can adjust the opacity of the current layer by dragging the Opacity slider to the left to decrease the current layer density or to the right to increase the density. Take a look at Figure 8-4. In both the image on the left and the image on the right, there are actually two photograph layers, with the bottom layer being a flowing fountain and the top layer being a floral lane. But in the image on the left, all you see is the floral lane layer because the opacity is at 100% and it doesn't allow any of the lower layer to peek through. On the right, the opacity of the top layer is set to a much lower 32%, so you can see some of the fountain in the underlying layer.

Figure 8-5 shows the Layers palette for the combined image. You can see the two individual layers, as well as the opacity setting for the selected (top) layer.

Figure 8-5
The Layers palette after adjusting opacity.

Figure 8-4
Images before and after adjusting opacity.

Naming Layers

As you add more layers, you can identify more easily what each layer represents by using the Rename feature to name each layer clearly. To rename a layer, right-click over it and choose Rename. The existing name appears highlighted, and you can type over the highlighted text with the new name. Press the Enter key when you're finished.

You can also rename layers through the Layer Properties dialog box. Double-click the layer you want to rename, and the Layer Properties dialog box appears displaying the existing layer name (see Figure 8-6). You can just type over the pres-elected existing name with a new descriptive name and click OK.

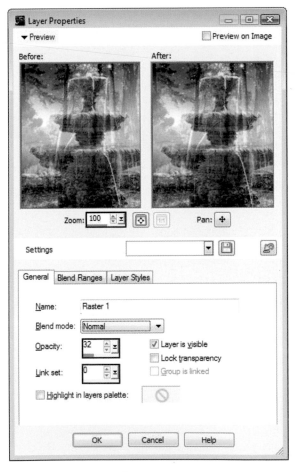

Figure 8-6
A sample Layer Properties box.

Duplicating Layers

For most simple image retouches and correc-tions, you do not have to add additional layers. However, you can duplicate the layer before applying actions such as the photo correction commands. By applying any changes to the duplicated layer, you always preserve the original image on its own layer. Another example might be if you created a layer just the way you want it, and you need another similar layer. Faced with this, you can duplicate the existing layer and modify the new one rather than re-create the layer.

From the Layers palette, right-click the layer you want to duplicate or click the Layers menu, and then choose Duplicate. By default, PaintShop Pro names the duplicated layer with the words *Copy of* and the original layer name. Optionally, you can rename the duplicated layer by following the instructions in the previous section.

Layer Dimensions

If you copy the layer to a different image, and the pixel dimensions of the two images are not the same, you may see the duplicated layer appear smaller or larger than you expect.

Reordering Layers

PaintShop Pro displays layers based on how they are stacked in the Layers palette, with the layer name on top being the top layer of your image. The order of layers within an image is critical to the appearance of the image, so if your layers are stacked differently from what you want, you can change their order. One exception is the background layer, which is always the lowest layer. You can move layers up or down one layer at a time, or you can move a layer to the top or bottom of the stack. Reordering layers is an option under the Layers ❯ Arrange menu, or you can simply place your mouse pointer on the Layers palette, on the layer name you want to move, and drag it to the desired order in the stack. The options under the Layers ❯ Arrange menu are as follows:

- ▶ **Bring to Top**: Moves the layer to the top of the layers.

- ▶ **Move Up**: Moves the layer up one level in the Layers palette.

- ▶ **Move Down**: Moves the layer down one level in the Layers palette.

- ▶ **Send to Bottom**: Moves the layer so it's directly above the background layer. If there is no background layer, Send to Bottom moves the selected layer to the bottom layer.

- ▶ **Move into Group**: Adds a layer to a layer group. See "Understanding Grouping and Merging" later in this chapter.

- ▶ **Move Out of Group**: Removes a layer from a layer group.

Bottom Layer Rules

Neither adjustment layers nor mask layers can be the bottom layer.

As an example, take a look at Figure 8-7. You see an image with two layers. For dramatic effect to show you moving layers, each layer consists of a totally different image. On the left side image, the fruit layer is on top of a little girl layer. After moving the little girl layer up one, it becomes the top image, as you see on the right. If I were to reduce the opacity of the little girl layer, you would be able to see some of the fruit underneath it.

Top layers

Figure 8-7
Changing layer order.

Moving Layers

If a particular layer isn't displaying the portion of the image where you want it, you can slide the layer into a different position. We're not talking about changing the stack order, but actually moving the entire layer content into a new position.

 From the Layers palette, click the layer name you want to move; then from the Tools toolbar, click the Move tool. It's the second tool down and shares space with the Pick tool. When you select the Move tool, the mouse pointer turns into a four-headed arrow, and the current layer is displayed.

Drag the layer and its contents around until they're in the position you want. In Figure 8-8, you see a photograph of a sunflower moved to the left and up. Because this image had another photo layer below it of a lighthouse, you see some of the lighthouse layer behind the sunflower.

You cannot move background layers. If you want to move something residing on a background layer, select the area you want to move and place it on its own layer, or promote the background layer to a regular raster layer. See "Promoting the Background Layer," later in this chapter.

Deleting Layers

If you've created a layer you no longer want, you can easily delete it from the Layers palette. If you delete the background layer, the background of the image becomes transparent.

As with other Layer commands, you can delete a selected layer by accessing the Delete command from the Layers menu or by right-clicking on the layer you want to delete and selecting Delete. A third method is to select the layer you want to delete and click the Delete button on the Layers palette. Whichever method you choose, PaintShop Pro displays the dialog box you see in Figure 8-9, which confirms that you really want to delete the layer.

Mouse pointer

Figure 8-8
Move layer elements for better positioning.

Figure 8-9
Confirming you really do want to delete the current layer.

One thing to remember about layers is that neither adjustment layers nor mask layers can be the bottom layer, so PaintShop Pro won't allow you to delete other layers if deleting them causes an adjustment or mask layer to become the bottom layer.

Use the Undo Function

If you delete a layer in error, don't forget that you can choose Edit ➤ Undo (or press Ctrl+Z) to reverse your last action.

Hiding Layers

On the Layers palette, you see an eye icon, called the *visibility icon*, next to each layer. When you see the eye, it means that you're seeing the layer in the editing screen. If you want to work on an image without seeing the effects of a particular layer, you can hide it by clicking the visibility icon. The icon disappears, and your image does not display the layer results. Click the gray area where the visibility icon was to redisplay the selected layer.

Hiding layers is especially helpful when you are working with adjustment layers and don't want the distraction of the adjustment on your screen. Technically, you can hide all layers in your image, but if you did, you would have nothing but a transparency on your screen.

Let's take a look. Figure 8-10 shows an image with three layers; a solid red layer; a solid blue layer, and a background layer of some vegetables. I've moved the layers so you can see all three layers on the image on the left, but in the image on the right, you see only the red layer and the vegetable layer because by clicking the visibility toggle, I've hidden the blue layer. When you want to redisplay a hidden layer, click the layer's visibility icon again.

Visibility icon (hidden)

Figure 8-10
Hide layers as desired.

Hidden Layers

Hidden layers do not print.

Promoting the Background Layer

As you've seen so far, a background layer, created when you open a new image with a nontransparent background, is a little different from the other layers. First, it is always the lowest layer in the stack. Second, it does not have opacity control like the other layers. If you want to control the opacity or transparency of the background layer, you must first promote it to a regular layer.

One-Way Conversion

You can promote background layers to standard raster layers, but you cannot change raster, vector, or any other layer type to a background layer type.

Choose Layers > Promote Background Layer, or right-click the layer in the Layers palette and choose Promote Background Layer. PaintShop Pro converts the background layer to a regular raster layer and renames it Raster 1 or whatever is the next available raster layer number.

Once you convert the background to a raster layer, you can apply blends and filters, change the stacking order, or do anything with it that you do with a standard raster layer.

Using the Background Eraser on a Background Layer

If you drag the Background Eraser tool on the background layer, PaintShop Pro automatically promotes the background layer to a raster layer, and erased areas become transparent. (See Chapter 10, "Discovering Drawing Tools," for more information on the Background Eraser tool.

Understanding Grouping and Merging

WHEN YOU GROUP LAYERS, you can perform steps to apply to the grouped layers, but you can then ungroup them and perform steps on the individual layers.

Most common graphics file formats, such as JPG, PNG, or TIF, do not support images with layers. Therefore, when you attempt to save your file in one of these formats, PaintShop Pro prompts you that it will merge the layers before saving. Merging takes multiple layers and compresses them into single layers.

Grouping Layers

After you merge layers, which you'll learn about in the next section, the elements are on a single layer and cannot be manipulated individually. Instead of merging the layers, you might want to group them. For example, you might want to group layers if you want to move items on one layer and want the items on some of the other layers to move along also. Each image can contain multiple layer groups. Think of grouping as a temporary way of merging layers. For example, if you want to change the layer opacity or blend mode of several layers, grouping them first allows you to apply the changes once. You can create as many layer groups as you want, and any group can have subgroups.

You have two different methods you can choose from to create a new layer group.

You can, from the main menu, choose Layers ❯ New Layer Group or from the bottom of the Layers palette, click the New Layers drop-down arrow and choose New Layer Group.

PaintShop Pro displays the New Layer Group dialog box seen in Figure 8-11, where you can optionally type a name for the group and then click OK.

Figure 8-11
Creating a new layer group.

Similar to creating a new layer, when you create a layer group, PaintShop Pro assigns a number or name to the group, and it appears on the Layers palette. The layer group begins with only the current layer, but you'll see in just a moment how easy it is to add additional layers to a group.

The new group appears on the Layers palette above the currently selected layer (see Figure 8-12).

Expand/Collapse icon

Figure 8-13
Adding additional layers to a group.

Figure 8-12
The new layer group consisting of one layer.

A group isn't much of a group with just a single layer, so you'll probably want to add other layers to it. In this example, I want to group the Butterflies and Raindrops layers. In the Layers palette, click the layer you want to move into the group and drag it under the Group layer label. You can see in Figure 8-12 that the moved layer (Raindrops) is now included in the group in Figure 8-13.

Also notice in Figure 8-13 that a minus sign, the Expand/Collapse button, appears next to the Group layer icon. You click the minus sign to condense the layers under the group. The minus sign then turns into a plus sign that you click to expand the group.

Removing Layers from a Group

To remove a layer from the group, click the layer you want to remove and choose Layers > Arrange > Move Out of Group. If you attempt to move the last layer in the group, a confirmation dialog box appears confirming that you want to delete the layer group.

Merging Layers

After you get your images in the correct position on their individual layers, you might want to merge two or more of the layers. When you create multilayered images, you must save them in PaintShop Pro's native format to maintain all layer information. When you save to most other file types, such as JPG, GIF, or PNG, PaintShop Pro prompts you that all layers are merged into one background layer since these formats allow for only a single layer.

Save Before Merging

After you flatten and merge your layers, other than using the Undo command, you cannot restore the individual layers. You might want to keep a copy of your images with all the layers. Save a copy of the file as a PaintShop Pro–formatted file before you merge the layers.

PaintShop Pro provides several types of merging:

▶ **Merge Down**: Selectively combines two layers that are adjacent to each other. The merged layer retains the name of the lower layer and contains images from both layers.

▶ **Merge All**: When you merge all the layers (called *flattening*), the image becomes nonlayered. If you have transparent areas in the image, PaintShop Pro fills them with white, and the image consists of a single background layer with all the components.

▶ **Merge Visible**: Merges all nonhidden layers into a single layer but leaves any hidden layers separate. This is helpful if you want to pick and choose which layers you want to merge, because the layers don't need to be adjacent to each other.

▶ **Merge Group**: Combines group layers into a single layer by merging the group. The single layer keeps the group name and contains the images from all the combined layers.

Adding Adjustment Layers

EARLIER IN THIS CHAPTER, I mentioned that the type of layer used most often by photographers is an adjustment layer. What are adjustment layers? Although they're similar to regular raster layers, adjustment layers are correction layers that modify an image color or tone without directly modifying the image pixels. You can't paint or add anything to an adjustment layer, but you can intensify or lessen its effect by adjusting its opacity or blend modes. (You'll learn more about blend modes later in this chapter.) You can also mask out areas of the layer that you don't want to adjust. (See "Masking with Layers" later in this chapter.)

You can, and should, place each correction type on its own layer to test various color corrections or to see how several corrections look when you combine them. Falling into three main types of corrections, PaintShop Pro provides several types of adjustment layers:

▶ To adjust the color balance, select Color Balance, Hue/Saturation/Lightness, or the Channel Mixer adjustment layers. Color Balance changes the color balance in the image shadow, midtones, and highlight areas. Hue/Saturation/Lightness manipulates the image colors. Saturation is the color strength, and Hue represents the color reflection. The Channel Mixer increases or decreases the red, green, or blue color channels. Use this adjustment layer when you want to adjust the individual color channels.

Layers Beneath Adjustment Layers

Adjustment layers affect all layers that are under them.

▶ To adjust the image brightness or contrast, select the Brightness/Contrast, Curves, or Levels adjustment layers. Brightness/Contrast lightens or darkens the image by controlling the lightness and number of color shades in the image. Curves adjusts the individual brightness levels in the image, and Levels, via a histogram, allows you to adjust image tones and color casts by manipulating the actual image color channels.

▶ To reduce or remove image colors, select the Invert, Threshold, or Posterize adjustment layers. An Invert layer creates a negative of the image based on brightness values. Threshold displays the image in true black and true white, which helps you locate the lightest and darkest areas. Posterize gives the image a flat appearance by reducing the number of brightness values, thus reducing the number of colors.

Change Layer Type

After you've created an adjustment layer, you cannot change its type. Simply delete the unwanted layer and create a different one.

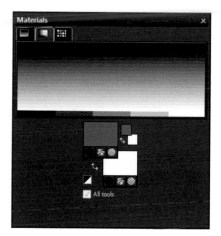

When you add an adjustment layer, you cannot add colors, so if you look at the Materials palette when you've clicked on an adjustment layer, all you see are shades of gray.

Follow these steps to add an adjustment layer to your image:

1. Select the layer on which you want to place the adjustment layer.

2. Choose Layers ❯ New Adjustment Layer or choose New Adjustment Layer after clicking the New Layer button on the Layers palette.

3. Select the type of adjustment layer you want. A dialog box relevant to the adjustment layer type you selected appears. The settings on the dialog box vary with the type of adjustment layer. In Figure 8-14, you see the Brightness/Contrast layer box where, like other PaintShop Pro dialog boxes, you see the Current View and the Preview panels so that you can observe the effect of your changes and adjustment until the image meets your preferences.

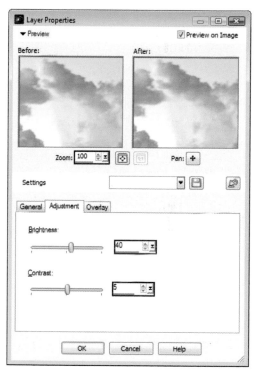

Figure 8-14
Adding adjustment layers.

4. On the Adjustment tab, you can choose settings for the adjustment you are making. Remember that you can also change these settings any time after you create the adjustment layer.

5. On the General tab, you can enter a different name for the layer and select a blend mode and opacity setting.

6. Click the OK button. The new layer appears on the Layers palette.

Figure 8-15 shows an image that was originally too dark, as you see on the left. On the right, after adding two adjustment layers—Brightness/Contrast and Color balance—you can see both the subject and the rich details of the sky more clearly.

Practice, Practice, Practice

In reality, modifying an image takes a lot of trial and error. Try a setting and see if you like it. If not, undo it or delete the layer. You'll find yourself doing a lot of "what-if" scenarios. Working with each correction on its own adjustment layer makes trying the "what-if" issue much easier.

Figure 8-15
Adding adjustments layers to lighten an image.

Masking with Layers

WE USE MASKS IN A LOT OF PLACES.
Obviously, at Halloween
you see masks that hide
your face but still allow
your eyes and mouth to
show through. When you
use a stencil to spray
paint some letters onto
a sign, you are using a
mask. When you paint
your living room and you
don't want to get paint
on the woodwork, you
tape the area that you want to protect with—what
else—masking tape. In the art world, watercolor
artists use a masking product to keep washes of
color from bleeding into particular areas of a
painting.

Similarly, PaintShop Pro supports masks, which
in reality, are grayscale layers that hide portions
of other layers without actually deleting them or
modifying them. You can use mask layers to hide
and show parts of a layer, fade between layers,
and create other special effects. You can create a
mask from a selection or from an existing image,
and the mask can completely cover a layer or
cover a layer with varying levels of opacity.

You can create a new mask layer that you can
paint on, use the mask layer to hide or show
underlying layers, or create a mask layer from an
image, a selection, or the luminance of an image.
In addition, you can use one of the sample masks
(stored in the Masks folder of the PaintShop Pro
program folder) and apply it as is or customize it.

Like other types of layers, you can turn the
visibility of the mask layer on or off, change
the overall opacity of the mask layer, or link the
mask layer to other layers.

When you save your image that includes a mask
in the PSPIMAGE format, the mask is saved as
well; however, if you save your image in another
format, such as JPEG or TIFF, PaintShop Pro flat-
tens the image and merges all layers, including
the mask layer. Additionally, you can save a mask
as a separate image file on a disk, which is bene-
ficial if you plan to use the mask again.

Using Standard Masks

PaintShop Pro comes with 26 uniquely designed
masks that you can use on your images as a
great time-saver. Additionally, you can add to the
predefined mask collection by creating your own
mask and saving it to a disk file, which you'll
learn about in the next section.

If you apply a mask to a background layer, the area being masked out becomes transparent, and when you save it to a file format that doesn't support transparency, PaintShop Pro turns the transparency to a solid color. For that reason, if you don't want transparency, you should start by creating a solid color background for your image. Make the background the same size as the photograph you are going to use.

A mask layer applies to all layers below it and that are at the same level, as follows:

> ▶ If a mask layer is in a layer group, it applies only to layers within the group that are lower in the stacking order.

> ▶ If the mask layer is at the main level (rather than in a layer group), it applies to all layers below it in the stacking order.

To change which underlying layers the mask applies to, on the Layers palette, drag the mask layer to a new position in the stacking order. Mask layers can never be the bottom layer in the image or in a layer group.

The following steps show you how to apply one of the standard masks provided with PaintShop Pro:

1. Open the image to which you want to apply a mask.

2. Change the background layer into a standard raster layer by clicking the layer and choosing Layers ❯ Promote Background Layer.

3. Create a new raster layer and fill it with the color you want to show through the mask. If you want the masked area to be transparent, you can skip this step. Remember, however, that some file formats, such as JPG and TIF, do not support transparency and convert the masked area to white.

4. Move the newly created raster layer so it's below the image layer. Figure 8-16 shows the Layers palette with an image and a filled raster layer.

Figure 8-16
Creating a filled raster layer for the mask.

5. Now you're ready to pick a mask. Make sure, from the Layers palette, that you have the image raster layer selected, and not a background layer. Choose Layers ❯ Load/Save Mask ❯ Load Mask from Disk. You see the dialog box shown in Figure 8-17.

Click here to view the different masks

Figure 8-17
When you create your own masks, they also appear in the drop-down mask list.

Figure 8-18
Adding a mask layer.

Automatic Conversion

If you apply a mask to a background, PaintShop Pro automatically converts the background layer to a raster layer.

6. Click the drop-down arrow next to the Mask box, and select the mask you want to use. For Orientation, you typically want Fit to Layer.

7. Click Load, and PaintShop Pro applies the mask to your image (see Figure 8-18). Additionally, if you take a look at the Layers palette, a mask layer appears above your image layer, and the two are grouped.

Creating Your Own Mask

PaintShop Pro certainly doesn't limit you to its selection of predefined masks. You can create your own and save it for future use. A mask can cover a layer completely or with varying levels of opacity. Where a mask is black, it completely covers the layer, and where it is white, it leaves the layer uncovered. If you use a gray value between black and white, the mask produces a semi-visible effect.

Although PaintShop Pro includes a number of masks and hundreds more are available on the Internet, you might want to design your own mask.

Close Other Open Images

It's easier to create a mask if you don't have other images open when you're creating it.

The following steps take you through creating your own mask:

1. Create a new raster image with a black background. When applied, the black portion of a mask blocks the image. The size of the image isn't too important; when you load a mask, you decide then what size it should be. Just make the new image a size that's easy for you to work with.

New Image

Presets:

Image Dimensions

Width : 800 Units :
                Pixels
Height : 800

Resolution : 200.000 Pixels/inch

Image Characteristics

◉ Raster Background
○ Vector Background
○ Art Media Background

Color depth : RGB - 8 bits/channel

Color:

☐ Transparent

Memory Required: 2.2 MBytes
Dimensions: 800 x 800 Pixels

OK   Cancel   Help

2. Next, you need to mark a portion of the black layer so that when you apply the mask, part of the image can show through. Click the Shape selection tool and from the Tool Options palette, pick a shape. For the example you will see shortly, I'm using the Hexagon shape.

Creating Soft Edges

Set Feathering to 4 or 5 for a nice edge-softening effect.

3. Draw a selection in the black image that displays the selection marquee. The size you select is the size of the masked area (see Figure 8-19).

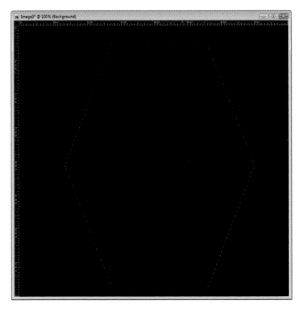

Figure 8-19
Draw a selection for the masked area.

4. Click the Flood Fill tool, and in the Materials palette, set the foreground color to white. Remember that whatever you paint in white appears through the mask. When you apply the mask to an image, the area in white is visible.

5. Click in the selected area, which turns it white (see Figure 8-20).

Flood fill

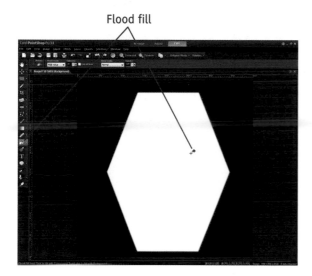

Figure 8-20
Creating a mask.

6. Deselect the mask area by choosing Selections > Select None or by pressing Ctrl+D. So far, you have an image consisting of a shape such as the hexagon. Next, you need to tell PaintShop Pro that the image is intended for a mask.

7. Click Layers > New Mask Layer > From Image. The Add Mask from Image dialog box appears, asking if the image you have onscreen is the one you want for a mask. (Now you know why the earlier Tip mentioned that it's easier to create a mask if you don't have any other images open.)

8. Click OK. PaintShop Pro now knows that the current image is a mask and turns the black area into a transparency, indicated by gray-and-white checks. Masks are made up entirely of black, white, or shades of gray. Notice the Materials and the Layers palettes on the right side of Figure 8-21.

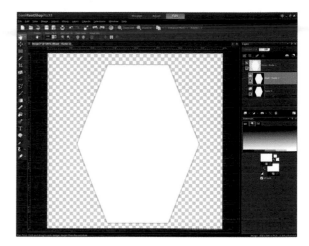

Figure 8-21
A newly created mask.

Set Transparency Preferences

Choose File > Preferences > General Program Preferences. Then click the Transparency and Shading tab to determine the way that PaintShop Pro displays a transparent area on your screen.

9. Now that you've created the mask, you probably want to save it for future use. Choose Layers > Load/Save Mask > Save Mask to Disk. The Save Mask to Disk dialog box shown in Figure 8-22 opens.

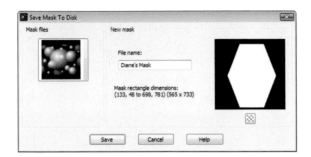

Figure 8-22
PaintShop Pro names mask files with a .pspmask
extension to identify them as masks.

10. Enter a descriptive name for the mask and
click Save.

Buttonize Effects

**See Chapter 9, "Adding Effects, Filters,
and Deformations," for more information
on adding effects.**

Now you can apply the mask whenever you want
it (see Figure 8-23).

Figure 8-23
In this example, I used a rainbow gradient bottom
layer and added a Page Curl effect to it.

Blending Layers

BY BLENDING LAYERS, you can change the mood of a photograph or create interesting abstract images. Just as the name implies, blends result from mixing. *Mixing,* in this case, refers to two or more layers blending together. Blend modes allow you to control how colors in one layer affect the underlying layers because the blend layer's pixels are blended into underlying layers without actually combining the layers. The way the pixels blend depends on which blend mode you apply.

PaintShop Pro includes a variety of blend modes. Table 8-1 illustrates an example of a field of star-gazer lilies with a solid yellow layer set at 50% opacity. You can see the image layers using each blend mode and a description of its effect.

Applying a Blend Mode

When you add a new layer, the New Layer dialog box includes a drop-down list where you can choose a blend mode. If you want to change the blend mode after creating the layer, select the layer and, from the top of the Layers palette, click the blend mode arrow and choose a different mode.

The blend modes are listed in alphabetical order.

Four of the blend modes (Color, Hue, Luminance, and Saturation) also have a Legacy blend mode that is more compatible with other applications.

Table 8-1   Blend Modes

Sample	Blend Name	Effect
	None	Original image with no layer blending.
	Burn	The lightness values of the selected layer reduce the lightness of underlying layers, which results in darkening the overall image.

Sample	Blend Name	Effect
	Color	Without affecting the lightness, Color applies the hue and saturation of the selected layer to the underlying layers. (Also has a Legacy mode.)
	Darken	Displays pixels in the selected layer that are darker than the underlying pixels. Any pixels lighter than the underlying layers disappear.
	Difference	Subtracts the selected layer's color from the color of the underlying layers.
	Dissolve	Creates a speckled effect by randomly replacing the colors of some pixels on the selected layer with those of the underlying layers.
	Dodge	The color's lightness values in the selected layer increase the lightness of underlying layers, which lightens the overall image.
	Exclusion	Similar to the Difference blend mode, subtracts the selected layer's color from the color of the underlying layers, but does so with a softer color difference.
	Hard Light	Adds highlights and shadows by combining the Multiply and Screen blend modes, depending on the color channel.
	Hue	Without affecting the saturation or lightness, applies the hue of the selected layer to the underlying layers. (Also has a Legacy mode.)
	Lighten	Displays pixels in the selected layer that are lighter than the underlying pixels. Any pixels darker than the underlying layers disappear.

Sample	Blend Name	Effect
	Luminance	Without affecting the hue or saturation, applies the lightness of the selected layer to the underlying layers. (Also has a Legacy mode.)
	Multiply	Darkens the image by mixing the colors of the selected layer with the underlying layers. There are two exceptions: multiplying any color with white leaves the color unchanged, and multiplying any color with black results in black.
	Normal	The default option; displays pixels of the underlying layers, based on the opacity of pixels on the selected layer.
	Overlay	Shows patterns and colors of the selected layer, but preserves the shadows and highlights of underlying layers. Similar to the Hard Light blend mode in that it combines the Multiply and Screen blend modes, depending on the color channel value.
	Saturation	Without affecting the hue or lightness, applies the saturation of the selected layer to the underlying layers. (Also has a Legacy mode.)
	Screen	Lightens the colors of underlying layers by multiplying the inverse of the selected and underlying layers, resulting in a lightened color of the selected layer.
	Soft Light	Adds soft highlights or shadows by combining the Burn and Dodge blend modes, depending on the channel value of the selected layer.

In most cases, the order of the layers becomes an important issue, because PaintShop Pro blends the pixels of the selected layer with all the underlying layers. The exceptions to this are the Multiply, Screen, Difference, and Exclusion blend modes, because they produce the same result no matter which layer is on top.

Alternative Blend Mode Method

You can also change the layer blend mode from the Blend section on the Layers palette.

You certainly don't have to apply a solid color layer to create blends. Let's take a look at another example, but this time we'll blend a beautiful sunset with a lake scene.

Copy Layer to Different Image

To duplicate a layer from one image to another, select the layer you want to copy and choose Selections > All; then choose Edit > Copy. Next, click the original image to activate it, and choose Edit > Paste as New Layer. When you are blending images, you should use photos of the same size or scale, one of which has an element that would look somewhat natural if placed in the second photo. In this example, we copied the Sunset picture and pasted it into the Lake photo as a new layer. In Figure 8-24, you see three completely different results from using a blend mode on the copied sunset layer. The image on the left is in Burn blend mode, the middle image is in Overlay blend mode, and the image on the right is in Screen blend mode.

Figure 8-24
Each blend mode gives the image a different look.

Chapter 8

If you aren't quite satisfied with the blend mode defaults, you have the option of adjusting any or all of the Grey, Red, Green, or Blue color channels. You can adjust channels for any layer. The Blend Ranges adjustments are a tab on the Layer Properties dialog box, as seen in Figure 8-25.

Figure 8-25
Adjust blend modes by channel color.

Being Creative with Layers

NOW THAT YOU'VE GOT A GOOD GRASP of what regular layers can do for you and how they operate, let's put it to some practical photographical use. In this example, by using layers, you see how you can convert a color image like the one shown in Figure 8-26 into one that is a combination of color and grayscale. To accomplish this, I need the Eraser tool, which erases pixels and makes them transparent.

Figure 8-26
Original image.

The following steps walk you through the process of creating the combination image.

1. To begin this project, you'll need two copies of the same image. You'll need to change one of the copies to a grayscale image, so you can't just duplicate the layer; you need to duplicate the image. Choose Window > Duplicate to duplicate the open image.

2. Next, take the duplicate image and change its color range to grayscale. Make sure the duplicate image is the active window, and choose Image > Greyscale (see Figure 8-27).

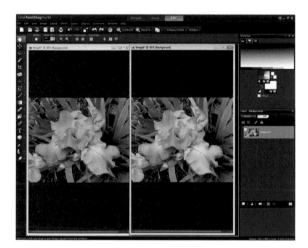

Figure 8-27
The original image and the grayscale image.

3. Now you're going to take the grayscale image and make it a layer in the original image. First, choose Selections > All or press Ctrl+A. Notice the marquee that appears around the entire image.

4. Choose Edit > Copy or press Ctrl+C. It doesn't look like anything happened, but it did. Windows and PaintShop Pro are keeping track of your steps.

5. Click the original image to activate it, and choose Edit > Paste as New Layer. The grayscale image appears as a new layer on the Layers palette. Your original image may look grayscale, too, but that's because the grayscale layer is on top of the background layer. That's okay, and as it should be. (You can now close the copy of the duplicated window if you want.)

Optional Paste Keystrokes

To paste the image as a new layer, you could also press Ctrl+V or Ctrl+L.

6. Now choose your favorite selection tool (for this example, I'm going to use the Freehand selection tool with the Edge Seeker selection type), and select the part of the image you want to be in color (see Figure 8-28).

Figure 8-28
Select the image portion you want to color.

Figure 8-29
The finished image.

 7. Click the Eraser tool on the Tools tool-bar. It's the eleventh tool from the top.

8. From the Tool Options palette, make sure that Opacity is 100%. Make the size large enough so that you don't have to spend too much time uncovering your colored image.

9. Using your mouse pointer, erase the complete area within the selection boundary. You don't have to worry about staying in the lines, because you selected the area you want to erase, and the Eraser tool will not go beyond those boundary lines. As you run the Eraser over the image, PaintShop Pro replaces the gray pixels with transparent pixels, and the color from the background layer begins to show through.

10. Deselect your selection boundary by pressing Ctrl+D or choosing Selections ❯ Select None. Take a look at the finished image in Figure 8-29.

Save as a PSPIMAGE File

Remember that if you save the image as anything other than a PaintShop Pro proprietary format, PaintShop Pro merges the layers, and you can't come back and easily bring out other colors in the image. You should save the image first as a PaintShop Pro image (PSPIMAGE); then when you're finished working on it, save it as another format, such as TIF or JPG.

9

Adding Effects, Filters, **and Deformations**

PICTURE YOURSELF AS AN ACTOR OR ACTRESS. Before you go on stage or in front of the camera, you spend time with a makeup artist. Changes are made—some subtle, others not. The makeup helps you get your message across to your audience. But you're still the same person underneath—you just have this layer on top of you making you look different. Consider that look a filter.

Filters are important correction and creativity tools. The function of a filter is to change the way the camera lens sees the subject. Some filters have a tint and can block certain colors; others can blur the image or even add distortion and special effects.

With digital image manipulation, you don't have to take your shots using those expensive and sometimes cumbersome filters. You can add the effect later using PaintShop Pro.

Working with Blur

YOU'VE ALREADY WORKED with some filters when you adjusted saturation, contrast, color balance, and noise. Most of those filters made corrections to your photographs in maintaining color and sharpness. The filters in this chapter have more to do with distorting your images into unique works of art. Some you may use a lot, and others rarely. This chapter takes a brief look at the many effects available with PaintShop Pro and demonstrates how they can easily give your images extra touches of character.

Interchangeable Terms

The terms *effects* and *filters* basically serve the same purpose, and you'll hear the words used interchangeably. The wonderful folks at Corel Software consider items under the Effects menu in the Edit workspace as effects and items under the Adjust menu as filters, but this is not a hard and fast rule, because often you hear effects referred to as filters. Complicate this rule by the fact that items from the Adjust menu appear within the Effect Browser, which you'll learn about later in this chapter, and you have total chaos. Confused? That's certainly understandable. For clarity, try thinking about all of them as *filters* and the names given under the Effects menu as results of filters.

Most good photographic images demand clarity. The Sharpening and Unsharp Mask adjustment commands help clarify your images, and you can remove noise with the Salt and Pepper filter, the Digital Camera Noise Removal (DCNR) filter, and JPEG Artifact Removal tools, just to name a few. Sometimes, though, instead of clarifying your image, you want to blur or soften all or part of the photograph. In Chapter 4, "Making Selections," you discovered one of the blur filters: the Gaussian filter. Other blur filters, which actually add noise to your image, include Average, Blur, Blur More, Radial, and Motion Blur.

Blur filters compare pixels to nearby other pixels and average their values, which, in turn, reduces the contrast between them. Most of the blur filters focus primarily on high-contrast areas, and all blur filters only work on grayscale and 16 million color or more images.

Blur and Blur More

You might use the Blur and Blur More filters to reduce graininess in your image. These filters remove noise by applying smooth transitions and decreasing the contrast in the image. As you might expect, the Blur More effect applies the blur effect with more intensity.

You apply the Blur and Blur More filters by clicking the Adjust menu, selecting Blur, and choosing Blur or Blur More. Neither filter provides you with options; each simply applies a preset amount of blur to the image.

Control Blur Area

Control the blur area by applying the filters to only selected areas of the image.

Figure 9-1 shows an image with no blur, Blur, and Blur More applied. Notice the detail change of the girls' eyes and curls in each image.

Original	Blur	Blur More

Figure 9-1
Decrease image contrast with the Blur and Blur More filters.

Average Blur

The Average Blur filter is really helpful at removing dithering that often occurs when you increase the color depth of an image. By reducing the contrast between pixels, you get less waffling and a smoother, more consistent appearance.

When you use the Average Blur filter, PaintShop Pro prompts you for an amount, measured in aperture. Aperture options run from 3 to 31, in odd numbers only. The higher the aperture setting, the more blur that PaintShop Pro applies.

Access the Average Blur filter by clicking the Adjust menu, selecting Blur, and then choosing Average Blur.

Gaussian Blur

Another type of blur is Gaussian Blur, which originates from German mathematician and astronomer Karl Friedrich Gauss. Mr. Gauss had many mathematical theories, some of which are what PaintShop Pro applies when you use Gaussian Blur. Gaussian Blur is similar to Average Blur, but Gaussian Blur is a little stronger and gives more realistic results. It works by controlling the amount of blurring applied to any given pixel or edge by an adjustable amount, making the blurring appear dense in the center and soft and feathery around the edges.

Like other blurring effects, you can apply the blur to an entire image or just a selected portion of it. Most of the time, you won't want to apply the blur to the entire photograph but only to a portion of it, which changes the depth of field.

You'll have the best results if you place the area you want to modify on its own layer and then add the Gaussian Blur to the selected layer. Follow these steps:

1. Promote the background to a raster layer. (Choose Layers > Promote Background Layer). (See Chapter 8, "Developing Layers," for information about working with layers.)

2. Select the area you want to blur. In the example here, I'll first select the dog using the Freehand Selection tool with Smart Edge. To give a softer edge, I set Feathering at 2.

3. Since it's not the dog I want to blur, but the background, I need to invert the selection. Choose Selections > Invert.

4. Move the selected area to its own layer by clicking Selections ❯ Promote Selection to Layer.

5. Now you can apply the blur. Again, making sure you are on the Promoted Selection layer, click the Adjust menu, select Blur, and then select Gaussian Blur. You see a Gaussian Blur dialog box like the one in Figure 9-2.

6. Set the blur radius you want, and click OK. Values range from 0 to 100, with 100 being totally blurred.

Figure 9-3 shows the image before and after adding a 10 radius Gaussian Blur. A setting of 10 is really too much blur for this image, but it does show you the dramatic effect of Gaussian Blur.

Reset button

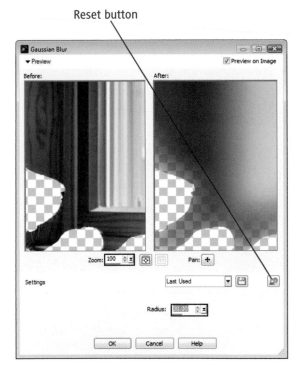

Figure 9-2
Set the amount of blur you want.

Figure 9-3
An image before and after applying Gaussian Blur to a selected area.

Reset Option

Don't forget that you can click the Reset button to reset all options to their default.

Motion Blur

Most of today's cameras have built-in features that reduce the chance of getting motion blur during a shot; however, there will be times when you *want* a motion blur, to add to the visual impact an object has on the image. PaintShop Pro includes a Motion Blur filter, which simulates taking a picture of a moving object using a fixed exposure time. This filter works best when used inside a selection.

Motion effects are placed in a directional manner to achieve the illusion of motion. You can adjust not only the intensity of the blur but also the direction in which the blur effect is applied.

Take a look at the car wheel shown in Figure 9-4. It's nice, but it lacks even a hint of motion. How boring is that? Let's add a little action to it, giving the impression of movement.

Figure 9-4
Put your wheels in motion with the
Motion Blur filter.

I want to add the blur to the wheel itself and not the area surrounding the wheel. Because I want to isolate the motion blur area, I have to make a selection first.

In this example, I chose the Freehand Selection tool. Then in the Tool Options palette, I set the Selection Type to Freehand, set Feather to 2, and enabled Anti-Alias. I selected a rough selection around the area I wanted to blur. See Figure 9-5 for the selected area.

Figure 9-5
Keeping the selection area rough prevents
the blur from looking too stiff.

Now you can apply the blur filter. Click the Adjust menu and select Blur. Next, select Motion Blur, which displays the dialog box you see in Figure 9-6.

217

Preset settings arrow

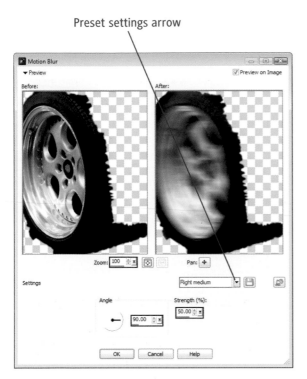

Figure 9-6
Use the dial control or enter in an Angle value
to set the blur direction.

Angle is a circular value ranging from 0 to 359
degrees. The Strength value is a percentage that
runs from 1 to 100, with 100% being a total blur.
For this example, I'll choose one of the Preset
values, so I click the Settings arrow and choose
Right Medium. The Right sets the motion
toward the right, and the Medium indicates the
amount of motion. In the case of the car wheel,
that's an Angle setting of 90 and a Strength
setting of 50%. One thing to remember is that
typically, if you are trying to blur a vehicle, you
won't want a high Motion Blur, because it would
be too much blur. Click OK after you've selected
your settings.

Additional Motion

**To add additional motion, apply a second
Motion Blur, but feather the selection size
first.**

Notice that the blur applied only to the selected
area. Since I don't need the selection anymore,
I click Selections ❯ Select None, or press Ctrl+D.

Figure 9-7 shows the wheel with motion.

Figure 9-7
Hot rodding anyone?

Radial Blur

One other type of blur you can achieve with PaintShop Pro is a Radial Blur. Radial Blur simulates blurring like spinning a camera in circles or zooming in quickly with a slow shutter speed. The Radial Blur filter can also give your image a twirling look.

Like many of the blur filters, you probably won't use the Radial Blur often, but with the right photograph, it produces a stunning effect, like the one you see in Figure 9-8.

Figure 9-8
Add a zoom blur effect with Radial Blur.

PaintShop Pro's Radial Blur filter provides three different blur types: Twirl, Zoom, and Spin. The Zoom type blurs pixels away from the center of the image, and the Twirl type blurs pixels in a spiraling manner.

The third type, Spin, blurs pixels circularly around the image center. Figure 9-9 shows the same image with a spin effect. Notice the circular motion.

Figure 9-9
Spin type Radial Blur makes the trees appear as if they are in the middle of a tornado.

The following steps walk you through applying the Radial Blur filter to your image:

1. Click the Adjust menu, select Blur, and then select Radial Blur. You see a dialog box like the one in Figure 9-10.

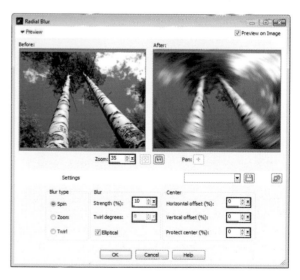

Figure 9-10
Twirl, zoom, or spin your image.

2. Select a Blur type: Twirl, Zoom, or Spin.

3. In the Blur section, choose a Strength value. Measured in percentages from 1 to 100, lower values lessen the effect, while higher values intensify the effect. If you choose the Twirl option, you can also set the Twirl degrees value from −90 to 90, which determines the tilt of the twirl.

4. Click the Elliptical check box if you have a rectangular image and want the radius squeezed to fit the image, which produces elliptical-shaped blurring, as opposed to circular.

5. The Center section contains settings that affect the center of the image. The horizontal offset sets the horizontal center point of the blur, whereas the vertical offset sets the vertical center point of the blur. Values for both center points range from −100 to 100. The last option, Protect Center, determines how much to diminish blurring at the image center. With values from 1 to 100, higher values increase the radius of the nonblurred center area.

6. Click OK after making your selection.

Experiment with the blur settings. You can even use blur to create some awesome backgrounds for other images.

Reviewing Effects and Filters

PAINTSHOP PRO INCLUDES many creative and sometimes mystical filter effects, designed to radically change the nature of your images. Some are subtle and barely detectable, while others make the image jump right out at you. As a photographer, you probably won't use these effects much, but in special situations, you may find them helpful, if not downright amusing.

Effects work on selections or the individual layers of an image, so you can apply a different effect for each layer, or you can apply multiple effects to a single layer. Like most filters you've already encountered, effects work only on raster images and only if the image is full (16 million) color or in certain grayscale settings. PaintShop Pro includes 88 different effects in 11 different categories, available from the Effects menu in the Edit workspace:

- ▶ Photo effects
- ▶ 3-D effects
- ▶ Art media effects
- ▶ Artistic effects
- ▶ Distortion effects
- ▶ Edge effects
- ▶ Geometric effects
- ▶ Illumination effects
- ▶ Image effects
- ▶ Reflection effects
- ▶ Texture effects

We won't be able to look at each one of the effects, but we'll review each category and the types of effects each category manages. Some effects, such as all of the edge category effects, simply apply without any dialog box or options. Others require input from you.

The dialog box you see in Figure 9-11 is one of the easier effects dialog boxes. Only a single option appears in this Artistic Aged Newspaper dialog box.

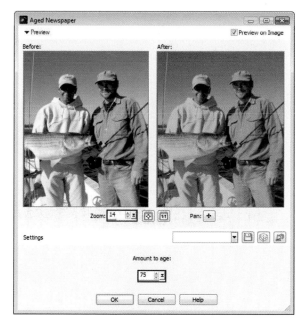

Figure 9-11
Select the number of years you want your image to appear aged.

Other dialog boxes provide you with options to make the effect develop the way you want it. For example, take a look at Figure 9-12. This is the dialog box for the Artistic Balls and Bubbles effect. You can see that there are four tabs for you to set options, and each tab has multiple selections. All these options may seem complex, but they provide you with lots of flexibility in applying the effect.

Figure 9-12
Click the Help button for a detailed explanation
of the dialog box options.

Apply to All or Part

You can apply most effects to the entire image or only to a selected area; however, some effects are unnoticeable unless you apply them to a selected area.

Photo Effects

The photo effects simulate some traditional film photograph processes and techniques, such as these:

▶ **Time Machine**: With this effect, you re-create some popular photographic styles from the debut of photography in the year 1839 to the 1980s. The Time Machine dialog box explains the different styles and why they were popular in their time.

▶ **Film and Filters**: With this effect, you can get effects similar to various camera film and filters. Choices include Vivid, Vivid Skin Tones, Muted Reds, Enhanced Reds, Vibrant Foliage, Warm Earth Tones, and Glamour.

▶ **Black and White Film**: Just as its name indicates, this effect emulates taking a photo with black-and-white film. You can optionally apply a colored filter effect as well.

▶ **Infrared Film**: This effect makes the image appear as if taken with black-and-white infrared film and an infrared pass lens filter. The dialog box Strength settings make greens appear brighter and blues appear darker. You can apply Flare controls for a halo effect to lighter areas in the photo. Grain controls add realistic infrared photo graininess.

▶ **Sepia Toning**: With this effect, you end up with images that are brown tone and somewhat aged looking.

▶ **Vignette**: New to PaintShop Pro X4, this effect fades the edges around the photograph. Through the vignette dialog box, you can control the edge color, shape, blur and glow.

▶ **Selective Focus**: Also new to PaintShop Pro X4, the Selective Focus effect (sometimes called a tilt-shift effect) makes an image scene appear somewhat surreal by focusing on the center and heavily diffusing the rest of the image. I see it as sort of a cross between blur and depth of field.

3D Effects

The 3D category includes six special effects designed to give your selection or image a sense of depth and dimension. Three of the effects—Chisel, Drop Shadow, and Outer Bevel—can only be used with a selection, not an entire layer. You can apply them to an entire layer by selecting the entire layer first. The other three effects—Buttonize, Cutout, and Inner Bevel—can be used on layers or selections.

Buttonize   Chisel

Sepia   Vignette

223

Art Media Effects

The six art media effects are an artist's dream. You can use them to make your image look as if it were hand-painted or drawn. Choices include Black Pencil, Brush Strokes, Charcoal, Colored Chalk, Colored Pencil, and Pencil.

Tools Versus Effects

Don't confuse the art media effects with the Art Media tools. With the Art Media tools, you create your own design, but with the art media effects, it only looks like you created the design.

Charcoal   Colored Pencil

Artistic Effects

The artistic effects are my favorite category, as well as one of the largest, with 15 possible effects designed to apply a variety of different results to your image:

▶ Aged Newspaper applies a yellowed, aging look to your image.

▶ Balls and Bubbles lets you create reflective transparent bubbles over your image.

▶ Chrome gives your image a metallic appearance.

▶ Colored Edges locates and enhances the edges in your photo.

▶ Colored Foil and Enamel gives the image a shiny, melded-together appearance.

▶ Contours presents an outline of your photograph.

▶ Glowing Edges applies a glow to the image edges and makes them look like they are under a black light.

▶ Neon Glow, similar to Glowing Edges, applies a glow to the image edges and applies a speckled pattern along with the enhanced colored edges.

▶ Halftone provides gradations of light as though the photograph was taken through a fine screen.

▶ Hot Wax Coating makes your image look as if a layer of melted wax was poured over the top of it.

▶ Magnifying Lens simulates placing a magnifying lens on a portion of the image.

▶ Posterize blends, smoothes, and compresses the image color to give a soft appearance.

▶ Solarize converts colors in an image into their inverse.

▶ Topography provides a graphic representation of the image surface features.

Balls and Bubbles

Chrome

Neon Glow

Magnifying Lens

Distortion Effects

Just like their name implies, the distortion effects distort your image. Another large category of effects, this one contains 13 choices, many of which can turn your image into a completely unrecognizable but artistic form. Select from Curlicues, Displacement Map, Lens Distortion, Pinch, Pixelate, Polar Coordinates, Punch, Ripple, Spiky Halo, Twirl, Warp, Wave, and Wind.

Wave

Ripple

Spiky Halo

Warp

Edge Effects

Only on the High Pass edge effect do you get a dialog box. On the other edge effects choices, PaintShop Pro simply applies the effect that you choose to clarify your image and put emphasis on your image edges. Select from Dilate, Enhance, Enhance More, Erode, Find All, Find Horizontal, Find Vertical, High Pass, and Trace Contour.

Find All

High Pass

Geometric Effects

Don't worry—you didn't have to pass your high school geometry class to use the geometric effects. This category includes eight options to transform your images into geometric shapes, including circles, cylinders, pentagons, and spheres.

Pentagon

Circle

Illumination Effects

The illumination effects category has only two choices: Lights and Sunburst, both of which add lighting to your image or selection area.

Sunburst   Lights

Image Effects

Think of the image effects category as the "everything else" category. There are three options available: Offset, Page Curl, and Seamless Tiling.

Page Curl   Seamless Tiling

Reflection Effects

From twisting your image into a kaleidoscope to using Feedback (sort of the old "mirror reflecting a mirror reflecting a mirror" routine), the four reflection effects make your current image appear as if you have multiple images. Choices also include Pattern and Rotating Mirror.

Blinds   Weave

Kaleidoscope   Feedback

Texture

Texture Effects

Enhance the essence of your image by using one of the 15 texture effects. Most of these effects make your image appear as if it were "top coated." Another of the larger categories, you can pick from 15 different texture effects, such as Blinds, Emboss, Fine Leather, Fur, Mosaic–Antique, Mosaic–Glass, Polished Stone, Rough Leather, Sandstone, Sculpture, Soft Plastic, Straw Wall, Texture, Tiles, and Weave.

Sculpture

Discovering the Effect Browser

WOW! THERE ARE SO MANY effects that it can be hard to choose the right one for your photograph. The easiest way to see what an effect applies to your image is by using the Effect Browser. The Effect Browser displays a thumbnail of your open image layer with a sample of each effect with its default and other preset settings. The Effect Browser is the first option under the Effects menu. Be patient; the Effect Browser (see Figure 9-13) takes a moment to load, but it is well worth the wait.

On the left side, you see a tree view of all the different categories of adjustments and effects. Click the plus sign next to any category to expand that category, or click the minus sign to collapse a category. When you locate and click the effect you want to use, click Apply, and PaintShop Pro automatically applies that preset option to your image. If the preset filter is close, but not quite what you want, click the effect thumbnail image and then click the Modify button. PaintShop Pro displays the dialog box appropriate to the effect you selected.

Figure 9-13
The Effect Browser can also show thumbnails of each Adjust filter.

Creating User Defined Filters

ALL IMAGE EDITING is a result of math. PaintShop Pro makes mathematical calculations for almost every command you issue, and filters are no exception. If you are a math wizard and really want a challenge, you can create your own effect filters. PaintShop Pro includes a User Defined Filter box where you can enter your own values. Click the Effects menu and select User Defined Filter. A dialog box like the one you see in Figure 9-14 appears.

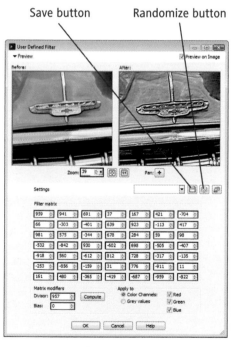

Figure 9-14
Create your own filters.

The Filter matrix allows you to enter the coefficients needed to process pixels for your needed effect. The Matrix modifier contains a Divisor number that PaintShop Pro uses to divide the Filter matrix values. It also contains a Bias number that can shift each color value by a specified amount. Sound difficult? It is. While you *could* calculate and enter a value for every factor in the User Defined Filter box, there's an easier way.

Click the Randomize button, which randomly changes all the values. Keep clicking until you find a look you like. If you only want this look one time and don't plan on using it again, just click OK, and PaintShop Pro applies the filter to your image or selection.

If, however, you think you might use this filter again, you can save the settings as a preset option. Click the Save button and enter a name for the custom filter in the resulting Save Present dialog box. The next time you want the same filter, you select it from the preset's list (see Figure 9-15).

Figure 9-15
Save your custom filters for future use.

Understanding Plug-Ins

IF THE OVER 80 FILTERS supplied with PaintShop Pro aren't enough, you can add others. Plug-in filters, by themselves, can't do anything, but combine them with PaintShop Pro, and you can create an even wider variety of functions and effects. The concept of plug-in filters originated long ago with Adobe Photoshop, and the success of the feature has many different software companies constantly trying to develop better and more unique filters.

Some are quite pricey, whereas others are free. Typically, you won't find filters available in your local software store, but they abound on the Internet, and in many cases, you can get a trial copy to evaluate.

Working with Plug-Ins

Most third-party filters are compatible with PaintShop Pro and typically have .8bf as the filename extension, such as swirleypop.8bf or bubblejets.8bf. The .8bf extension is not, however, a requirement in PaintShop Pro.

> ## Note
>
> Many older Adobe Photoshop plug-ins are compatible with PaintShop Pro.

Look around on the Internet, and I think you'll be quite pleased with what you find. Whether you choose Flaming Pear's SuperBladePro, Corel's KPT Collection, Alien Skin's Eye Candy, or one of the hundreds of others, you'll find unique special effects in each application. Here are a few places you can begin your search:

▶ www.corel.com: Enter KPT in the Corel search box. The folks who bring you PaintShop Pro offer the KPT Collection, one of the first third-party filter sets, originally called Kai's Power Tools.

▶ www.alienskin.com: The creator of the award-winning Eye Candy filters provides a variety of photo-realistic textures, such as snake and lizard skin, while its Xenofex 2 collection simulates natural phenomena such as lightning and clouds or even filters that can transform your photos into jigsaw puzzles or constellations.

▶ www.andromeda.com: Andromeda software provides many excellent filter collections, several of which are aimed at photographic correction and adjustments.

▶ **www.flamingpear.com**: The Flaming Pear family of filters includes the powerful SuperBladePro and a number of other unusual filters, such as ones that create images of planets or the illusion of flooding (see Figure 9-16). They also have several free filters for download.

▶ **www.thepluginsite.com**: This popular site offers free and commercial plug-ins, including their own Colorwasher and Focal Blade. The best part of this website is that it provides reviews of a variety of third-party filters and a master index to them.

▶ **www.autofx.com**: Auto FX software carries a variety of plug-in packages with some really unique effects, including edges, wrinkle, tape, and gels.

▶ **www.humansoftware.com**: There are lots of great plug-ins available here, including a variety of frames and textures that are great for working with photographs.

▶ **www.avbros.com**: AV Bros. has some fantastic page curl and puzzle filters. Even if you don't need extra filters, take a look at its website and see some of its examples.

▶ **www.namesuppressed.com**: The plug-ins available include Plaid Lite, Softener, and Autochromatic.

Figure 9-16
A photograph before and after applying the Flaming Pear's Mr. Contrast filter.

Installing Plug-In Filters

Each filter manufacturer provides its own method and directions to install its filters. When you install the filters, make a note of their file location, because you need to tell PaintShop Pro where you keep those filters on your computer. PaintShop Pro stores instructions to file locations in its Preferences area. Follow these steps to install plug-ins:

1. Click the File menu and select Preferences.

2. From the Preferences submenu, click File Locations. You see a File Locations dialog box like the one in Figure 9-17.

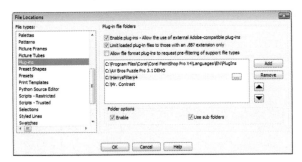

Figure 9-17
Tell PaintShop Pro where to locate your plug-in filters.

3. Click Plug-Ins from the File Types section. A list of plug-in file locations displays.

4. Click Add to display the Browse for Folder dialog box.

5. Locate and click the folder where the plug-ins are located; then click OK twice.

Choose your plug-in by clicking Effects ▸ Plugins and choosing the plug-in you want (see Figure 9-18).

Last used plug-in filter

Figure 9-18
Select from any installed plug-in filter.

Inventing Image Imagery

WHILE NOT TRULY DISTORTION effects or filters, two other items you might find interesting are the two Flip commands. Flip Vertically turns the image upside down on its head, and Flip Horizontally reverses the picture left to right as if looking in a mirror.

Both commands are located on the Image menu in the Edit workspace and can be applied to an entire image, a layer, or a selection. If your image has multiple layers and you want to mirror all or multiple layers, before mirroring, make the layers part of a layer group.

Not many photographs would be appropriate for a Flip Vertically command, but many images could benefit from the Flip Horizontally command. In Figure 9-19, you see a woman in a beautiful headdress. In the original image on the left, the woman is facing right, but after flipping the image on the right horizontally, you see she is now facing left.

Figure 9-19
Flip your image horizontally.

Figure 9-20 demonstrates hands. In the original image on the left, the hands are reaching upward. After flipping the image vertically, you see on the right that the hands are reaching downward.

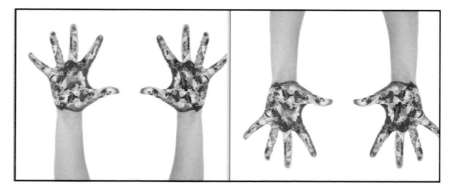

Figure 9-20
Flip your image top to bottom.

233

Discovering
Drawing Tools

PICTURE YOURSELF A SKILLED CRAFTSPERSON: a carpenter, for example. Whether you're building a birdhouse or a beach house, you know you need to use the right tools to get the job done. So it is with PaintShop Pro. Different tasks require different tools, and it's important to use the right tool for the job.

In this chapter, we're going to use more of these tools to work with creating images from scratch. If you're a web designer or artist, you may find the drawing tools quite useful when creating drawings, logos, and other web elements. As a photographer, you'll find more tools to use for photo retouching or manipulation. As you work with PaintShop Pro, you may find that you use some of the tools a lot and other tools rarely. I'm sure you'll find yourself looking at one of your photographs and thinking, "Aha! I can use the (*xyz*) tool to accomplish this." Let's take a look at some of these tools.

Identifying the Tools

IN CHAPTER 1, "GETTING ACQUAINTED,"
I mentioned the PaintShop Pro Tools toolbar, and
you used some of those tools in earlier chapters.
Let's take a moment to look at the tools you
haven't used much yet and define each one.

Position the mouse over each tool to display the
tool name along with any assigned shortcut key
while additional information about each tool
displays in the status bar located at the bottom
of the window. Click on a tool to select it, or
click on any tool arrow to see the additional tools.

The list that follows indicates the drawing-related
tools on the Tools toolbar and describes their
functions. Some of these tools you've used in
earlier chapters. Throughout this chapter, you'll
discover how to use more of them.

Figure 10-1
The Tools toolbar.

View Tools

 Pan tool: Changes the focus of the
view area of a zoomed-in image.

 Zoom tool: Increases or decreases
the image magnification.

Movement Tools

 Pick tool: Moves, resizes, or rotates
canvas elements, including entire layers.

 Move tool: Moves a selection to a
different image area. You used this
tool briefly in Chapter 8, "Developing
Layers."

Using Movement Tools

You learn how to use the movement tools in various other chapters of this book.

Selection Tools

 Selection tool: Selects a geometrically shaped image area you want to edit. You'll often use this tool and all the selection tools.

 Freehand Selection tool: Selects an irregularly shaped area you want to edit.

 Magic Wand tool: Selects an image area with similar colors or other similar features.

Dropper tool: Selects a foreground or background color from the image. You briefly used this tool in Chapter 7, "Understanding Color." Left-click to select a foreground color, and right-click to select a background color.

Using Selection Tools

Discover how to use the selection tools in Chapter 4, "Making Selections."

Painting Tools

 Paint Brush: Paints areas of your image as though using a paintbrush.

 Airbrush: Paints areas of your image as though using a spray can.

Enhancement Tools

 Lighten/Darken Brush: Lightens or darkens image areas. You left-click to lighten and right-click to darken.

 Dodge Brush: Lightens image areas. This tool is similar to the Lighten brush but has different options.

Burn Brush: Darkens image areas. This tool is similar to the Darken brush but has different options.

 Smudge Brush: Smears pixels and blends colors as though smearing wet paint.

Push Brush: Smears pixels but does not blend colors as the Smudge brush does.

 Soften Brush: Softens image pixels. Useful for softening edges around a cloned or moved area.

Sharpen Brush: Makes pixel areas sharper and more focused.

 Emboss Brush: Semi-hides color and blackens edges, creating an embossed look.

Saturation Up/Down Brush: Makes the image colors brighter or paler. You left-click to saturate more and right-click to lessen the saturation.

 Hue Up/Down Brush: Shifts image color hues. Left-click and then brush to change the hue in one direction on the color wheel, and right-click and brush to change the hue in the other direction.

 Change to Target Brush: Changes pixels based on how you click. You left-click to change the area to the foreground color and right-click to change the area to the background color.

 Color Replacer tool: Replaces the foreground color with the background color or vice versa. When you click and drag with the left mouse button, it replaces the background color with the foreground color. When you use the right mouse button, it replaces the foreground color with the background color.

Eraser Tools

 Eraser tool: Changes image's pixels, replacing them with transparency. You briefly used this tool in Chapter 8.

 Background Eraser tool: Replaces image areas with transparency. Similar to the Eraser tool but with softer edges.

Color Tools

 Flood Fill tool: Fills an area with a color, pattern, or gradient. You briefly used this tool in Chapter 8.

 Color Changer tool: Replaces color without changing shading and luminosity. You briefly used this tool in Chapter 5, "Making Quick Fixes."

Shape Tools

 Picture Tube tool: Paints predefined images and shapes.

 Text tool: Creates text areas on the image.

 Preset Shape tool: Draws fun shapes, such as callouts, arrows, and starbursts.

 Rectangle tool: Draws squares, rectangles, and rounded rectangles.

 Ellipse tool: Draws circles and ovals.

 Symmetric Shape tool: Draws multi-sided shapes, such as polygons and stars.

Pen tool: Draws lines, polylines, Bézier curves, and freehand lines.

Distortion Tools

 Warp Brush: Produces the effect of warping and deforming image areas.

 Mesh Warp tool: Produces the effect of warping and deforming based on a grid.

Art Media Tools

 Oil Brush: Simulates painting with wet oil paint.

 Chalk tool: Simulates drawing with dry chalk.

 Pastel tool: Simulates painting with dry pastel paints.

 Crayon tool: Simulates drawing with crayons.

 Colored Pencil: Simulates drawing with colored pencils.

 Marker tool: Simulates drawing with a wet marker.

 Palette Knife tool: Simulates using a sharp edge to smear pigments.

 Smear tool: Simulates smearing pigments, as with finger painting.

 Art Eraser tool: Erases areas created with the Art Media tools.

Discovering the Drawing Tool Options

EACH TIME YOU SELECT A TOOL, the Tool Options palette changes to reflect options for the selected tool. For example, when you select a Brush tool, you see options for brush size and shape, but when you select the Crop tool, you see options pertaining to cropping the image.

After you select the tool you want to use but before you actually use it, select from the available options on the Tool Options palette. In Figure 10-2, at the top of the window you see the Tool Options palette for the Pen tool, whereas on the bottom you see the Tool Options palette for the Eraser tool.

Creating with Brush and Art Media Tools

Now that you know the various tool names, we will take a brief look at using some of the tools along with their options. The first tools we'll review are the brushes that apply paint or other media to a canvas. Typically, you apply them to create works of art on a blank canvas. Leonardo da Vinci I'm not, but we can still have fun trying out the various brush and Art Media tools. Start with a blank canvas by choosing File > New and then clicking the OK button.

PAINT BRUSH

Begin using the PaintShop Pro Paint Brush tool in a freehand style as you would if you were using a real brush. Don't worry if your drawing doesn't look like much to begin with. With just a little practice, perhaps by drawing a mustache on your Great Aunt Lucy, you'll learn how to use your mouse to control the brush.

Pen tool options   Eraser tool options

Figure 10-2
Tool Options choices vary with the selected tool.

Just follow these simple steps:

1. Select the Paint Brush tool. The mouse pointer appears as a paintbrush tip. The circle surrounding the mouse pointer illustrates the stroke size.

Paint Brush Tool Shortcut

Just press the letter B to activate the Paint Brush tool.

2. In the Tool Options palette, select a brush size. Either type a value in the size box, or use the up and down arrows to select a size. A higher value results in a wider brushstroke, whereas a lower value produces a thinner line. Sizes range from 1 for the thinnest line to 999 for the widest line.

3. Click a color from the Materials palette. If you don't see your Materials palette, press F6. The color you select appears in the color swatch box. You discovered more about the Materials palette in Chapter 7.

4. Click and drag the mouse across a section of the canvas. Your brush line appears on the canvas. That's it! You just painted with the Paint Brush tool. See my example in Figure 10-3.

Laugh Away!

Please feel free to laugh at my examples in this chapter. I told you I am not an artist!

Figure 10-3
Using the Paint Brush tool.

Combining different brush options can provide a variety of different effects. Try changing other Paint Brush options and drawing another line to see what happens. For example, if you use a round shape brush and set the thickness to 25, the rotation to 45, and the hardness to 100, you get a brushstroke that is similar to a ribbon or calligraphic stroke.

Table 10-1 describes some of the brush options and their uses.

Other Tools Use the Same Options

Many Paint Brush options are the same options that are available in a number of the other drawing tools.

Table 10-1   Paint Brush Options

Tool	Use
Shape	Identifies whether the brush tip is rounded or squared. Rounded tip brushes create a smoother edge, whereas squared tips create a firmer edge.
Size	Determines the size of the brush in pixels. Values range from 1 to 999.
Hardness	Defines how the painted item edges blend into the background or other items. A higher value, which represents a harder brushstroke, produces a crisper edge, whereas a lower value produces a softer edge. Hardness ranges are from 0 to 100.
Step	Labels the distance between brushstrokes. A higher value decreases the frequency of the paint drops as the brush tip touches the image, whereas a lower value produces a smoother and denser effect. Step ranges are from 1 to 200.
Density	Designates the number of pixels that the brush paints. A higher value paints a more solid line, whereas a lower value produces a speckled stroke effect. Density values are from 1 to 100.
Thickness	Selects the thickness of the brushstroke. A lower value draws a thinner stroke, whereas a higher value creates a heavier, thicker stroke. Thickness values range from 1 to 100.
Rotation	Turns the angle of the brushstroke. Rotation is measured in degrees from 0 to 359.
Opacity	Displays the density of a brushstroke. A higher value applies a more solid color effect, whereas a lower value results in softer, more transparent color. Opacity is measured from 1 to 100.
Blend Mode	Determines how pixels blend with other pixels, usually on other layers. See Chapter 8 for more information on blend modes.
Stroke	Allows paint to build up on existing strokes. This feature is active only if the next feature, Continuous, is checked and only has an effect if the opacity is less than 100.
Continuous	When checked, specifies whether paint builds up when applying multiple brushstrokes over the same area.
Wet Look Paint	Simulates wet paint, showing a softer color inside and a darker ring near the outside edge.

Figure 10-4 illustrates painted lines drawn with various selected options.

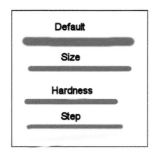

Figure 10-4
Applying different Paint Brush tool options.

SELECTING PRESET OPTIONS

If you don't want to select all those options each time you want to use the tools, you can select from a variety of unique brushes included with the Paint Brush tool. Click the Brush Tips drop-down list, which displays a gallery of presaved brushes. Some are simple, and others are more elaborate, as you see in Figure 10-5. As you float your mouse over any of the presets, a ToolTip appears showing the brush settings. Click the preset brush you want, and then click the OK button. Choose the color you want, and paint away.

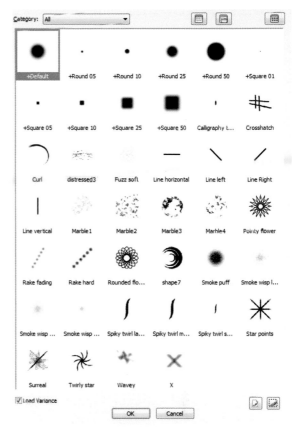

Figure 10-5
Choosing from predefined brush tips.

Default Brush Tip

Click the first brush tip to quickly reset your brush to the PaintShop Pro default options.

More Brush Tips

Scroll down through the list of preset brushes. Some unique brush tips are included.

Airbrush

Although using the Airbrush tool is similar to using the Paint Brush tool, you'll also find that using the Airbrush tool is similar to painting with a spray can. When you're spray painting, if you stay in one place for a moment, the paint builds up. The same reaction occurs when you use the Airbrush tool. You'll notice this behavior even more if you set the Opacity fairly low in the Tool Options palette. Using the Airbrush tool is different from spray painting in one big way: the Airbrush tool doesn't drip!

The Airbrush tool is really a variation of the Paint Brush tool, so PaintShop Pro lists it under the Paint Brush button. The following steps show you how to use the Airbrush tool:

1. Click the arrow next to the Paint Brush tool and click the Airbrush tool. The mouse pointer turns into an airbrush tip.

2. Set any desired options from the Tool Options palette. You'll find mostly the same options for the Airbrush tool that you have with the Paint Brush tool. One exception is that the Airbrush tool includes an option for Rate, which sets the spray flow. With values from 0 to 50, a higher value applies more paint when you pause or slow down while using the Airbrush tool.

3. Click a color from the Materials palette.

4. Click and drag the mouse pointer across the canvas to spray paint your image. The example in Figure 10-6 uses the default Airbrush settings.

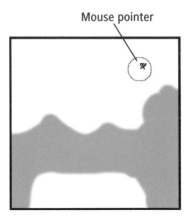

Figure 10-6
Paint with the Airbrush tool.

Art Media Tools

Wikipedia.com describes art media as "The artistic methods, processes, or means of expression, used by an artist to produce a work of art." In the drawing sector of the art world, this includes choosing between wet pigment media such as oil paints or markers or dry pigment media such as chalk or crayons. PaintShop Pro includes a variety of Art Media tools you can use to express yourself on the electronic canvas.

Art Media Layers

When you use the Art Media tools, PaintShop Pro automatically places them on a separate layer called an art media layer. Learn more about layers in Chapter 8.

PaintShop Pro groups the Art Media tools together on the last tool of the Tools toolbar. Click the arrow next to the last tool to choose your favorite Art Media tool (see Figure 10-7).

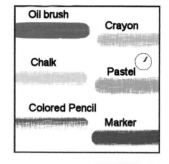

Figure 10-8
Art media samples.

Figure 10-7
Art Media tools.

Note

Don't confuse the Art Media tools with art media effects. You use the Art Media tools to draw on a canvas, and you apply the art media effects to an existing image to change its appearance. See Chapter 9, "Adding Effects, Filters, and Deformations."

Most Art Media tools contain options primarily for the shape, size, thickness, and brush rotation. They also include an option for Head tracking, which determines whether you want the brush head to bend as it follows a stroke path or to remain at a fixed angle. After you select the tool you want and choose the desired options, click and drag in the canvas to draw with the tool. Take a look at Figure 10-8, which illustrates a few examples drawn with the Art Media tools.

In addition to the actual Art Media drawing tools, PaintShop Pro includes several items to assist you when working with art media. One of my personal favorites is the Smear tool, which allows you to soften a stroke made with an Art Media tool. It's often used with a dry medium, such as the chalk or pencil stroke, to simulate using your finger or a rag to soften out the stroke. It's not limited, however, to only chalk or pencil. You can also use it with a wet medium such as oil. It gives the appearance of smearing wet paint.

In Figure 10-9, you see an example of an oil brushstroke smeared on the edges as well as a colored pencil stroke that was smeared in the center.

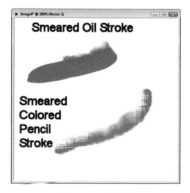

Figure 10-9
Smearing brushstrokes.

Using Shape Tools

You don't have to be an incomparable artist to draw shapes and other items, because PaintShop Pro includes many common shapes, such as rectangles, ellipses, triangles, and stars, as well as fun shapes, such as lightning bolts, musical notes, or paw prints. Keep the following facts in mind when you're drawing shapes:

▶ If you click and drag from the top of the canvas toward the bottom, the image shape will be drawn from corner to corner.

▶ If you click and drag from the bottom of the canvas toward the top, the image shape will be drawn upside down.

Vector Layers

By default, PaintShop Pro draws shapes on a vector layer. You learn about layers in Chapter 8, and you learn about vector graphics in Chapter 11, "Constructing Vector Objects."

DRAWING A RECTANGLE

When you're drawing a shape such as a rectangle, you can select the color, thickness, and style of the outer lines, as well as the roundness of the corners. Rectangle tool options also include whether to draw a rectangle or a perfect square. The following steps walk you through drawing a rectangle or square:

1. Click the arrow next to the Preset Shape tool (fourth tool from the bottom) and choose Rectangle. The mouse pointer takes the shape of a large black arrowhead with a small black plus sign under it.

Rectangle Tool Shortcut

Just press the letter G to activate the Rectangle tool.

2. From the Tool Options palette shown in Figure 10-10, in the Mode section, click Rectangle or Square.

Figure 10-10
Shape tool options.

3. From the Horizontal and Vertical Radius sections, select a radius setting for the amount of curvature desired around the edges of the object. Enter a 0 in both sections if you want squared corners, or enter a higher value such as 15 if you want slightly rounded corners. The higher the value, the more rounded the object corners.

4. If you want other than a single line for the outside edge of the object, click the Line Style drop-down arrow and make a selection. As you see in Figure 10-11, PaintShop Pro provides quite a variety of line styles.

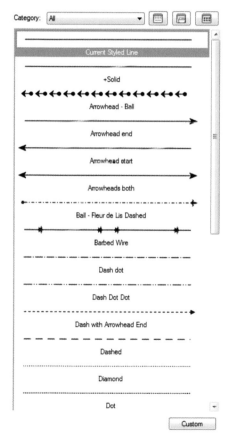

Figure 10-11
Line styles.

Can't See Line Style

Depending on your monitor size and display resolution, you may not see all the tool options available for some tools. If you don't see the Line Style option, click the arrow to the right of the Tool Options palette.

5. From the Materials palette, click a color for the line, and then right-click a color for the object inside fill area. (See Chapter 7 for more information about using the Materials palette.)

6. Click and drag in the canvas to draw your shape.

7. Click the Apply button to accept your drawing. Figure 10-12 illustrates a canvas with several different objects drawn using the Rectangle tool.

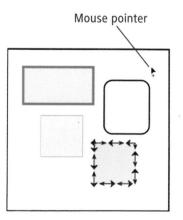

Figure 10-12
Drawing rectangles and squares.

Draw Circles

Click the Ellipse tool and draw ellipses or circles. Many of the same options appear as with the Rectangle tool.

CREATING SYMMETRICAL SHAPES

Would you like to draw symmetrical multisided shapes such as stars or polygons? Yes? Well, PaintShop Pro has a tool for that, too. Using the Symmetric Shape tool, you can choose the number of sides the object should contain as well as the amount of rounding you want at the inner or outer points of the object.

Follow these steps to create a symmetrical object:

1. After selecting the Symmetric Shape tool, which shares a space with the Rectangle tool (fourth from the bottom) use the left mouse button and, in the Materials palette, click the color you want for the object's outer edge.

2. Use the right mouse button and click the color you want for the object's interior fill.

3. In the Tool Options palette, in the Mode section, choose whether you want to draw a polygon or a star (*stellated*) shape.

4. Select the number of sides you want for the object. For example, if you want a standard 5-point star, choose 5.

5. If you want the object to have rounded inner corners, click the Round Inner box, and if you want the object to have rounded outer corners, click the Round Outer box (see Figure 10-13).

> ### Note
>
> The Rounded Inner box is not available for polygons.

6. Select a line style and width.

7. At the far right of the Tool Options palette, you may see choices for Joins and Miter limits. If you do not see these options, click the Line Style Options arrow at the right end of the Tool Options palette. The Line Options expand, as you see in Figure 10-14.

Figure 10-14
The expanded Line Style options.

Figure 10-13
The Symmetric Shape Tool Options palette.

8. If you are drawing a stellated object, choose the types of corners you want your object to take. The corners are called the *join*, indicating how you want the corners joined (see Figure 10-15). Join choices include these:

- Mitered corners

- Rounded corners

- Beveled corners

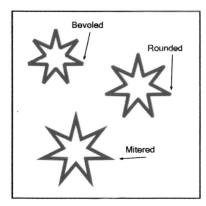

Figure 10-15
Corner join examples.

 9. Click and drag on the canvas to draw the object, and then click the Apply button.

Using Preset Shapes

The Preset Shape tool, similar to the Rectangle, Ellipse, and Symmetric Shape tools, allows you to select from over 100 distinctively shaped objects. Choices range from fancy arrows, callout balloons, gears, paw prints, hearts, and musical notes to shapes you *could* create with the other shape tools, such as octagons, circles, and stars.

Select the Preset Shape tool, which shares a space with the Rectangle, Ellipse, and Symmetric Shape tools. Then from the Tool Options palette, click the Shape List, which displays a gallery of choices. Select the shape you want, and draw it on the canvas. Figure 10-16 illustrates several of the shapes you can draw using the Preset Shape tool.

Figure 10-16
Preset shapes.

Retain Style

If you want the shape to be the same color as you see it in the Shape List, leave the Retain Style box checked. If, however, you want to choose your own foreground and background color, remove the check from the Retain Style check box.

DRAWING LINES WITH THE PEN TOOL

The Paint Brush tool you used earlier allowed you freedom in drawing by emulating a real paintbrush, relying on manual brush actions. The Pen tool is more like a drafting tool, drawing straighter, more distinctive lines. Using the Pen tool, graphic designers and illustrators can create almost any type of shape or line object they can imagine.

Using the Pen tool in the Draw Lines and Polylines mode, you can easily create straight lines, thick lines, thin lines, and even lines with arrows. Follow these steps:

 1. Click the Pen tool, which turns the mouse pointer into a black arrowhead with a plus sign below it.

2. From the Tool Options palette, select the Draw Lines and Polylines button located in the Mode section.

3. Choose the line style and the width (thickness) you want to use.

4. From the Materials palette, select a color for the line.

5. Click and drag on the canvas to draw your line.

Draw Straight Lines

To constrain your lines and make them perfectly straight or at 45-degree angles, hold down the Shift key while you're drawing.

 6. Click the Apply button. Figure 10-17 illustrates several drawn lines.

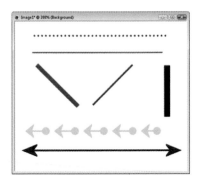

Figure 10-17
Drawn lines.

DRAWING POLYLINES AND POLYGONS

If you want to draw polylines, or polygons, you still use the Pen tool, but you need to tell PaintShop Pro you want to connect the line segments. When creating a polygon using the Pen tool, you need to decide if you want the interior of the polygon filled with a color or with no color, called *transparency*. Use the following steps:

1. Follow steps 1 through 3 in the previous section, "Drawing Lines with the Pen Tool."

2. Click the Connect Segments option on the Tool Options palette.

3. From the Materials palette, left-click on a color to select the line color.

4. If you are going to create a polygon and want the interior of the shape to have a color, right-click the color you want on the Materials palette. If you want the polygon interior to be transparent, click the Transparent button on the Materials palette (see Figure 10-18). Chapter 7 contains more information about the Materials palette.

Transparent buttons

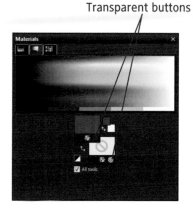

Figure 10-18
The Materials palette.

5. Select a corner Join preference. You can choose from mitered, rounded, or beveled corners.

6. On the canvas, click your mouse where you want the first line to begin.

7. Click your mouse in another location on the canvas. A second line will appear, connected to the first line. If you have a color selected for the object fill, the space between the lines fills in with the background color.

8. Continue clicking for each point of your line or polygon. Each line will connect to the previous one.

9. Click the Apply button. Figure 10-19 shows a couple of examples.

Figure 10-19
Polylines and polygons.

DRAWING FREEHAND

Another option with the Pen tool is freehand drawing. Drawing freehand with the Pen tool is similar to using the Paint Brush tool, except that the Pen tool lines appear crisper and sharper than with the Paint Brush tool.

Click the Pen tool and any desired options for your line. Additionally, click the Freehand mode, which is on the Tool Options palette, under the Mode section. It is the last tool. Click and draw freely on your canvas, clicking the Apply button when you are finished.

Bézier Curves

Bézier (pronounced bez'-ee-ay) curves are curved lines, created based on mathematical calculations. They have at least three points to define the curve. The two endpoints of the curve are called the *anchor points*, while the other point or points, which define the actual curvature, are called *handles*. Moving the handles lets you modify the shape of the curve. See Chapter 11 to discover how to draw and manipulate a Bézier curve.

PAINTING WITH PICTURE TUBES

If there were such a prize, picture tubes would win the gold medal as the "most fun feature" of PaintShop Pro. Picture tubes are amusing little pictures that are created with a click of your mouse button. Use them in combination with other images, and you can create quite a masterpiece. You'll probably use them most if you do digital scrapbooking. You discover more about digital scrapbooking in Chapter 16, "Making Digital Scrapbooks."

If you run down to Walmart and look in the scrapbooking supplies section, you're bound to see lots of ink stamps. You know—the kind that creates an image that you can stamp on the paper over and over again. Well, the PaintShop Pro picture tubes are similar to those stamps, but even better. You can actually paint images with these tubes. In addition, whereas the stamps you find at the store can each produce only a single image, that's not necessarily the case with tubes. Some tubes might contain only a single image, but many produce several variations of a single image or several different images with a common theme.

Place Tubes on Their Own Layer

For ease in editing the image after it is drawn on the screen, you should place each tube on its own raster layer. See Chapter 8.

Follow these steps to use the Picture Tube tool:

1. Click the Picture Tube tool, which makes the mouse pointer look like a tube of paint.

2. Click on the preview arrow in the Tool Options palette, and select the tube you want to use. A selection of tubes similar to Figure 10-20 appears. Your selections will vary from the ones displayed in this figure.

Figure 10-20
Picture tubes are fun!

3. Similar to the Paint Brush tool, click the canvas to place a single tube, or drag across the canvas to achieve the look you want. Depending on the tube you select, another identical or related image will appear each time you click.

Straight Line Tubes

Draw your picture tubes in a straight line by clicking once at the beginning of the line. Then hold down the Shift key and click a second time at the end of the tube line. PaintShop Pro draws a straight line using the tube between those two points.

If you find that a picture tube is painting an image that is too large or too small, too far apart, or too close together, you can edit the settings. You must change the settings before you paint the image. There are four settings you will probably use with picture tubes:

▶ **Scale**: Adjusts the size of the tube, from its originally created size of 100%, down to 10% of its original size or up to 250% of its original size.

Increase Size Decreases Quality

As you scale an image larger, image quality generally decreases.

▶ **Step**: Modifies the distance between the intervals in which the tubes appear. The larger the step, the more distance between the tubes. Values range between 1 and 500.

▶ **Placement mode**: Choices are Continuous or Random. Continuous spaces the images evenly according to the step size you selected, and Random randomly spaces the images with intervals ranging from 1 pixel to the step size.

▶ **Selection mode**: This option tells PaintShop Pro how to select which image to use from the currently selected picture tube. The default option, Random, randomly selects an image. Incremental paints the images as they are created in the picture tube from the top left to the bottom right. Angular selects an image based on the direction you drag the mouse. Pressure applies only when you are using a pressure-sensitive tablet and chooses the image based on the amount of pressure you apply. Finally, Velocity chooses which image to paint based on the speed you drag the mouse.

Try drawing with the different tubes. Many of them are more exciting than they appear in the Preview panel. The Piano Keys, Yarn Red, and Spiral Garland tubes are perfect examples of the actual tube, looking tremendously different from the sample in the Preview panel. Every image you see in Figure 10-21 is from a PaintShop Pro–provided picture tube.

Figure 10-21
Happy tubing!

ADDING NEW PICTURE TUBES

Many picture tubes come with the PaintShop Pro application, and even more are available on the CD. You can even find thousands of free picture tubes on the Internet. In most cases, PaintShop Pro automatically reads the picture tubes, provided that you copy them to one of the locations specified in File ❯ Preferences ❯ File Locations.

When you download any picture tubes, you need to tell PaintShop Pro where they are located. By default, the picture tubes that are supplied with PaintShop Pro are located in the Picture Tubes folder where you installed the PaintShop Pro program. Typically, this would be C:\Program Files\Corel\Corel PaintShop Pro X4\Corel_10.

Tubes that you create or import are typically stored in a folder under your Documents folder, such as C:\Users*Your Name*\Documents\Corel PaintShop Pro\14.0\Picture Tubes.

Additional File Locations

You can specify additional file locations under File ❯ Preferences ❯ File Locations.

Sometimes, however, you might want to save your own files as picture tubes. A picture tube is really a drawing or a series of drawings that is created and saved in a special format. The images are created on a transparent background so that all you see is the image. Here are a few other stipulations required by PaintShop Pro for picture tubes:

▶ The image must be grayscale or have a color depth of 24 bit (16 million colors).

▶ The image must be on a single raster layer.

▶ The background of the image must be transparent.

▶ If your file has multiple images on it, the items should be symmetrical in position, dividing the canvas space equally between the items. PaintShop Pro saves picture tube files in a row and column pattern.

The following steps show you how to save your own file as a picture tube:

1. Create or open the file that contains the picture tube.

2. Click on File ❯ Export ❯ Picture Tube.

3. In the Export Picture Tube dialog box, specify the number of cells across and down in the image. In the example you see in Figure 10-22, the image consists of three cells across and three down. Be sure to follow the guidelines for picture tubes.

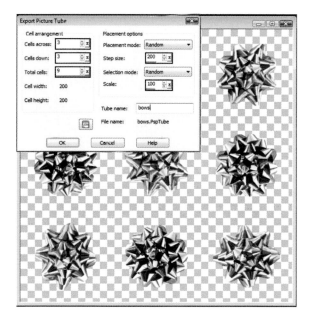

Figure 10-22
Creating your own picture tube files.

4. Type a name for the tube, and then click OK. PaintShop Pro saves picture tube files with a file extension of .psptube.

Figure 10-23 shows an image created with the newly saved picture tube (along with a couple of other tubes).

Figure 10-23
It's a party!

Using the Enhancement Tools

Unless you are drawing a diagram that requires crisp edges, you will probably not want to leave the drawn lines and shapes in their natural state. When drawing complete images, which typically consist of many different shapes and elements, you'll want to lighten or darken certain areas or soften the edge of a section. Fortunately, PaintShop Pro includes a variety of enhancement tools. You can use these tools on a drawing you create or a photograph that you are retouching. See Chapter 5 and Chapter 6, "Manually Editing Images."

Select the enhancement brush you want (as seen in Figure 10-24), and choose any size, hardness, and other desired options from the Tool Options palette. The Tool Options palette choices vary from tool to tool (see Figure 10-25).

Figure 10-24
Enhancement brush tools.

Figure 10-25
Enhancement brush Tool Options palette.

Take a look at Figure 10-26. I used the Lighten/Darken brush to create a light spot on the horse's nose. I then used the Soften brush to better blend the light spot, making it look more natural.

Converts to Raster Layer

If you use the Eraser tools on a background layer, PaintShop Pro automatically converts the background layer to a standard raster layer. See Chapter 8.

Mouse pointer

Figure 10-26
Images before and after using enhancement brush tools.

Clearing with the Eraser Tools

When you are practicing your drawing techniques, you might decide that it would be easier to start over. You can close the current file without saving it and start again with a new file, but you can also erase your canvas and start over. Of course, most of the time you won't be drawing in PaintShop Pro, but working with photographs; however, you can use the PaintShop Pro erasers for working with photo images. PaintShop Pro includes two different Eraser tools: the standard Eraser and the Background Eraser.

CLEANING UP WITH THE ERASER

The Eraser tool works similarly to a regular pencil eraser, except that you have options you can select. Eraser options are similar to the Brush options that you discovered earlier in this chapter. The Eraser tool works by changing the pixels in the image as you drag through them. If you are working with a background layer, using the Eraser tool converts the background layer to a raster layer and then replaces the erased pixels with a transparency. See Chapter 8 for more information on layers.

Follow these steps to use the Eraser tool:

1. With the image you want to edit open on your screen, select the Eraser tool. The mouse pointer looks like a pencil eraser.

2. From the Tool Options toolbar, select a brush tip style and thickness (see Figure 10-27).

Brush tip styles

Figure 10-27
Eraser options.

3. Select the opacity at which you want to erase. The default is 100%, which means a complete total erase of an area. If you set the opacity low, say at 15%, the area will be only lightly erased.

4. Click and drag the mouse pointer over the area you want to erase. The erased area is replaced with transparency. In Figure 10-28, you see some sunflowers. As I erase part of the sunflower, the transparency shows through.

Undo Eraser

If you erase an area in error, drag over the area while holding down the right mouse button. The erased pixels are restored.

Mouse pointer

Figure 10-28
Erase an unwanted area.

Restrict Erasure Area

To restrict the Eraser to a specific area, select the area before you use the Eraser tool. See Chapter 4.

Using the Background Eraser

The Background Eraser, while similar to the regular Eraser and often used in conjunction with the regular Eraser, works more from the center of the brush, resulting in softer edges. The tool works best on images with higher contrast between the background and the foreground. For example, if you have a picture of a poppy growing wild in the grass, and you want just the flower, the Background Eraser is the tool you want to use.

The Background Eraser determines which pixels to erase by finding similarly colored pixels under the mouse pointer and then makes the erased pixels transparent.

Raster Layers Only

Both the Eraser and the Background Eraser tools work only on raster layers and do not work on the background layer. If your image is on a vector layer, PaintShop Pro displays a dialog box prompting you to promote it to a raster layer. Click OK and then proceed with the Eraser tools.

As with the standard Eraser, the center of the Background Eraser tool is the key to using this feature, so it works best if you can easily see the center. To make the center easier to spot, turn on the Precise Cursor option. Both erasers center on the mouse pointer crosshairs; however, the Background Eraser erases to a softer edge, while the Eraser tool erases across a harder edge.

Follow these steps to turn on the Precise Cursor option and use the Background Eraser tool:

1. Click File ❯ Preferences ❯ General Program Preferences. The Preferences dialog box opens.

2. Click Display and Caching and click Use Precise Cursors. The option will have a check mark indicating that the feature is activated. See Figure 10-29.

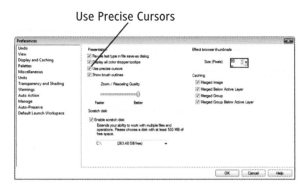

Figure 10-29
Activating the Use Precise Cursors option.

3. Click OK to accept the change. You're now ready to begin using the Background Eraser tool.

4. Choose the Background Eraser tool. The mouse pointer will appear as a circle with centering sights.

5. Select an eraser size and any other desired options from the Tool Options palette. If you have a large area to erase, you might want to start with a larger size, such as 50 or 110. You will probably need to change the brush size frequently.

6. Click and drag the mouse pointer over the area you want to erase. However, instead of using the brush edge, as you would with the regular Eraser tool, don't worry about anything but the center of the brush where the crosshairs are located. PaintShop Pro replaces the erased area with a transparency.

Restore Erased Areas

To restore an area completely and quickly, hold down the spacebar and then drag the right mouse button over the erased area.

Figure 10-30 illustrates an image with some of the background removed by the Background Eraser.

Precise cursor mouse pointer

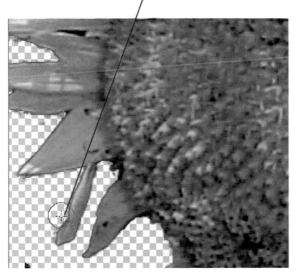

Figure 10-30
Erasing a background area.

Having Fun with the Deformation Tools

The deformation tools, which include the Warp brush and the Mesh Warp tool, allow you to push, twist, and twirl portions of your image, creating a surreal look such as an underwater effect. You use the tools for reshaping areas so they appear to fit seamlessly in the image.

Using the Warp Brush

One of the most powerful paint brushes, the Warp Brush tool is akin to finger painting with your mouse. Applied in the same manner as a regular paintbrush, the Warp Brush bends and warps the pixels under the brush.

Where can you use the Warp Brush? Well, some photography editors use the Warp Brush to increase eye size, giving the subject a wide-eyed appearance. Other uses might be to reduce and straighten facial details. Still others just use the Warp Brush as a stress reliever by distorting an image of someone they are angry at! Often you use the Warp Brush just to have fun.

The Warp Brush shares space on the Tools toolbar with the Mesh Warp tool. When you select the Warp Brush, the Tool Options palette displays brush settings such as size, hardness, and strength (see Figure 10-31).

Figure 10-31
The Warp Brush Tool Options palette.

The Warp Brush can apply the warp in any of several different modes. Push smears the pixels in the direction you brush; Expand smears the pixels away from the center of the brush; and Contract smears the pixels into the center of the brush. You can also Twirl the pixels clockwise or counterclockwise around the center of the brush, or you can use Noise mode to smear the pixels randomly. Both Iron Out and Unwarp remove a warp.

Because of the computing power involved in using the Warp Brush, you may see some lag time between when you brush and when you see the results. Use the Warp Brush slowly, and give the computer a chance to catch up with your brush.

 Click the Apply button to accept a warping action.

Look at Figure 10-32, where on the top you see a picture of my beautiful friend. She is…really! But after using the Warp Brush on her, she may never speak to me again.

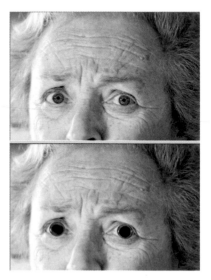

Figure 10-32
Go ahead…play a little. The Warp Brush is fun!

WORKING WITH THE MESH WARP TOOL

The Mesh Warp tool warps the current layer or interior of a selection to a mesh frame, which can give the image dimension and depth.

When you select the Mesh Warp tool, PaintShop Pro places a grid called a *deformation map* over the image. You can modify the grid size through the Mesh horizontal and Mesh vertical options on the Tool Options palette. The values indicate the number of mesh lines within the frame, not including the border lines. See Figure 10-33.

Figure 10-33
Mesh Warp Tool Options palette.

At each grid intersection, you see a small node box that acts as a handle to drag and deform sections of the image. You can use these nodes in one of several ways:

▶ Click and drag a node to move it.

▶ Press Shift while dragging a node to move the entire row or column.

▶ Press Ctrl while dragging a node to deform the row or column into a smooth curve.

Because of the power involved in using the Mesh Warp tool, you may see some lag time between when you move a node and when you see the results. If needed, you can change the grid size as you work. Entering new Mesh values reconfigures the grid and returns it to the original position, but the image retains any deformations you have already made.

Click the Apply button to accept a warping action.

Take a look at Figure 10-34. By moving the nodes on the warp grid, I took a worktable, used the Mesh Warp tool on it, and ended up with an interesting distortion.

Deformation grid

Figure 10-34
Using the Warp Mesh tool.

Viewing Your Work

IT'S ALL IN YOUR PERSPECTIVE, RIGHT?
When you're working creatively, sometimes you
need to see the finest detail, and sometimes
you need to stand back and check out the overall look. Well, at the top of the Tools toolbar are
tools you can use to change the way you look at
your image. Both the Zoom and Pan tools pertain
to how and what you see on your screen. Neither
of these tools actually physically modifies your
image in any form; they only change how you
view it on the screen.

Turn Off Precise Cursors

**If you still have your precise cursors acti-
vated from earlier in this chapter, you may
find this section easier to review without
the precise cursors. Deactivate them.**

Zooming In and Out

 The Zoom tool increases or decreases
image magnification, and you'll find you
use it quite a lot while working in PaintShop
Pro. When you select the Zoom tool, the Tool
Options toolbar you see in Figure 10-35 appears,
and your mouse pointer looks like a magnifying
glass.

Figure 10-35
Zoom tool options.

With the Zoom tool active, you have quite a few
different methods you can use for zooming in or
out on the image:

Zoom Tool Shortcut

**Press the letter Z to activate the Zoom
tool.**

▶ Click the image to zoom in. Each time
you click on the image, it zooms in for
greater intensification, allowing you to
perform close-up detail work. You can
continue to zoom in until you get to a
pixel-by-pixel depiction of the image at
5000% of the normal 100% view. Right-
click the image to zoom out to a smaller
percentage.

▶ On the Tool Options palette, click
the magnifying glass with a plus in it.
Each click zooms in to a greater
percentage. Click the magnifying
glass with a minus sign to zoom out.
You can zoom out until the image is
only 1% of the 100% normal view.

Zoom Faster

To zoom in larger increments, click the Zoom More options.

- ▶ On the Tool Options palette, enter a zoom percentage in the Zoom (%) box. Optionally, click the up/down arrows on the Zoom (%) box.

- ▶ Press the plus sign (+) on the numeric key pad to zoom in or press the minus sign (–) on the numeric keypad to zoom out.

- ▶ If your mouse has a scroll wheel, you can roll the scroll wheel to zoom in or zoom out.

- ▶ From the PaintShop Pro menu bar, choose View ❯ Zoom In, View ❯ Zoom Out, or View ❯ Zoom to 110%.

Quickly Change to 100%

Click the Actual Size button to quickly change the zoom percentage to the normal 100%.

Panning Around

When you select the Pan tool, your mouse pointer changes to a small Hand tool. Use the hand to click and drag to view different areas of your image. It's especially helpful to use when you are zoomed in or working with a large image.

You can zoom to a high percentage yet still see other areas easily. It's similar to using the horizontal or vertical scrollbars.

Seeing the Overview Palette

Although it's not actually a tool on the toolbar, the Overview palette seen in Figure 10-36 provides you with the best of both worlds. You can zoom tightly on the image detail and still see the image in its entirety on the Overview palette. Turn the Overview palette on or off by choosing View ❯ Palettes ❯ Overview or by pressing the F9 key.

The Overview palette appears displaying the entire image, but with a rectangle around the currently viewed area (see Figure 10-36). To move from one area of your image to another quickly, drag the rectangle in the Overview palette to the area you want to view.

Overview palette

Figure 10-36
Using the Overview palette.

Constructing

Vector Objects

PICTURE YOURSELF HIRING AN ARCHITECT to design your new home. You have some ideas that you want incorporated into the new home, but you need to make sure your thoughts are well laid out so they are fully functional. After seeing the architect's blueprints, you may decide to expand an area or move it somewhere else.

Up to this point, you've worked primarily with raster graphics, which use pixels to store image information. Vector objects, the other type of PaintShop Pro graphic, are stored as separate items with information about each item's position, starting and ending points, width, color, and curve information. Working with vector objects provides you with greater flexibility in moving and editing individual objects.

You'll find vector objects especially useful when you're designing logos and making line drawings.

Understanding Vector Versus Raster Graphics

COMPUTERS ONLY UNDERSTAND 1s and 0s. When it comes to displaying art on computers, the computer must convert what you draw on the screen into those 1s and 0s. Vector graphics use lines, points, and polygons based on mathematical equations to represent images. Therefore, the computer can easily convert the numerical instructions from the vector graphic into an image it displays on the screen.

Seeing the Differences

Photographs and scanned images are always raster images. Raster images use a grid system of individual pixels, where each pixel can be a different color or shade and the image contains a value for every pixel on the screen. Because the pixels are such small rectangular blocks, like mosaic tiles, the colors from one pixel to the other can appear softly blended.

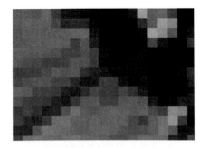

You use vector graphics instead of raster graphics. Most people find vector graphics ideal for line art drawings and illustrations, drawings that contain text, and images that do not need a photo-realistic appearance. Fonts are a type of vector object.

Some advantages of vector graphics include the following:

▶ Vector graphics are more flexible because they are easily resized and stretched without losing quality.

▶ Vector graphics typically require less computer memory than raster graphics.

▶ Because of their smaller size, vector graphics are fast to download and are ideal for web use.

▶ Vector graphics look better on monitors and printers with higher resolution.

▶Vector graphics are not restricted to the rectangular shape of a pixel.

▶ Vector object properties such as outline or fill color are easily changed.

▶ Changing the vector object attributes does not affect the object.

As you can see, vector images have many advantages, but their primary disadvantage is that they're unsuitable for producing photo-realistic images. Vector images are usually made up of solid areas of color or gradients, but they cannot depict the continuous subtle tones of a photograph. That's why most of the vector images you see tend to have a cartoon-like appearance.

Even so, vector graphics are continually becoming more advanced, and we can do a lot more with vector drawings now than we could just a few years ago. PaintShop Pro has many tools available that allow you to apply raster textures to vector objects, giving them a more tonal appearance, and you can now create blends and subtle shading that once were difficult to achieve in a vector image.

Creating a Vector Layer

A single image can contain both raster objects and vector objects; however, vector objects and raster objects cannot be mixed on the same layer. Vector objects must be on a vector layer. If you try to create a vector object on a raster layer, PaintShop Pro automatically creates a vector layer for you. If the current layer is already a vector layer, PaintShop Pro adds the new object to the current layer. PaintShop Pro files can have many vector layers, and each vector layer can have multiple vector objects.

Saving File with Layers

As mentioned in Chapter 8, "Developing Layers," many file types do not support layers. The PSPIMAGE file format does save layers, so it's a good idea to save your file in the PSPIMAGE format and not merge your layers until you are completely finished working with the image.

To create a new vector layer, either click the Add Layer icon on the Layers palette and select New Vector Layer from the resulting drop-down list or choose Layers ❯ New Vector Layer. The New Vector Layer dialog box seen in Figure 11-1 appears.

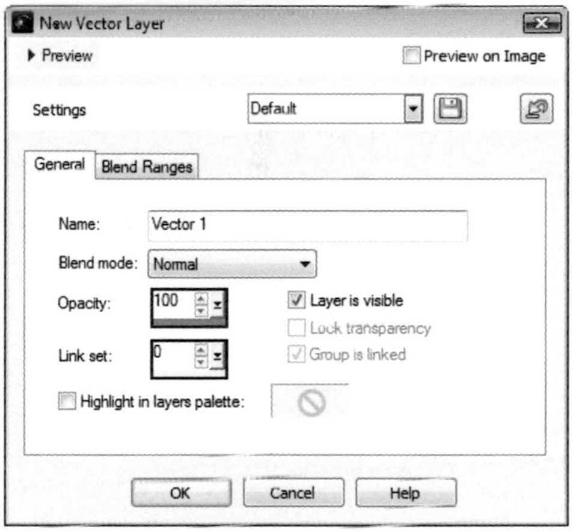

New Layer Shortcut

You can bypass the New Vector Layer dialog box by holding down the Shift key while you select New Vector Layer.

Figure 11-1
Creating a new vector layer.

From this dialog box, you can give your vector layer a name, select a blend mode, or establish an opacity setting. After you click the OK button, PaintShop Pro places the new vector layer above the last selected layer, and the new layer becomes the active layer.

Converting Layers

You can later convert a vector layer to a raster layer, but you cannot convert a raster layer to a vector layer.

Drawing Vector Shapes

IN CHAPTER 10, "Discovering Drawing Tools," you learned about drawing basic shapes, but it's a good idea to review them here as well. Vector shapes include the rectangle, square, ellipse, circle, symmetrical shape, preset shape, and lines drawn with the Pen tool. This section covers drawing the shapes, and drawing with the Pen tool is covered in the next section, "Adding Vector Lines."

Vector Text

Text is also a vector object. See Chapter 13, "Working with Text," for more information.

First, from the Tools toolbar, select the shape tool you want to use from the choices seen in Figure 11-2.

Figure 11-2
Select a shape tool.

Next, choose your options from the Tool Options palette. On all of the shape tools, to create a vector shape, make sure the Create on Vector option is checked. If the Create on Vector option is not checked, PaintShop Pro draws the shape as a raster object. The other Tool Options palette choices vary depending on the tool you selected. Table 11-1 lists the other shape tool options and their function.

Can't See All Options

Depending on your monitor size and display resolution, you may not see all the tool options available for some tools. If you don't see all the options, click the arrow to the right of the Tool Options palette.

All the shape tools have line options, including setting the line style, width, anti-alias, joins, and miter limits. See Chapter 10 for more information.

After you choose the desired shape tool options, you need to choose a foreground and background color. From the Foreground and Stroke properties box on the Materials palette, choose an outline color, and from the Background and Fill properties box, choose a fill color. If you don't want the shape to have a fill, click the Transparent button on the Background and Fill properties box.

Table 11-1   Shape Tool Options

Option Name	Shape Used With	Function
Mode	Rectangle, Ellipse, Symmetrical	Allows you to choose between rectangle, square, ellipse, circle, polygon, or stellated shape
Shape List	Preset	Allows you to choose from 99 different predesigned shapes
Show Nodes	Rectangle, Ellipse, Symmetrical	Displays the nodes, which are the points on line and curve objects.
Retain Style	Preset	When checked, draws the shape with the default color; when unchecked, the shape picks up the foreground and background color in the Materials palette
Radius X	Ellipse	Sets curve amount on horizontal corners
Radius Y	Ellipse	Sets curve amount on vertical corners
Center X	Ellipse	Manually sets the center horizontal position
Center Y	Ellipse	Manually sets the center vertical position
Horizontal Radius	Rectangle	Sets the amount of horizontal curve for the shape corners
Vertical Radius	Rectangle	Sets the amount of vertical curve for the shape corners
Number of sides	Symmetrical	Determines the number of sides ranging from 1 to 1,000
Radius	Symmetrical	On a stellated shape, sets the distance from center to its outermost points
Round Inner	Symmetrical	Provides rounded inner curves
Round Outer	Symmetrical	Provides rounded outer curves
Transformation	Symmetrical	Provides settings for corner and side variations
Left	Rectangle	When Show Nodes is active, determines rectangle left edge location
Top	Rectangle	When Show Nodes is active, determines rectangle top edge location
Width	Rectangle	When Show Nodes is active, determines rectangle width
Height	Rectangle	When Show Nodes is active, determines rectangle height

Click and drag on the canvas to draw the selected shape. As you drag the mouse, an outline of the shape appears. When you release the mouse button, the completed shape appears.

Draw from Center

If you right-click and drag, PaintShop Pro places the center point of the shape where you click.

Figure 11-3 shows a canvas with three different vector objects. Notice the vector layer on the Layers palette.

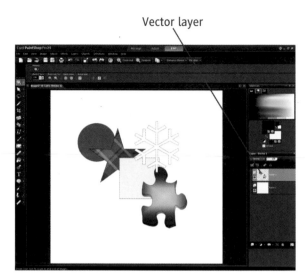

Vector layer

Figure 11-3
Drawing shapes.

Adding Vector Lines

THE PREVIOUS SECTION SHOWED you how you can create various shaped vector objects. Another type of PaintShop Pro vector object is lines. You can draw straight lines or lines with multiple segments. You can also create Bézier curved lines with PaintShop Pro. Finally, you can draw freely using your mouse to create vector lines.

Use a Drawing Tablet

If you like to draw freehand, check into using an electronic pressure-sensitive drawing tablet. Drawing tablets help you draw with better precision. PaintShop Pro supports most drawing tablets on the market today.

Drawing Vector Lines

You use the Pen tool to draw lines. When you activate the Pen tool, the Tool Options palette seen in Figure 11-4 appears. Notice that many of the options are the same ones available with other vector shapes, with a couple of exceptions.

One option is the Connect Segments check box. When you draw multiple lines, you can have them connected into a polyline. If you click the Connect Segments option, when you finish drawing one line, PaintShop Pro automatically connects it to the next line you draw. Connected lines continue until you click the Apply button. See Figure 11-5 for an example.

The following steps show you how to draw vector lines:

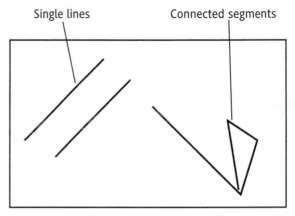

Single lines   Connected segments

Figure 11-5
Connecting multiple lines.

1. From the Tools toolbar, select the Pen tool.

2. From the Materials palette, choose a Foreground and Stroke color. If you are going to draw polylines and you want them filled in making a polygon, choose a Background and Fill color. If you do not want the center filled, click the Transparent button on the Background and Fill color swatch.

3. Choose options from the Tool Options palette, including the line style and width. If you want to draw polylines, click the Connect Segments option. Also make sure that Create on Vector is checked.

4. From the Tool Options palette, select the Draw Lines and Polylines button or the Draw Freehand mode.

Curve Tracking

If you are using the Freehand mode, you can set Curve Tracking, which allows you to set the distance in pixels between nodes.

Connect Segments check box

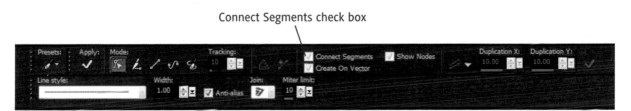

Figure 11-4
Pen tool options.

5. Click and drag on the canvas until the line is the length you want. As you draw, a light gray line with small boxes on the ends appears.

6. If you checked the Connect Segments box, click and drag to draw the next line.

7. If you are drawing polylines, after you draw your connected lines, you have two additional options. You can choose to close the open lines or start a new line. Click the Close Selected Open Contours button to create a closed loop, or click the Start New Contour – Move To button (immediately to the right of the Close Selected Open Contours button) to leave the lines as you drew them—with a start-point and an endpoint. See Figure 11-6 for an example of each.

8. Click the Apply button.

Working with Bézier Curves

Bézier (pronounced bez-ee-ay) curves are handy little drawing nodules that give you much more control over your lines, paths, and curves. The curves were first developed in 1959 by Paul de Casteljau using de Casteljau's algorithm, a numerically stable method to evaluate curves. The mathematics behind these curves is classical, but it was the French automobile engineer Pierre Bézier who introduced their use in 1962 with computer graphics. Bézier used them to design Renault automobile bodies, creating a smooth contour to its modern cars.

A Bézier curve may be smooth and streamlined, but it may also have very sharp turns. It may have one or two bends, and it may even form loops. Bézier curves use four points to define the curve: two endpoints and two control points. The endpoints are called the *anchor points*, while the other point or points, which define the actual curvature, are called *nodes* or *handles*. Moving the nodes lets you modify the shape of the curve. Figure 11-7 illustrates sample Bézier curves.

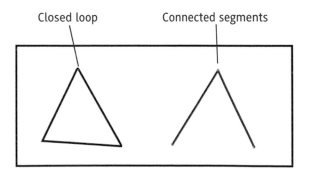

Figure 11-6
Creating open and closed segmented lines.

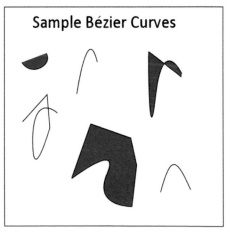

Figure 11-7
Sample Bézier curves.

The following steps show you how to draw a Bézier curve.

1. Click the Pen tool on the Tools toolbar.

2. From the Materials palette, choose a color for the outline with the Foreground and Stroke box.

3. If you are drawing a closed shape and want a fill color to the curve, click the Background and Fill properties box, and select a fill color; however, if you don't want a fill, click the Transparent button.

4. In the Tool Options palette, click the Draw Point to Point button.

5. Mark the Show Nodes check box. You need this feature visible when working with the Bézier curves.

6. If your curve will have multiple segments, check the Connect Segments box.

7. Choose a line style and width.

8. Draw a straight line by clicking where you want the curve to begin, which creates your first anchor point.

9. Drag the mouse to where you want the curve to end. As you drag, the arrow end of the control arm handle points in the same direction. Release the mouse button when the first control arm reaches the desired length, which then creates the second endpoint (see Figure 11-8). You see only the outline of your line segment. You're not finished yet.

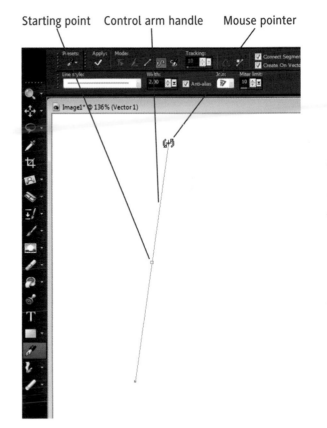

Figure 11-8
Drawing a Bézier curve.

Control Arms

The control arms and their arrow end handles help you manipulate nodes. Chapter 12, "Editing Vector Objects," explains more about working with nodes.

10. Click the mouse pointer in the direction you'd like to warp the curve, and then drag the mouse pointer until you get the curve you want. When you release the mouse pointer, the control point is set in place. As you see in Figure 11-9, as you drag the mouse pointer, the curve segment appears on the image canvas. If you marked the Connect Segments option, you can continue adding segments in this manner.

11. On the Tool Options palette, click either the Start New Contour – Move To button, which creates an open shape where the first and last segments are not connected, or click the Close Selected Open Contours button, which creates a closed shape where the first and last segments are connected.

12. Click the Apply button. Figure 11-10 illustrates open and closed Bézier curves.

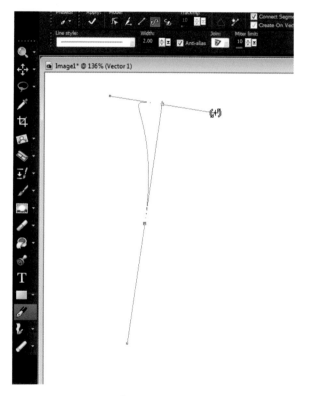

Figure 11-9
Adding a second curve node.

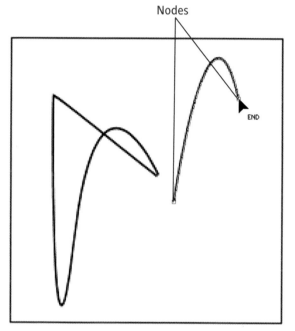

Figure 11-10
Bézier curves can be open or closed.

Bézier curves can be frustrating, especially at first. But with practice, they will be your friends. They are extremely useful tools that help you draw more accurately. The easiest way to learn Bézier curves is to practice, practice, practice.

Managing Vector Graphics

PAINTSHOP PRO FILES CAN HAVE many vector layers, and each layer can have many objects. Because vector objects are independent elements, you can modify, move, reshape, or delete any of them without affecting the rest of the image objects.

Selecting Vector Objects

Before you can modify a vector object, you must select it. You begin by selecting objects from the active layer, and you can select additional objects that exist on different layers at the same time. When selecting multiple vector objects, you pick and choose which individual objects you want using the Pick tool.

Deleting Objects

To delete a vector object, select the object and press the Delete key.

One method of selecting individual vector objects is by using the Pick tool. Choose the Pick tool by clicking it from the Tools toolbar (it's the second tool from the top) or by pressing the letter K. You won't need to select options from the Tool Options palette before using the Pick tool because most of them pertain to aligning multiple objects. You'll discover later in this chapter about managing and aligning vector objects.

When the Pick tool is active, the mouse pointer has a small box beneath it. With the Pick tool active, make sure the layer containing your object is active, and position the mouse pointer over the object. If the object has no fill, you need to position the mouse over an edge of the object. When your mouse pointer turns into a four-headed arrow like the one you see in Figure 11-11, click to select the object. Eight selection handles appear around the selected object.

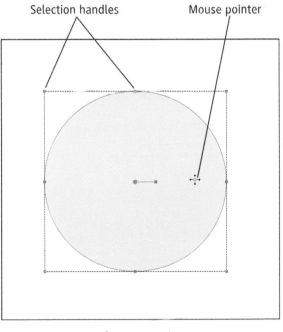

Figure 11-11
Selecting vector objects.

Hold down the Shift key and click to select additional objects. (The mouse pointer displays a plus sign.) If you want objects on a different layer, click the layer, and then select the additional objects. See Figure 11-12, where three of the four vector objects are selected and surrounded by the selection box.

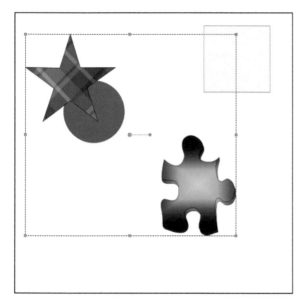

Figure 11-12
Selecting multiple vector objects.

Deselect Objects

To deselect individual objects, hold down the Ctrl key and click. To deselect all objects, choose Selections > Select None or press Ctrl+D.

Resizing a Vector Object

Changing the size of a vector object is simple. You can change the object size from a selected side, in an equal conformed amount, or you can skew or distort the object. Additionally, if you created several objects, you can make them equal in size.

RESIZING OBJECTS

You use your mouse and the selection handles around an object to change the object size. After using the Pick tool to select the object you want to resize, choose one of these options:

▶ Drag a corner handle to resize the object width and height at the same time, keeping the object's proportions.

▶ Drag a left- or right-side handle to resize the object width.

▶ Drag a top or bottom handle to resize the object height.

▶ Right-click and drag a corner handle to resize both the height and width disproportionately.

When your mouse pointer is on top of a selection handle, it turns into a white either two-headed or four-headed arrow. The arrow directions indicate the resizing direction. As you click and drag, an outline of the resized object appears (see Figure 11-13). When you release the mouse, the vector shape takes the new size.

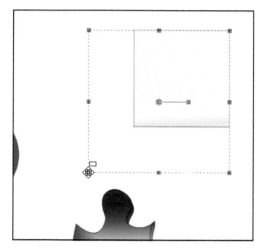

Figure 11-13
Resizing a vector object.

DEFORMING VECTOR OBJECTS

When you deform an image, you distort its original shape. Technically, resizing an image is a form of deforming an image, but other types of deformation include Skew, Distort, Change Perspective, and Shear. You can use any of these types of deformation with vector shapes, lines, and vector text objects. Just follow these easy steps:

1. Using the Pick tool, select the object you want to deform. The object appears with selection handles.

2. Position the mouse over an image handle. Whether you select a corner handle or a side or top handle depends on how you want to deform the object. Deforming a vector object is similar to resizing it, but you need to hold down one or more additional keys before dragging a selection handle:

   - To change the image perspective, hold down the Ctrl key and drag a corner handle.

   - To skew the image, hold down the Shift key and drag a corner handle.

   - To distort the image, hold down both the Ctrl and Shift keys and drag a corner handle.

   - To shear the image, hold down the Shift key and drag a side or top handle.

3. Hold the appropriate key and drag the selection handle until the selected object outline displays the shape you want.

4. Release the mouse button, and the selected object retains the new shape. See Figure 11-14 for examples of each distortion.

Figure 11-14
Deforming a vector object.

MAKING OBJECTS A UNIFORM SIZE

If you have multiple objects and you want them to be the same size, PaintShop Pro includes a tool to quickly resize them. You can make the objects the same height, the same width, or both the same height and width.

The secret to working with most multiple object features is the order of selection. The object you select first is considered the "base" object—the one the others will adjust to. This applies to alignment, spacing, and resizing features. The following steps show you how to make multiple objects the same physical size:

1. Using the Pick tool, select the object you want the objects to imitate in size.

2. Hold down the Shift key and click the objects you want to resize. A selection box surrounds the selected objects. In Figure 11-15, the larger paw print was the first object selected, and then three additional paw prints were selected.

3. Click a resize button from Make Same Size buttons on the Tool Options palette. The selected objects will be uniform in size to the first selected object.

   - Make the selected objects the same width.
   - Make the selected objects the same height.
   - Make the selected objects the same width and height.

In Figure 11-16, the paw print on the right did not resize because it was not included in the selection.

First selected object   Make Same Size buttons

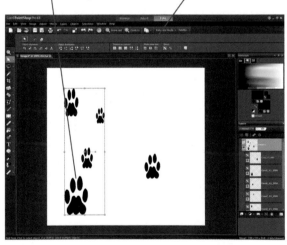

Figure 11-15
Selecting the objects you want to resize.

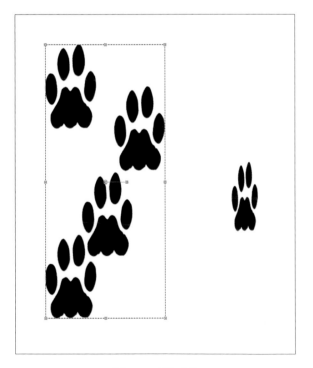

Figure 11-16
Making multiple objects uniform in size.

Moving a Vector Object

If an object is not in the position you require, move it easily by using your mouse. Moving vector objects is a little different from moving raster objects. With raster objects, you use the Move tool, but with vector objects, you don't use the Move tool; instead, you simply use your mouse.

Using the Pick tool, select the object you want to move. If you want to move multiple objects, hold down Shift and select the objects. The object(s) appears with selection handles. Position the mouse in the center of the object, over the move circle. The mouse pointer turns into a black four-headed arrow. Click and drag the object to the new position. As you drag the object, an outline indicates the move location (see Figure 11-17). When you release the mouse button, the object moves into the new position.

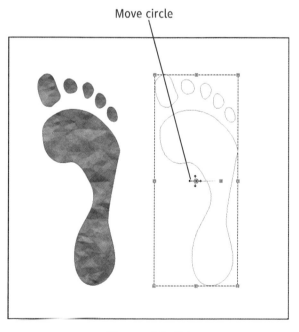

Move circle

Figure 11-17
Dragging vector objects to a new position on the canvas.

You can also use the keyboard to move the object. Often this gives you more precise control over the movement, especially if you only want to nudge the object short distances. Keyboard methods to move a selected vector object include these:

▶ Pressing an arrow key moves the object one pixel at a time.

▶ Holding down the Ctrl key and pressing an arrow key moves the object 10 pixels at a time.

▶ Holding down the Shift key and pressing an arrow key moves the object 50 pixels at a time.

▶ Holding down both the Shift and Ctrl keys and pressing an arrow key moves the object 100 pixels at a time.

Altering Vector Properties

Even after you create a vector object, you can easily change its line style, color, style, thickness, and other properties. Also, as you place your objects on a layer, you might find it helpful to give the individual object a name to help you easily identify each object. When you create the object, PaintShop Pro assigns a name that corresponds to the shape, such as Ellipse, Rectangle, or Star, but you can easily rename the object to something more to your liking.

Select the object or objects you want to modify, and then click the Properties button. Optionally, right-click the object and choose Properties. The Vector Property dialog box seen in Figure 11-18 opens.

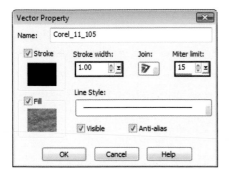

Figure 11-18
Changing vector object properties.

Rotating a Vector Object

You can freely rotate any vector object to any angle by using the rotation handle. Using the Pick tool, select the object you want to rotate. Along with the selection handles, you see a rotation handle, which is a small square box. Position the mouse pointer over the rotation handle to change the mouse pointer into two curved arrows, as you see in Figure 11-19. Click and drag the rotation handle until the image rotation outline appears in the position you want. When you release the mouse button, the image moves into the new rotated position.

From the Vector Property dialog box, you can click the Stroke materials box and select a different color for the object outline, or click the Fill materials box and choose a different option for the object center fill. You can change the line style, thickness, and corner options. You can also give a more meaningful name to the vector object. The object name appears on the Layers palette.

As you change any options, the changes immediately reflect on the object. Click OK when you're finished.

Multiple Object Properties

If you have multiple objects selected, all objects take on the property change except for the name. You can rename only one object at a time.

Rotation pivot point   Rotation handle

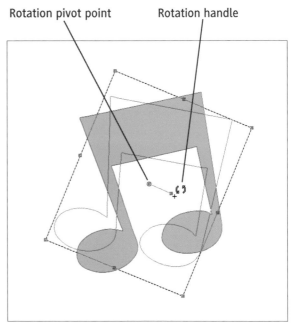

Figure 11-19
Rotating objects.

280

Change Rotation Center

To change the center of rotation, hold down Ctrl and drag the rotation pivot point to a new location.

Arranging Multiple Objects

PaintShop Pro includes several handy features for working with positioning objects. You'll find features to line up object edges, to create equal spaces between objects, and even to combine multiple objects into one.

REORDERING OBJECTS

When a vector layer has multiple objects, the elements are stacked according to their order in the Layers palette. The element at the top of the list is at the top of the other elements as well, making it visible in front of all other objects on that layer. The object at the bottom of the layer is at the bottom of the stack and might appear to be behind the other objects.

Using the Pick tool, select the object you want to reorder. Click Objects ❯ Arrange, and then click an arrangement option. The selected object moves to the new order in the stack of objects.

Arrangement options include the following:

Optional Method

Optionally, right-click the object, choose Arrange, and select one of the arrangement options.

- ▶ **Bring to Top**: Moves the selected object to the top of the stack
- ▶ **Send to Bottom**: Moves the selected object to the bottom of the stack
- ▶ **Move Up**: Moves the selected object up one level
- ▶ **Move Down**: Moves the selected object down one level

Optional Reorder Method

You can also arrange vector objects by dragging them up or down in the Layers palette.

On the top of Figure 11-20, you see the objects in their original stacking order. On the bottom, you see a copy of the objects as they are restacked. Notice on the reordered objects that the black arrow moved on top of the blue box.

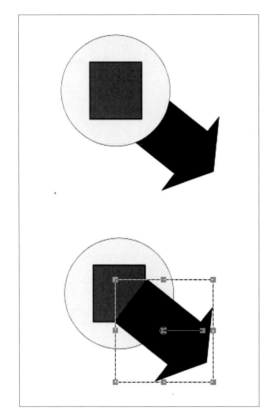

Figure 11-20
Restacking vector objects.

ALIGNING OBJECTS TO EACH OTHER

Suppose that you have two or more objects and you want them to be at the same vertical position on the image, or you want one (or more) of the objects to be centered in another. Well, you could use your mouse to move the objects, but sometimes it can be difficult to visually align them. Instead, let the alignment feature do the guesswork for you.

Just remember that the secret is in the order in which you select the objects. The first selected object is the one that the other selected objects will match up to. Just follow these easy steps:

 1. Using the Pick tool, select the object you want the others to line up to. Selection handles appear around the selected object. In the example seen in Figure 11-21, to line up the star even with the circle, select the circle first and then select the star. As in previous examples, the top circle and star are the originals, and the ones on the bottom are aligned copies.

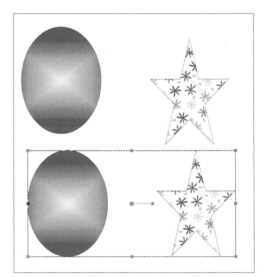

Figure 11-21
Aligning vector objects.

2. Hold down the Shift key and select the remaining objects you want to line up to the first object. A selection box appears around the selected objects.

3. Select an alignment option from the Object Alignment section of the Tool Options palette. The objects align together. In this example, the top edges of the star and circle align. The following list explains each option:

- **Align Top**: All selected objects match up to the top edge of the first selected object.

- **Align Bottom**: All selected objects match up to the bottom edge of the first selected object.

- **Align Left**: All selected objects match up to the left edge of the first selected object.

- **Align Right**: All selected objects match up to the right edge of the first selected object.

- **Align Vertical Center**: All selected objects match up vertically to the center of the first selected object.

- **Align Horizontal Center**: All selected objects match up horizontally to the center of the first selected object.

Some alignment choices might take two steps. In the example you see in Figure 11-22, aligning the star in the center of the circle is accomplished in two steps. First the objects were aligned Vertical Center, and then they were aligned Horizontal Center.

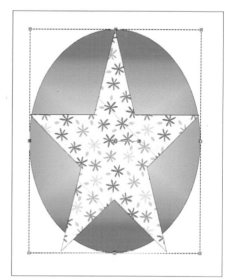

Figure 11-22
Making multiple alignment choices.

Optional Alignment Method

You can also set alignment through the Objects > Align menu or by right-clicking the object, choosing Align Objects, and making a selection.

POSITIONING OBJECTS ON THE CANVAS

You just learned how you can align objects together, but you can also align one or more objects to the canvas. For example, you created a button, and you need it in the middle of the image. You could turn on the ruler and the grid and visually move the button until it looks like it is in the center of the canvas, but by using the Align to Canvas feature, you only need to make a mouse click and let PaintShop Pro do the work for you.

 Using the Pick tool, select the object(s) you want to line up, and click an option from the Position on Canvas buttons:

- **Center on Canvas**: Moves all selected objects to the exact center of the canvas
- **Horizontal Center in Canvas**: Moves all selected objects horizontally in the center of the canvas, but not vertically center
- **Vertical Center in Canvas**: Moves all selected objects vertically to the center of the canvas but not horizontally center
- **Space Evenly Horizontal**: Used with two or more objects, places all selected objects so that there is equal horizontal canvas space between the objects
- **Space Evenly Vertical**: Used with two or more objects, places all selected objects so that there is equal vertical canvas space between the objects

In Figure 11-23, you see a triangle centered on the canvas.

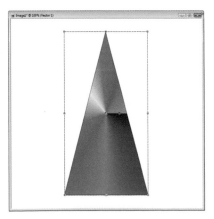

Figure 11-23
Positioning objects on the canvas.

DISTRIBUTING SPACE BETWEEN OBJECTS

Anytime you have multiple objects, PaintShop Pro can distribute the space between the objects evenly, either horizontally or vertically.

At least three objects should be selected to distribute space evenly. If you choose to distribute evenly three or more objects horizontally, the objects that are closest to the left and right boundaries of the group become the two target objects. When you distribute evenly three or more objects vertically, the objects that are closest to the top and bottom of the group boundaries become the target objects. The distance between these target objects determines the spacing of the objects between them.

 Using the Pick tool, select the object(s) you want to line up, and click an option from the Object Distribution buttons:

- **Distribute Vertical Top**: Spaces objects evenly between the top edges of the top and bottom targets
- **Distribute Vertical Center**: Spaces objects evenly between the centers of the top and bottom targets
- **Distribute Vertical Bottom**: Spaces objects evenly between the bottom edges of the top and bottom targets
- **Distribute Horizontal Left**: Spaces objects evenly between the left edges of the left and right targets
- **Distribute Horizontal Center**: Spaces objects evenly between the centers of the left and right targets

- **Distribute Horizontal Right**: Spaces objects evenly between the right edges of the left and right targets

- **Space Evenly Horizontal**: Divides horizontal space on the canvas equally between all selected objects

- **Space Evenly Vertical**: Divides vertical space on the canvas equally between all selected objects

As you see in Figure 11-24, the five circles at the bottom are evenly distributed horizontally.

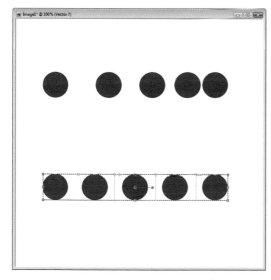

Figure 11-24
Distributing space evenly between objects.

Optional Distribution Method

You can also distribute object space through the Objects ➤ Distribute menu or by right-clicking the object and choosing Distribute Objects and then making a selection.

GROUPING MULTIPLE OBJECTS

Grouping multiple objects is like linking the objects for easier manipulation. Grouped objects can be ungrouped at any time. When you select multiple objects, PaintShop Pro treats them as a temporary group but then ungroups the objects when you deselect them. Using the grouping feature, however, keeps them grouped until you decide to ungroup them. Grouping objects makes them easier to move, resize, reshape, and change their lines and materials. The following steps show you how to group multiple objects:

1. Using the Pick tool, select the objects you want to group. Selection handles appear around the objects.

2. Click Objects. The Objects menu appears.

3. Click Group. The multiple objects meld into a single selected object.

Optional Group Method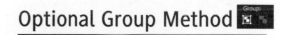

Optionally, click the Group button on the Tool Options palette, or right-click and choose Group.

Ungroup objects by clicking on the Ungroup button on the Tool Options palette or by selecting Ungroup from the Objects menu.

Editing
Vector Objects

PICTURE YOURSELF AS A CUSTOM FASHION DESIGNER and a tailor. You're well known for your chic arrangements and attention to the finest detail. No garment leaves your shop unless it fits perfectly. Whether you need to take the fabric in or let it out, the results are always exactly as your client wants. When tailoring, you need to consider the seams, hems, shoulder lines, waistbands, and other fine clothing aspects. That's what makes you so good—you pay attention to the detail.

After you create your vector objects, you may notice they need a little tweaking here or there. In Chapter 11, "Constructing Vector Objects," you discovered how to perform minor modifications to the objects, but in this chapter, you'll discover how to manage the minute details, called the *nodes*, that make up the vector object.

Understanding Vector Terms

VECTOR OBJECTS ARE COMPOSED of a mathematical data array laid out in such a way that together you see an editable object. Vector graphics use lines, points, and polygons based on equations to represent images, making it easy for your computer to convert the numerical instructions from the vector graphic into an image it displays on the screen. To understand working with vector objects, such as the one shown in Figure 12-1, you should acquaint yourself with a few terms:

- **Object**: An *object* is any item that you can individually select or manipulate. In PaintShop Pro, you create objects with the Shape tools or with the Pen tool. When selected, each object is represented by its own box and has properties you can control, such as line style and fill color. Each object contains one path made up of contours and nodes.

- **Node**: A *node* is a square point indicating the starting or ending points or joints of an object. A combination of nodes defines an object shape.

- **Curve handles**: These are the directional lines that describe the angle and length of a curve. Curve handles have an arrow with a point at one end and a circle at the other. They appear over the node showing the direction that the curve or line is going at that point.

- **Line segment**: A *line segment* is the portion of a line delimited by two points or nodes. Segments can be either straight or curved, and nodes define the segment ends.

- **Contour**: *Contours* are the lines or curves in a line segment. A single set of nodes makes up a contour, which can be open or closed. The object's properties, such as line style, fill color, and anti-aliasing, determine some of a contour's properties.

- **Path**: The *path* is the sequence that an object follows, including all the contours. The object's nodes and segments control it. A path's direction flows from its start-point to its endpoint. Some paths are closed, which means that their start-points and endpoints are the same.

The direction of the path always goes from the startpoint to the endpoint. For circles, squares, ellipses, and rectangles created with the Shapes tool, the direction of the path is clockwise by default. For lines, the path starts where you first click and goes to the end of the line. For curves, you can find the specific direction at a particular node by selecting it while in Edit mode. The curve control arm handle arrow appearing over the node indicates the direction that the curve or line is going at that point.

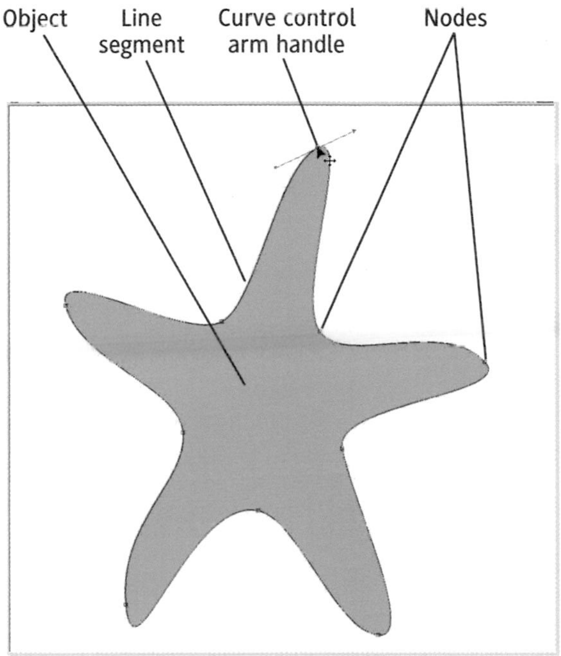

Figure 12-1
Understanding vector components.

Convert Shapes to a Path

Some vector shapes, such as circles, don't easily lend themselves to editing the individual nodes. You must first convert the vector object to a path, which makes it as though the shape were drawn with the Pen tool. See the section "Converting Vectors to a Path."

Working with Nodes

A HANDY FEATURE WHEN YOU'RE working with vector graphics is the ability to create new shapes from an existing vector object. Each vector graphic has nodes, which are control points for the vector object. By adjusting the nodes, you change the shape of the vector graphic.

Nodes are square and are often at a joint or edge in a straight or shaped object. You'll also find them where curves change direction. You change the shape of a line or curve object by dragging one or more of its nodes.

All vector objects, whether lines or closed shapes, have certain features. They all have a startpoint and a path direction. Shapes have a closepoint, and lines have an endpoint. To edit vector shapes, you must go into node editing mode and if, while in node edit mode, you move your mouse pointer over some nodes, you'll see a small tag appear indicating whether the node is a startpoint, endpoint, or closepoint.

There are several node types. The node type controls the behavior of the lines before and after the node:

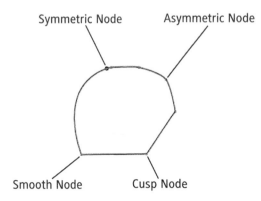

Symmetric Node   Asymmetric Node

Smooth Node   Cusp Node

▶ **Symmetric**: You use symmetric nodes to create smooth, flowing curves on either side of a node. Neither curve handle can be moved without the other moving in an equal and opposite direction, maintaining handles of equal length and opposite direction.

▶ **Asymmetric**: You use asymmetric nodes to obtain a different amount of curve on each side of the node but keep a smooth flow through the node. You can lengthen or shorten the control arm handles independently of each other, but if you try to change the direction of one, the other follows, keeping both handles in a straight line.

▶ **Cusp**: A cusp node makes a sharp corner. You can adjust the length and direction of each control arm handle independently. You can use cusp nodes to create extreme changes in direction.

▶ **Smooth**: Use a smooth node when you have a curve segment on one side and a line segment on the other. A smooth node gives a smooth transition from the curve to the line by constraining the curve handle to the same direction as the line.

Easily View Nodes

From the Layers palette, click the Visibility icon next to the vector object you are working on. Hiding the object hides the fill and outline, leaving only the nodes visible.

Selecting Nodes

Before you can modify a vector object by its individual nodes, you need to select the node you want to edit. When drawing many vector shapes, you have the option on the Tool Options palette to show the nodes. If you draw the object and later decide you want to edit the nodes, you can use the Pen tool to select the individual nodes. The following steps show you how to select individual nodes:

1. From the Tools toolbar, select the Pen tool.

2. On the Tool Options palette, click the Edit Mode button.

3. Click the vector object on which you want to see nodes.

4. Click an individual node to select it or, if you want to select multiple nodes, hold down the Shift key and click the individual nodes. The first selected node appears with a solid gray fill. If you select multiple nodes, a rectangular selection box encloses them (see Figure 12-2). If you select a start or end node, pausing your mouse pointer over the node displays the word *Start* or *End*.

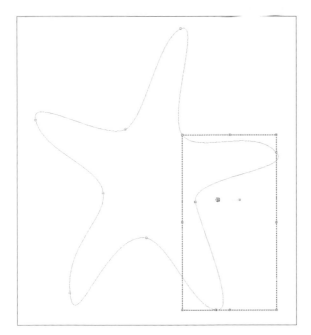

Figure 12-2
Selecting nodes.

Select All Nodes

To select all the object's nodes, right-click any node and choose Edit > Select All. To deselect all nodes, click anywhere outside the selection box.

Moving Nodes

Once you select the node you want to edit, you can perform a number of different actions, including moving the node. Moving a node reshapes the entire object, whether a curved or a straight line, or a filled or an unfilled object. You move a node by following these steps:

1. From the Tools toolbar, select the Pen tool.

2. Click the Edit Mode button from the Tool Options palette.

3. Select the object you want to modify.

4. Click and drag the node you want to modify until it reaches the position you want. As you drag the node, you can see the original node location as well as the new node position (see Figure 12-3).

5. Click the Apply button.

Original node position

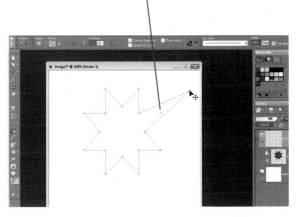

Figure 12-3
Moving a node.

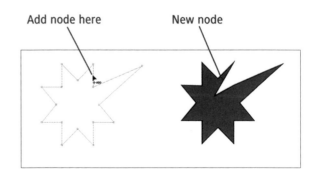

Add node here   New node

Figure 12-4
Adding a node.

Constrain Segments

Hold down the Shift key as you drag a node to constrain the movement to 45-degree increments.

Adding Nodes

You can easily add nodes to your vector object. Adding more nodes gives you further control over the object by providing additional control points you can edit. Follow these steps:

1. From the Tools toolbar, select the Pen tool.

2. Click the Edit Mode button from the Tool Options palette.

3. Select the object you want to modify.

4. Hold down the Ctrl key and click where you want to add a node. As you see in Figure 12-4, the mouse pointer displays +ADD.

5. Drag the new node to a desired location.

6. Click the Apply button to accept the change.

Deleting Nodes

If you want to remove a node, you can. Deleting a node in the middle of an open contour forces the object into two separate contours. If you delete a node in a closed contour, the object remains a single object but becomes an open contour.

Select the node you want to delete and press the Delete key. In Figure 12-5, I began with a starfish shape and deleted one of the nodes, which left the shape open.

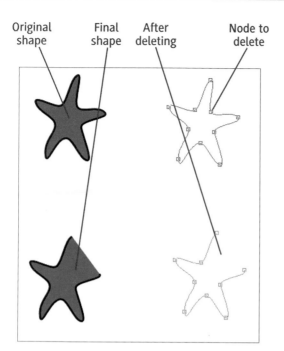

Figure 12-5
Deleting a node.

Merging Nodes

You can merge one or more selected nodes to remove the control points. When you merge nodes, the selected nodes disappear, and the nodes on both sides of the merge connect. Follow these steps to merge nodes on a vector object:

 1. From the Tools toolbar, select the Pen tool.

2. Click the Edit Mode button from the Tool Options palette.

3. Select the object you want to modify.

4. Hold down the Shift key, and click each node you want to merge. A selection box appears around the selected nodes.

5. Click Objects ❯ Edit ❯ Merge or optionally right-click over the selected nodes and choose Edit ❯ Merge. The selected nodes merge into a single node (see Figure 12-6).

6. Click the Apply button to accept the change.

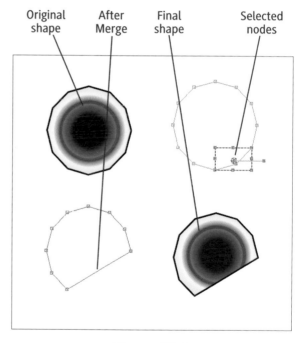

Figure 12-6
Merging nodes.

Working with Curves and Contours

SO FAR IN THIS CHAPTER, you've seen where you can add, delete, and otherwise modify nodes on vector shapes. But what happens when you want to work with nodes on a curve? PaintShop Pro provides the options you need to adjust or straighten curves.

Adjusting Curves

If you want to modify the curve of a line, such as making it a wider or narrower curve, you do so using the node control arm handles. Follow these steps:

1. From the Tools toolbar, select the Pen tool.

2. Click the Edit Mode button from the Tool Options palette. Also, if it's not already checked, click Show Nodes.

3. Select the object you want to modify. The individual nodes appear around the object.

4. Click the node you want to adjust. The node control arm handles appear.

5. Move the mouse pointer over a control arm handle until the mouse pointer displays two rotating arrows, such as you see in Figure 12-7.

Control arm handle   Mouse pointer

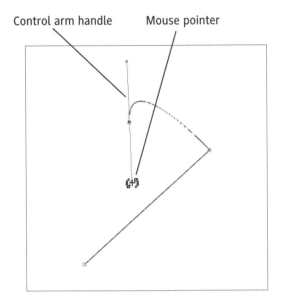

Figure 12-7
Selecting a control arm handle.

6. Drag the control arm handle until the curve takes the shape you want. In Figure 12-8, you see the shape after adjusting the curve.

Adding Control Arm Handle

If the node you want to adjust does not display a control arm handle, choose Objects > Node Type and choose a different node type.

294

7. Click the Apply button to accept the change.

4. Click one of the end nodes of the line you want to straighten. Then hold down the Shift key and click on the next consecutive node of the line you want to straighten (see Figure 12-9).

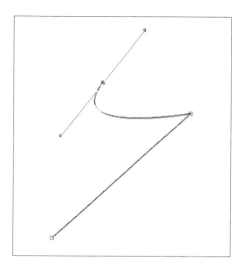

Figure 12-8
The line after adjusting the curve.

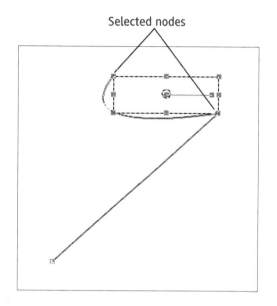

Figure 12-9
Selecting curve nodes to straighten.

Straightening a Curve

Sometimes you begin with a curve and then decide you'd rather have a straight line. You can easily convert any curve to a straight line by following these steps:

 1. From the Tools toolbar, select the Pen tool.

 2. Click the Edit Mode button from the Tool Options palette. Also, if it's not already checked, click Show Nodes.

3. Select the object you want to modify. The individual nodes appear around the object.

5. Choose Objects ❯ Node Type ❯ Convert to Line or right-click either selected node and choose Node Type ❯ Convert to Line. The curved area turns into a straight line.

 6. Click the Apply button to accept the change.

Closing Contours

If you originally drew an open curve and later decide you want the curve to be closed, you do not have to add nodes and draw in the contour yourself. You can tell PaintShop Pro to close the contour by drawing a segment from the start node to the end node. Just follow these easy steps:

1. From the Tools toolbar, select the Pen tool.

2. Click the Edit Mode button from the Tool Options palette. Also, if it's not already checked, click Show Nodes.

3. Select the object you want to modify. The individual nodes appear around the object.

4. Click the start node to select it and then, holding down the Shift key, click the end node. A selection box appears around the two nodes, as shown in Figure 12-10.

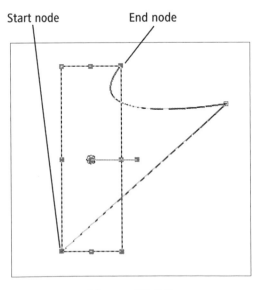

Start node   End node

Figure 12-10
Selecting the start and end nodes.

Determine Start or End

If you pause the mouse pointer over the individual nodes, PaintShop Pro displays *Start* or *End* when you hover over the start or end node.

5. From the Tool Options palette, click the Close Selected Open Contours button. You see a new line segment between the start node and the end node (see Figure 12-11).

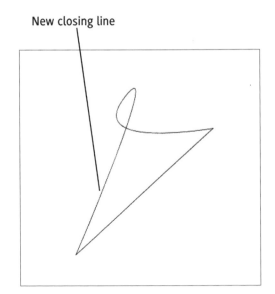

New closing line

Figure 12-11
Closing an open contour.

6. Click the Apply button to accept the change.

Breaking a Curve

This command takes a selected node and breaks a curve or line in two at that point. Where one node was, PaintShop Pro creates two unconnected nodes, which you can then move independently of one another. Follow these steps to break a curve:

1. From the Tools toolbar, select the Pen tool.

2. Click the Edit Mode button from the Tool Options palette. Also, if it's not already checked, click Show Nodes.

3. Select the object you want to modify. The individual nodes appear around the object.

4. Select the node where you want to break the contour.

5. Choose Objects ➤ Edit ➤ Break or right-click the selected node and choose Edit ➤ Break. The contour breaks, and PaintShop Pro adds a new node on top of the current node. The node square changes to a node-on-node indicator.

6. Select one of the nodes in the node-on-node indicator, and drag it to a desired position.

7. Repeat if desired for the other broken node (see Figure 12-12).

8. Click the Apply button to accept the change.

Original contour with selected node — Node-on-node indicator — Contour after moving one node

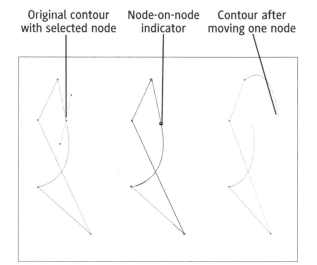

Figure 12-12
Breaking a contour.

Converting Vectors

ONE SIZE DOESN'T FIT ALL. Although vector graphics are fun to create and easy to manipulate without losing quality, sometimes the vector graphic may need a little more fine tweaking. For example, some vectors don't have individual editable nodes. That's not a problem, though. PaintShop Pro can fix that for you. Also, if you are working with complicated drop shadows or other effects, PaintShop Pro only applies effects to raster layers. Again, that's not a problem. You can convert the vector layer to a raster layer.

Converting Vectors to a Path

You've probably noticed that many vector shapes don't seem to have a path with individual editable nodes. Fortunately, PaintShop Pro provides a method in which you can convert any vector object to a path with nodes you can individually edit using the Pen tool. You can easily convert text, shapes, or any vector object to a path.

 Begin by using the Pick tool from the Tools toolbar to click the vector object you want to convert.

Pick Tool Keyboard Shortcut

Optionally, press the letter K to activate the Pick tool.

Choose Objects ❯ Convert to Path, or right-click the selected vector object and choose Convert to Path.

In Figure 12-13, you see a circle on the left that I converted to a path. After conversion, I moved one node to create the object you see on the right.

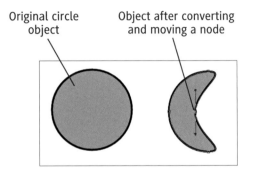

Original circle object

Object after converting and moving a node

Figure 12-13
Converting shapes to a path.

Figure 12-14 shows text before and after converting to a path. As you can see on the character on the right, you can edit many nodes. You'll learn about creating text in Chapter 13, "Working with Text."

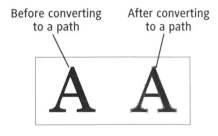

Before converting to a path

After converting to a path

Figure 12-14
Text converted to a path.

Converting Vector Layers to Raster Layers

The main drawback to vector objects is that you cannot apply effects and filters to vector layers. Don't give up hope, though! PaintShop Pro includes a feature to convert vector objects on vector layers to raster images on raster layers. This process is called *rasterizing*. From there, you can apply effects and filters. Also, if you are planning to use the image on the web, you'll need to convert it from a vector graphic to a raster graphic.

Another common reason to convert a vector graphic to a raster graphic is file size. A raster file might be smaller than a vector file if the image has several vectors and many areas of uniform color. The following steps guide you through converting vector graphics to raster objects:

Save in PaintShop Pro Format First

It's a good idea to save a copy of your original vector file in its native PaintShop Pro format before converting it to a raster. Once you convert the vector to a raster, you can no longer resize and modify the image without losing image quality.

1. From the Layers palette, select the vector layer you want to convert to a raster layer.

2. Choose Layers ❯ Convert to Raster Layer. The vector layer becomes a raster layer.

3. Apply any desired effect or filter. Figure 12-15 illustrates taking a simple vector shape, a musical note, and after converting it to a raster layer, applying the warp, glowing edges, and drop shadow effects.

Original vector shape

After converting and applying effects

Figure 12-15
A converted vector object after applying effects.

Working with Text

PICTURE YOURSELF AS A SMALL CHILD SINGING the ABC song. Now you are old enough to begin learning what each of those letters looks like, so your mother shows you how each letter has lines that are different from each other. You take your pencil and practice until the letter looks just the way you want it.

We've been told that a picture is worth a thousand words, and PaintShop Pro has certainly proven that true. But, sometimes you just *have* to spell it out. You can create text with PaintShop Pro's text feature.

Creating Text

YOU USE THE TEXT TOOL in the Edit work-space to create text in PaintShop Pro. Similar to the other tools you've used so far, when you select the Text tool, you will have additional options on the Tool Options palette that you can use to determine items such as font, size, style, alignment, kerning, and leading, as well as the method you want PaintShop Pro to use when placing the text on your image.

From the Tools toolbar, click the Text tool. The mouse pointer resembles a cross with the letter *T* beside it, and the Tool Options palette displays options for working with text.

As with other PaintShop Pro tools, once you select the tool, the Tool Options palette appears with choices pertaining to the selected tool. The Text tool is no different except that the Tool Options palette associated with it has three major areas that you can work with. In fact, there are so many options that they can't fit easily on a single bar. Depending on your screen size and resolution, you may have to click the right arrow on the far right side of the Text Tool Options palette to display more Text Tool options.

In some situations, you'll find additional options, such as the text style or the text positioning, on a second toolbar beneath the first one. (You'll learn about the text style and positioning options later in this chapter.) Figure 13-1 shows you the Text Tool Options palette.

Selecting a Text Object Type

PaintShop Pro provides three types of text objects: vector, floating, and selection. The type you choose determines what kind of editing you can do. You can't change the text object type once the text object appears on the image. PaintShop Pro places vector text on a vector layer and selection text on a background or raster layer. Floating text is placed on a floating layer above a background or raster layer.

 From the Tool Options palette, click the Create As arrow, which displays a list of text types. Then select the text type you want to create.

Figure 13-1
The Text Tool Options palette.

The option you select appears in the Create As box.

▶ **Vector**: Creates the text as a vector object and adds a new vector layer, if necessary. Remember that you can easily move or edit vector objects, but you cannot add effects.

▶ **Floating**: Creates the text as a selection that floats above the current layer. You can move the text and you can apply effects, but you cannot modify the text. After you apply effects, you can "defloat" the text, which places it on the next lowest raster layer. After you return the text to the raster layer, you can no longer easily move the text.

▶ **Selection**: Creates the text as an empty selection on the current layer. You cannot move or edit the text without leaving behind the background color, although you can apply a few effects to the text. For example, you can create selection text from a photograph and paste it into the same image or a different image.

Create as Vector Text First

You will probably find it most practical to create the text as vector text, until you are absolutely sure you are finished with the placement and appearance of the object. You can then convert the vector layer to a raster layer and apply any desired effects. See Chapter 9, "Adding Effects, Filters, and Deformations," for more information about adding effects.

Choosing Text Options

Later in the chapter, you will see that you can change text options after you create the text object, but it's much easier to select the text options prior to creating the text. PaintShop Pro includes options for the font, font size, font style, alignment, and material. Follow these steps in preparation for creating text:

1. With the Text tool selected, from the Tool Options palette, click the Font list box. A list of available fonts appears (see Figure 13-2).

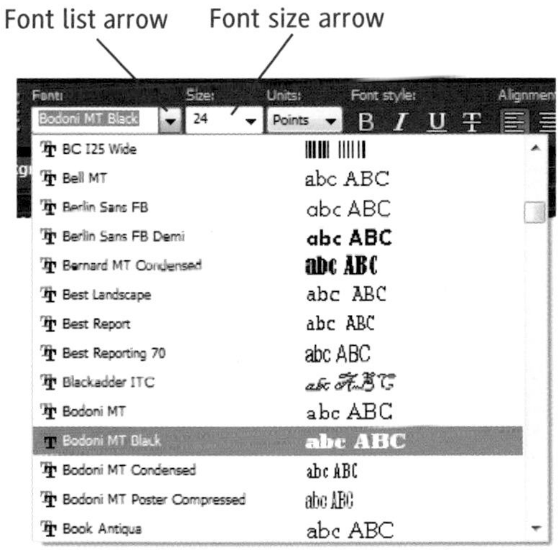

Font list arrow   Font size arrow

Figure 13-2
Choose the font you want to use.

> **Note**
>
> Your fonts may vary from the ones shown here.

2. Choose the font you want. You can select any font installed on your computer.

3. Click the Size list box. A list of font sizes appears.

4. Click a font size. As a general rule of measurement, when printing, a 72-point font is 1 inch tall; however, when viewing text on a computer screen, the sizes vary depending on the screen resolution.

5. Click an Alignment button. Alignment determines how multiple lines of text line up with each other (see Figure 13-3). Alignment choices include

   • **Left**: The left edges of each text line align.

   • **Center**: Each line centers to the one above it.

   • **Right**: The right edges of each text line align.

6. PaintShop Pro provides text styles such as bold, underline, italic, or strikethrough on any portion of your text. Click one or more of the four available text enhancements. Figure 13-4 shows you a sample of each font style type. Font styles include

   • **Bold**: Makes the text characters darker and thicker.

   • *Italic*: Makes the text characters slightly slanted.

   • Underline: Draws a line under each character and space.

   • ~~Strikethrough~~: Draws a line through the middle of each character and space.

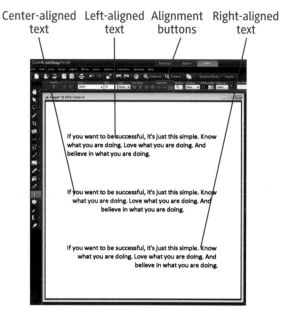

Figure 13-3
Choose a text alignment option.

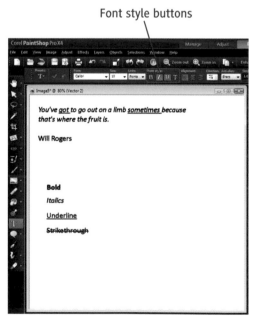

Figure 13-4
Select a style for all or part of your text.

7. When working with text, you have the same materials options available as with other PaintShop Pro objects. The stroke style is the color of the edge around the letters, while the fill style is the center or body of the letters. Select a color, gradient, or pattern for the foreground and stroke and the background and fill of your text. Your current selections appear on the Materials Properties swatches.

8. Optionally, select a stroke width. When you have a stroke width of 1 or greater, your text will take the foreground and stroke appearance and form a line around the text characters. In Figure 13-5, you see text with a stroke and text without a stroke.

Stroke width

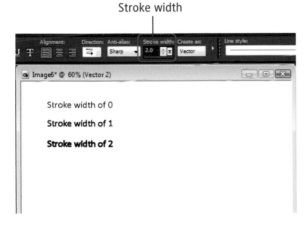

Figure 13-5
Choose text materials options.

Choosing Null

You cannot choose Transparent for both the stroke and the fill. Choosing Transparent for the fill creates outlined text.

Setting Kerning, Tracking, and Leading Options

Three additional features available when working with text are kerning, leading, and tracking. *Kerning* refers to the spacing between two specific letters, and *tracking* refers to the amount of space between individual letters. The two are similar and often confused.

Leading (pronounced like *sledding* without the *s*) refers to the space between lines of text. Positive kerning, tracking, or leading values increase the amount of space between characters (kerning and tracking) or lines (leading), while negative values decrease the amount of spacing. The following steps show you how to adjust text kerning, tracking, and leading options:

1. With the Text tool selected, from the Tool Options palette, click the Text positioning options arrow. It's the last arrow on the right. Kerning, Tracking, and Leading options appear, as seen in Figure 13-6.

Figure 13-6
Select from kerning, leading, and tracking options.

2. Click a Kerning or Tracking arrow. Click the up arrow to increase the distance between the characters, or click the down arrow to decrease the distance. Figure 13-7 shows you examples of kerning and leading.

No kerning or tracking

Kerning set to 50

Tracking set to 0.100

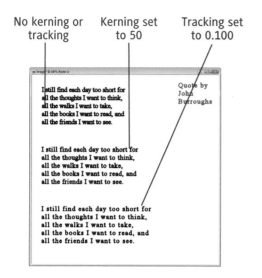

Figure 13-7
Kerning and tracking samples.

3. Click up on the Leading arrow to increase space between lines of text or down to decrease space between lines of text (see Figure 13-8).

No leading

Leading set to 0.600

Figure 13-8
Leading examples.

4. Click the Text format options arrow. The Text format Tool Options palette reappears, and the Text positioning options hide.

Typing Text

Now that you have set your options, you are ready to create the text. Different from using a word processor, the text does not automatically wrap to the next line. You need to tell PaintShop Pro when you want the text to begin on a new line. The following steps show you how to enter your text:

1. Select the Text tool. Your mouse pointer becomes a plus sign with a T next to it.

2. Select the text options you want, including type, font, size, styles, stroke, or any others.

3. Click the canvas where you want the text to appear. A blinking cursor appears.

4. Type the text you want. The text appears on the canvas (see Figure 13-9). If you chose to create vector text, PaintShop Pro automatically places the text on a vector layer.

5. If you have more text to add under the first line, press the Enter key, which drops the insertion point to the next line.

6. Type the additional text. Add as many lines of text as you would like.

7. Click the Apply button..
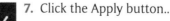

Apply button   Press Enter here to start the next line   Vector text type   Vector layer

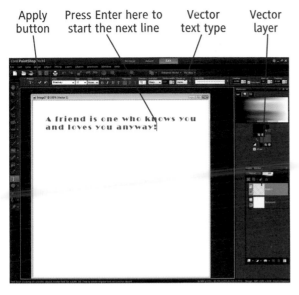

Figure 13-9
Type the desired text.

Cancel Button

If you don't want to keep what you've typed, instead of clicking the Apply button, click the Cancel button.

Alternatively, and I think this is the easier way, you can enter your text into a Text Entry dialog box. After selecting the Text tool, instead of clicking on the canvas, press the Shift key and then click on the canvas. The Text Entry dialog box seen in Figure 13-10 appears. You can type your text and then click the Apply button in the Text Entry dialog box.

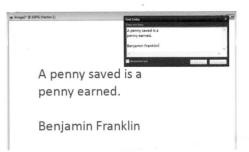

A penny saved is a penny earned.

Benjamin Franklin

Figure 13-10
Using the Text Entry dialog box.

If you chose a floating text type, your screen looks similar to Figure 13-11. Notice the Floating Selection layer on the Layers palette.

Floating Selection layer

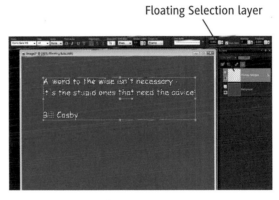

Figure 13-11
Creating floating text.

In Figure 13-12, you see Selection text selected from a solid white background.

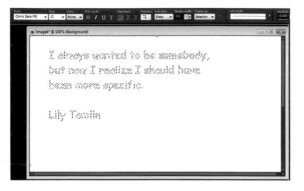

Figure 13-12
Creating Selection text.

You'll learn lots more about scrapbooking in Chapter 16, "Making Digital Scrapbooks."

You may be asking, "Why would I ever use Selection text?" Well, it's typically not that great on a solid color background. But it can look great on scrapbook pages and other items where you've created the text on a patterned background.

Editing Text

SUPPOSE THAT AFTER YOU CREATED your text, you see a problem; perhaps you misspelled a word, or you want a different font or style. Depending on the text type you created, you may be able to edit the object.

Modifying Vector Text

You can only modify the actual text or the text properties on vector text type objects, not selection or floating text types.

Follow these steps:

1. From the Tools toolbar, choose the Pick tool and select the text object. Make sure you are on the vector layer where the text resides and that your mouse pointer is positioned over the text and displays as a four-headed arrow like you see here.

Cannot Select Text Object

If you cannot select the text object, you may have to click the Apply button to finalize your previous action.

2. Click the right mouse button while the mouse appears over the selected text. A shortcut menu appears.

3. Choose Edit Text, which displays the blinking cursor at the beginning of your text.

Display the Text Entry Box

If you hold down the Shift key when you choose Edit Text, you can edit your text through the Text Entry dialog box.

4. If you want to delete text, click and drag across the unwanted text and press the Delete key. If you want to add or edit the text, move the insertion point into the desired position and add or change the text.

5. If desired, drag across and highlight (select) the portion of the text you want to modify and then, from the Tool Options palette or the Materials palette, change the font, size, attributes, or materials. The text in the Preview panel reflects the changes, as does the text on the screen.

6. Click the Apply button, which accepts the changes and reselects the entire text object.

Resizing a Text Object

You can only resize vector type text; you cannot resize selection text or floating text. Resize vector text in the same manner that you resize any vector object—by using the object selection handles. Use these steps to resize a vector text object:

1. From the Tools toolbar, choose the Pick tool and select the text object. Make sure you are on the vector layer where the text resides.

2. Position the mouse over a selection handle until you see the mouse pointer turn into a white two- or four-headed arrow. If you position the mouse over a corner handle, you see the four-headed arrow and can resize the height and width of the text. If you position the mouse over a middle handle on the top or bottom, you see the two-headed arrow and can resize the text height. And if you position the mouse over a middle handle on the left or right, you see the two-headed arrow and can resize the text width.

3. Click the selection handle. As you drag the handle, an outline of the text appears (see Figure 13-13).

4. Release the mouse button. The text object remains at the new size.

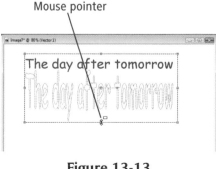

Figure 13-13
Resizing vector text objects.

Changing Floating and Selection Styles

Although you cannot easily edit the font size or the actual text on floating or selection type text, you can edit the style by using the Paint Brush tool.

 From the Tools toolbar, click the Paint Brush tool. From the Materials palette, select a foreground color, gradient, or pattern, and then paint over the text (see Figure 13-14). Because the text is selected, the paint doesn't go over the boundaries of the selection. (See…you really *can* color within the lines!)

Click Apply

If your tools are unavailable, click the Apply button to finalize your previous action.

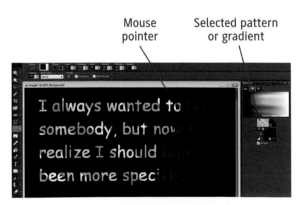

Figure 13-14
Easily paint over floating or selection type text.

Moving Text

If text isn't placed where you intended, you can move it. You can move either vector type text or floating type text. You cannot move selection type text without moving the entire layer that the selection is on.

MOVING VECTOR TEXT

You move vector text in the same manner that you move any vector object. The following steps show you how to move vector text:

1. Using the Pick tool, click the vector text object.

2. Position the mouse over the center move circle until the mouse pointer turns into a four-headed arrow.

3. Click and drag the text to a new position. As seen in Figure 13-15, as you drag across the canvas, an outline of the text appears.

4. Release the mouse button. The text moves to the new position.

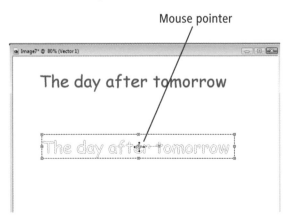

Figure 13-15
Moving vector text.

MOVING FLOATING TEXT

You cannot easily move raster objects. However, even though floating text is raster-style text, you can move it anywhere on the image as long as the text is still floating. Once you defloat the text, you cannot easily move it.

 1. Click the Move tool. The mouse pointer resembles a four-headed arrow.

2. Position the mouse anywhere over the floating text object until the mouse pointer turns into a four-headed arrow.

3. Click and drag the text to a new position. The text moves along as you drag the mouse (see Figure 13-16).

Mouse pointer

Figure 13-16
Moving floating-style text.

4. Release the mouse button. The text remains selected in the new position.

Copying Selected Text

Although you cannot move selected text, you can copy or cut it and paste it into a different location on the same image or onto a different image. This is a particularly nice feature if you want your text to take on the appearance of a specific image. Look at Figure 13-17. It shows a row of beautiful vegetables, and I've created some selection text (Healthy Living) on the image.

Figure 13-17
Creating selected-type text from an image.

Now I'll copy (Edit ❯ Copy or Ctrl+C) the selection and create a new image. By pasting (Edit ❯ Paste as New Layer or Ctrl+V), you see in Figure 13-18 how the selection text appears on a new blank image. Of course, you don't *have* to paste the text to a blank image. You could paste it to any existing image as well.

Figure 13-18
After pasting selected-type text to a new image.

Deselect Selection Text

To deselect the selection text, choose Selections, Select None or press Ctrl+D.

Defloating Text

ONCE YOU'VE PLACED THE FLOATING text where you want it, you'll need to defloat it to the next lowest raster layer. If you want special effects applied to the text only, apply the effect before you defloat it. Once you defloat the text, you cannot apply effects only to the text; any new effects apply to the entire layer. Click Selections ➤ Defloat. The text no longer floats above the layers and merges with a raster layer; however, the text is still selected and surrounded by a marquee. Notice that the Layers palette no longer displays "Floating Selection." See Figure 13-19, which shows the floating text after applying the Inner Bevel and Drop Shadow effects.

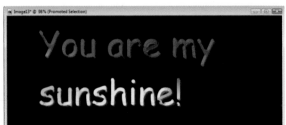

Figure 13-19
Apply effects before defloating text.

Deselect Floated Text

To deselect the text, choose Selections ➤ Select None or press Ctrl+D.

Deleting Text Objects

THE METHOD TO DELETE TEXT OBJECTS depends on the type of object. Deleting vector text is different from deleting floating text or selection text.

Deleting Vector Text

 You can delete vector text in the same manner that you would delete any vector object. Click the Pick tool, and then click the text object to select it. Press the Delete key to delete the text object.

Select Floating Layer

If the floating text doesn't disappear, make sure you've selected the floating selection layer.

Deleting Floating Text

As long as the floating text is still floating, you can easily delete it. If the floating text has been defloated, you can't just delete it. You'll need to paint over the area with a desired background color. To delete floating text, make sure you select the floating selection layer and then choose Edit > Clear. The floating text disappears.

Deleting Selection Text

Deleting selection text is a little different because it isn't really a text object; it's a selection. Choose Selections > Select None or press Ctrl+D. The area outlined with the marquee will disappear; however, this method works only if the selection text has not been painted or moved.

Deleting Painted or Moved Selection Text

If the selection text has been painted or moved, deselect the text and then paint over the entire image with your desired background color.

Wrapping Text

NOW THAT YOU KNOW HOW TO create the text, get your cape and magic wand ready, because you can add some creative elements to your text to make it stand out on the image. Perform magic such as wrapping your text around a shape or wiggling your text along a squiggly line.

You learned in Chapter 11, "Constructing Vector Objects," and Chapter 12, "Editing Vector Objects," about working with open and closed shapes. One text magic trick you can do is fitting your vector text so that it appears around a specific closed shape such as a circle, square, or rectangle. And while technically you can wrap text around preset or stellated shapes, text wrapped around those shapes doesn't look very good. Follow these steps to wrap text around a shape:

1. Create a vector shape such as a circle, ellipse, rectangle, or square. Leave room around the shape for your text.

2. Select the Text tool, make sure the Create as Text type is set to Vector, and position the mouse pointer along the shape where you want the text to begin. You'll know you're in the right position when the mouse pointer changes into a *T* over a semicircle with an *X* on top of it (see Figure 13-20).

3. Click the mouse, which displays a blinking cursor.

Mouse pointer

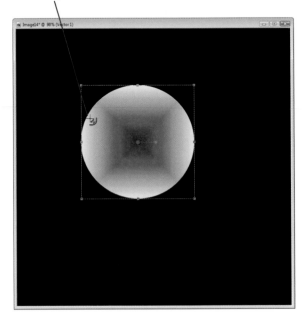

Figure 13-20
Creating text around a path.

Where to Begin?

Where you begin the text depends on the text alignment choice you make. Left-aligned text starts where you click; centered text is centered at the spot where you click; and right-aligned text ends where you click.

4. Set any desired text options such as font, size, and color.

5. Type the desired text and click Apply (see Figure 13-21).

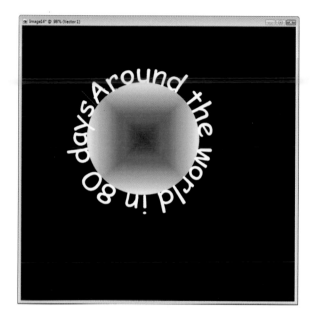

Figure 13-21
Type the text to wrap around the shape.

Adjust Text

To make the text fit as you want around the shape, you may need to adjust the text size as you are typing. Text longer than what will fit around the shape overlaps itself.

Open paths are those such as lines or curves or where the start and end nodes do not meet. You can also create text along an open path using the same steps as when wrapping text around a shape. Simply draw the line and add the desired text.

Separating Text from the Shape

If you create the shaped text but determine you do not want to keep the shape you used to wrap the text, you can delete the shape object and still have the text retain the distinctive shape.

When you create text around a shape, both the text and the shape you wrapped the text around appear as vector objects on the vector layer; however, PaintShop Pro internally links the two objects. Therefore, you cannot delete just one of the objects. You need to separate them before you can delete the vector shape.

When the two sublayers are linked, the text layer icon on the Layers palette displays the letter *T* with a semicircle under it, but when you unlink them, the text layer icon changes to an oddly shaped teardrop (see Figure 13-22).

Linked text icon   Unlinked text icon

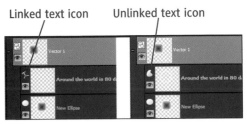

Figure 13-22
The Layers palette with text objects.

From the Layers palette, click one of the vector sublayers and then choose Objects ❯ Convert to Path. PaintShop Pro unlocks the internal link, and the two objects become separate objects. You can now select the unwanted shape object and press Delete to get rid of it.

Separating Multiple Text Objects

If more than one text object is attached to the shape, you must separate each one individually.

Attaching Previously Created Text to a Path

If you previously created a vector text object and then later decide you want it placed on a shape or other path, you do not have to re-create the text. You can tell PaintShop Pro to fit the text object along the shape or path.

 Using the Pick tool, click the text object and then hold down the Shift key and click the shape or line you want. A selection box surrounds both objects, as you see in Figure 13-23.

Selected objects   After choosing Fit Text to Path

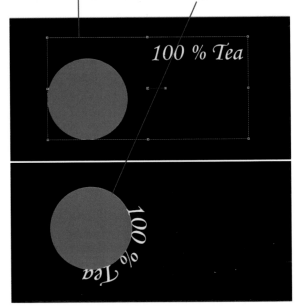

Figure 13-23
Select both vector objects.

Choose Objects ❯ Fit Text to Path. The text wraps around the shape, curve, or line.

Adjusting Shaped Text Position

If you're not completely pleased with the position of the text in relation to the shape, you can make some adjustments. One adjustment you can make is to shift the text object left or right so it better fits the shape. In Figure 13-24, you see where the text should begin further to the left on the shape.

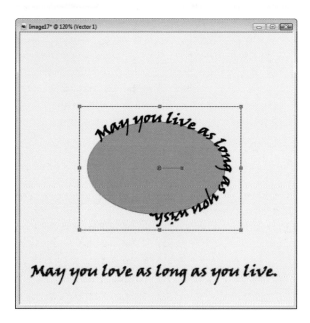

Figure 13-24
This text is not centered over the shape.

Using the Pick tool, click the text object. Position the mouse over the outer, lower-right selection handle center circle until the mouse pointer is a curved double-headed arrow. Then rotate the text to the left or right. Release the mouse button when the text is in the desired position. You'll probably need to move the text several times until you get it just where you want it.

If you want to move the text closer or farther away from the shape, you must adjust the offset amount. Follow these steps to adjust the offset:

1. Right-click the text object and choose Edit Text. The blinking insertion point appears in your text, and the Tool Options palette reappears with text options.

Display the Text Entry Box

If you hold down the Shift key when you choose Edit Text, you can edit your text through the Text Entry dialog box.

 2. Set a value in the Offset control. Positive values position the text above the path; negative values position the text below the path.

3. Click Apply. Figure 13-25 shows the text moved above the shape with an offset of 10.

Offset space

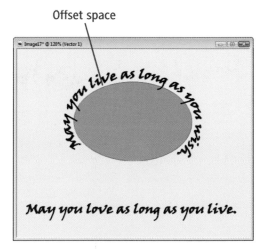

Figure 13-25
Adjusting vertical offset spacing.

14

Printing

and Sharing Images

PICTURE YOURSELF AS A SMALL BOY playing catch all by yourself. Or imagine you are a little girl alone in a room, playing dress up. There's no one else around. It's quiet—too quiet. That doesn't sound like a lot of fun, does it? Children like to share their fun with other children, and while sometimes it's wonderful to keep small delights to yourself, more often than not, it's much better to share the pleasure with others. Sharing is what this chapter is all about.

You've finally reached the summit. You've snapped, downloaded, corrected, enhanced, resized, and done all kinds of things to your photographs. It's time to share, either on paper or electronically, some of the memories that your photographs hold. Although you probably won't want to share all your photographs with others, there are some that you just can't keep to yourself. Sending pictures to family members or friends makes those images become priceless treasures to others.

If you plan to print your photos, you establish *what* you print, as well as *how* you print. You can print items on your own printer, have them printed online by professionals, print them to the web, or email them to others.

Understanding Resolution

ONE OF THE MOST MISUNDERSTOOD topics in the digital realm is resolution. A writer once said that trying to understand resolution is easier than spit-roasting jellyfish—but only marginally. Unfortunately, that's true.

In Chapter 2, "Working with PaintShop Pro Files," we discovered that digital images are made up of pixels (short for *picture elements*), which are the small sections of color and light that make up a digital image like pieces of a mosaic. A digital image is really a grid of those pixels, and when the pixels are viewed together, the image is formed. When there are enough pixels and they are small enough so as not to be individually discernible, the digital image can achieve photo quality.

A *digital image*, as it is stored on a hard drive or a flash card, is simply an informational record of the image pixels; it has no physical size. But when an image is displayed on a monitor or printed, it takes on physical form. At that point, the image has spatial dimensions of width and height. The physical dimensions are the number of pixels that a digital image is made up of, and they are expressed in pixel dimensions such as 1600 × 1200.

The *resolution* of a digital image is defined as the number of pixels per inch it contains. So, when considering resolution, you need to determine what you intend to do with the image. Are you going to use it on a webpage? Are you going to print it? If so, what size? Fine detail is rendered by having an ample number of pixels. Too few, and the picture appears jagged or pixilated.

Let's take a look at the two principal types of resolution measurements and how they are used.

PPI

PPI, which stands for *pixels per inch*, is a measurement of how many pixels can fit into one square inch of your image. If they are large pixels, obviously you won't get as many into an inch as you would if they were smaller. Think of it as how many peas you can fit into a sandwich bag, versus how many plums you can fit into that same sandwich bag.

PPI actually has a dual purpose. One place that uses PPI is your screen display, which is called *monitor resolution*. Settings you select for your computer monitor resolution affect all programs that you run on your computer, including web-pages. The options you choose are based on the graphics card installed in your computer, your overall monitor size, and the quality of your eyes. You access the monitor resolution through your Windows control panel. When you are setting the monitor resolution, remember that as you increase the number of pixels, you can display more information on your screen, but the information, including text and icons, becomes smaller.

The use of PPI we are going to discuss in this chapter refers to how PPI is used in *image resolution* and how it relates to the photo dimensions. People often get confused about how many inches a digital image is. To understand digital image size, you simply have to understand that pixels are more tightly packed for printing than for display on a computer screen.

A combination of the image size and pixels determines how large you can print your image. Obviously, you can physically make your image any size you want, but that doesn't mean it will print well. Images that are printed too large for the number of pixels they contain lose their quality.

We will show you later in this chapter how you can change your image size.

Units of Measure

We're using the term PPI here, but besides pixels, PaintShop Pro allows you to optionally measure your image in inches, centimeters, or millimeters.

Unlike conventional photographs, where we refer to a 4 × 6-inch or 8 × 10-inch print, the overall size of a digital image is measured by its number of pixels. The image's final destination, whether to a good printer or to the screen, also factors into the image size. Check the actual dimensions, as well as the resolution of your image, to know how the image will print.

For example, if you have an image that is 1200 × 1500 pixels, and the resolution is set at 300 PPI, the image will print at 4 × 5-inch size, but if the image resolution is set at 200 PPI, the image will print at approximately 6 × 7 inches.

Required pixel dimensions for a given print size can be calculated by multiplying the print size by the resolution, so an 8 × 10-inch print at 300 PPI requires an image size in pixels of 2400 × 3000. Or, let's look at it from another perspective and divide the size by the resolution. If we know the image size in pixels and we know the resolution, what size print can we get? If we know our image is 2400 × 3000 and the resolution is 300, we'll take 2400 and divide it by 300, and then we'll take 3000 and divide it by 300, which gives us a print size of 8 × 10 inches. Got it?

DPI

DPI represents *dots per inch* and refers to your *printer resolution*. Printer resolution is independent of and unrelated to screen image resolution. DPI is the measure of how many dots of ink or toner a printer can place within an inch (or centimeter) on paper. The maximum value is determined by your printer and cannot be changed through PaintShop Pro, although most printers provide settings where you can select low, medium, or high settings from within the printer's DPI range. DPI affects the quality of your printed image, but it does *not* affect the size of your printed image.

Most printers print the same number of dots horizontally and vertically, so a 600 DPI printer prints 600 tiny dots horizontally across one inch of space and 600 dots vertically, creating a one-inch square. The lower the DPI, the less fine the detail it will print and the fewer shades of gray it will simulate.

Better printers are capable of a higher DPI resolution. For photographs, you will probably want to print between 300 and 1000 DPI. Anything less than 300 DPI can produce spotty, pixilated images, and DPI over 1000 provides little extra benefit. In addition, the paper you use can have some bearing on the outcome. We'll talk about paper types later in this chapter. With good printer resolution, you get better tones, especially in areas that have uniform color and density, such as the sky. Good printer resolution also provides a smoother transition from one color to another. In general, the more dots, the better and sharper the image will be.

Let's now take a look at PaintShop Pro and how it handles image sizes.

Manipulating Image Size

IF YOU NEED TO MANIPULATE your image size for printing, start big and work your way down the scale. When you shoot your image, use a high-resolution setting on your camera, which provides the largest number of pixels in the image. That way, you will start with a larger physical image that you can scale down if needed without losing image detail. The problem arises when your image is too small for the size you want to print. You can make your image larger, but there's no way for PaintShop Pro to add details that aren't in the image to begin with, which can result in the image losing crispness and becoming fuzzy or pixilated.

Viewing Image Information

PaintShop Pro includes a dialog box that tells you all about your image, including type, size (both physical and digital), color depth, resolution, number of layers, and all sorts of other information. From the Edit workspace, you can view the image information by clicking Image **>** Image Information. Optionally, you can press Shift+I. Both options display the dialog box you see in Figure 14-1.

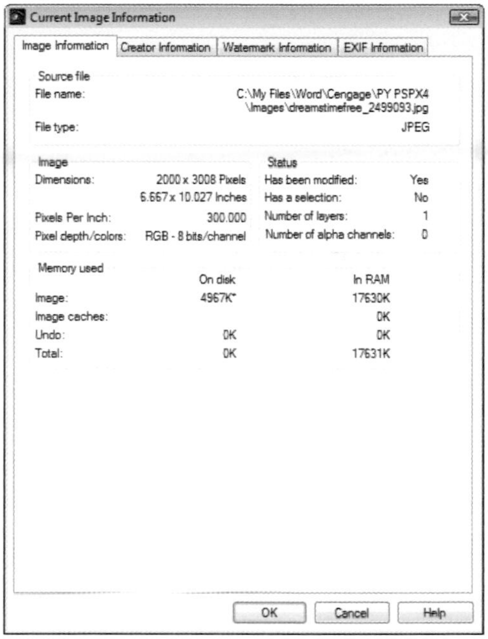

Figure 14-1
The Image Information tab does not have editable boxes, but it contains image information.

Another piece of valuable information regarding your images is the EXIF information. The EXIF information, which stands for *Exchangeable Image File*, includes information such as the date and time a photograph was taken, but more importantly, it displays the camera settings when the image was taken, including resolution, exposure, focal length, white balance settings, metering mode, and color space. Click the EXIF Information tab to view the EXIF information (see Figure 14-2).

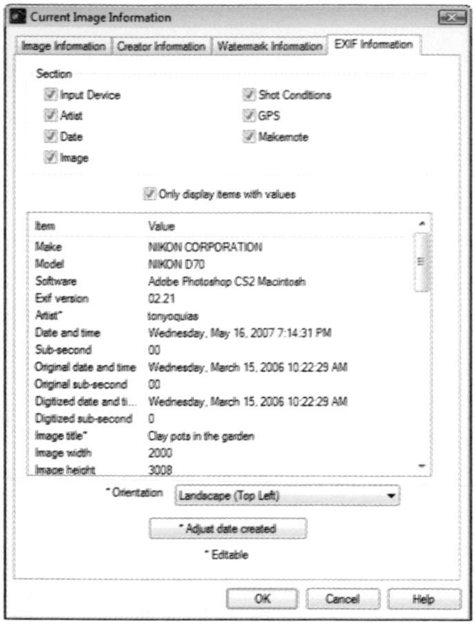

Figure 14-2
Viewing Image EXIF information.

For More Information

See Chapter 3, "Becoming More Organized," for more information on ways to view image EXIF data.

Resizing Versus Resampling

Adjusting an image resolution's PPI, or its size in inches, has no effect on the actual pixels. This is called *resizing* or *scaling,* and it involves specifying the printing resolution if and when the image is printed. The image retains the same grid of pixels with the same pixel dimensions and pixel data.

However, if you change the image's size in pixels, changing the actual pixel dimensions, this is called *resampling*. Resampling changes the actual image file, which results in a different number of pixels, and it alters some pixel color and tonal data to maintain the same appearance over the altered amount of pixels.

The bottom line is that there are two different ways to make the same digital image print at different sizes. You can resize it, which changes the print resolution to yield the desired physical dimensions without changing the existing pixel dimensions, or you can resample it, which changes the existing pixel dimensions to yield the desired physical dimensions at a given output resolution.

Resampling changes the number of pixels contained in the image, whereas resizing changes how many pixels are being printed per inch. Resampling affects the nature of the digital image; resizing affects only the printing of the image.

Table 14-1 illustrates an example of what happens to an image when you modify your image size.

Table 14-1 Resizing Results

	Dimensions in PPI	Print Size	Resolution PPI	Resize Type	Result
Original image	900 × 600	6 × 4	150	N/A	N/A
Increase size only to 200%	1800 × 1200	12 × 8	150	Resize	Increases print size but decreases quality
Increase resolution only to 300 PPI	900 × 600	3 × 2	300	Resample	Decreases print size but improves quality
Increase size to 200% and resolution to 300 PPI	1800 × 1200	6 × 4	300	Resize	Maintains same print size but improves quality*
Decrease resolution only to 100 PPI	900 × 600	9 × 6	100	Resample	Enlarges print and decreases quality
Decrease size only to 50%	450 × 300	3 × 2	300	Resize	Reduces print size and maintains quality

* Best option

More pixels per inch create the effect of packing more printed pixels in a space and a smaller printed image, while fewer pixels per inch create the effect of more loosely packed printed pixels in a space and a larger printed image. As you can see, as the output resolution becomes smaller, the quality of a larger print decreases. It sounds strange and in a way it is, but that's how the image sizing process works.

Resizing an Image

As stated earlier, when you resize an image, you change the image dimensions. PaintShop Pro provides a dialog box where you can change your image size.

Click Image > Resize, or press Shift+S. You'll see a Resize dialog box like the one in Figure 14-3. The Pixel Dimensions area is where you resize your image, and the Print Size area is where you resample your image.

Advanced   Resolution   Select Pixels
Settings   or Percent

Lock Aspect Ratio

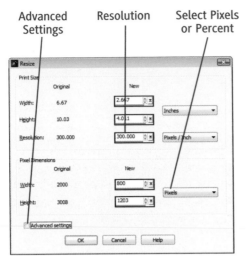

Figure 14-3
Change an image's dimensions in pixels either
by a percentage or by pixel amounts.

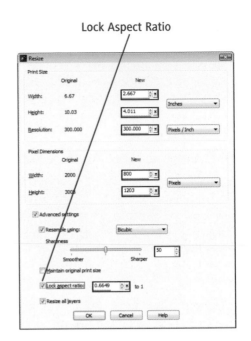

Figure 14-4
The Resize dialog box with advanced settings.

For tighter image resize control, click the
Advanced Settings box. The Resize dialog box
expands, as you see in Figure 14-4. When you
make a change, you should make sure Lock
Aspect Ratio is on. As you make changes to the
image width, PaintShop Pro also changes the
height, maintaining image proportions. If you
change the aspect ratio, it can distort your
image by making it larger or smaller in one
dimension than the other. If you need specific
heights and widths, try using the Crop tool after
you resize the image.

Resize Once

**For best results, to retain as much quality
as possible, resize your image only once.
If you resize it and aren't happy with it,
use the Edit > Undo Resize command and
try it again.**

Resampling an Image Up

When you resample an image to a larger size,
PaintShop Pro must do some interpolation. In
photography, *interpolation* is the process of
upsizing a photograph by adding pixels that
were not there originally. Because every pixel
must have a color, this process usually involves
assigning a color to the newly created pixels
based on the colors of the preexisting pixels
surrounding the new ones. The result is a larger
image in terms of resolution, but one that now
has less clarity and less accuracy because you
simply cannot produce something from nothing.

PaintShop Pro has several resampling type methods to calculate the interpolation. All of them are based on mathematical calculations:

▶ **Smart Size**: Smart Size is the option you should use in most cases. It lets PaintShop Pro determine, based on current image information, which of the other four resampling types is best for your image.

▶ **Bicubic**: Bicubic is similar to the Weighted Average calculation in that it does use a weighted average, but the Bicubic method uses a larger area of pixel samples to calculate the new pixel values. The Bicubic method generally takes a little more time, but it usually produces a more accurate sample.

▶ **Bilinear**: The Bilinear method determines new pixels by using the two pixels nearest each existing pixel.

▶ **Pixel Resize**: The Pixel Resize resampling type duplicates or removes pixels, as needed, to reach the desired image's width and height. This method works best with line drawings and other simple graphics.

▶ **Weighted Average**: When creating new pixels, this option looks at nearby pixels and then, by calculating a weighted average color value, uses that result to create the new pixels.

Like the resizing options, you make your resampling choices through the Resize dialog box. Make sure the Resample Using check box is selected and you have selected a resampling type (see Figure 14-5). The resampling options are in the Advanced Settings area of the Resize dialog box.

After you resample an image, you should run the Unsharp Mask filter. Click Adjust ❯ Sharpness ❯ Unsharp Mask. See Chapter 6, "Manually Editing Images," for more information.

Resample Once

For best results and to retain as much quality as possible, only resample your image once. If you resample it and aren't happy with it, use the Edit ❯ Undo Resize command and try it again.

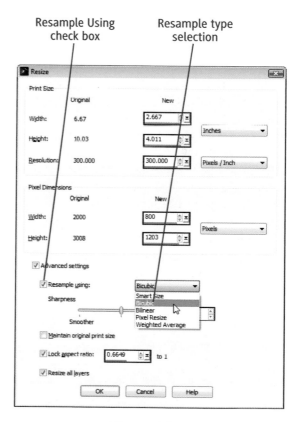

Figure 14-5
Select a Resample type.

Determining Printing Options

FOR MANY SITUATIONS, the end product
for your photographs will be prints. Many of the
images will remain on your hard drive or CD,
but those special ones look their best when you
print them.

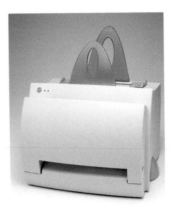

After all the work you did to manipulate your
images in PaintShop Pro, you want to make sure
you get the best output. You can print your
images in a number of different ways. Some
options include nonprinting sources such as
emailing your images, posting them to a webpage,
or simply storing them on a CD for personal
viewing or distribution. But the type of output
we will examine here is the actual physical print
options of your color images from your printer.

Ink-Jet Versus Laser Printers

The two main types of printers are ink-jets and
laser printers. The technology behind each is
distinctly different from the other.

INK-JET PRINTERS

Ink-jet printers are slower than laser printers
but are typically cheaper to buy. They work by
shooting tiny sprays of colored wet dyes through
microscopic holes in a print head onto pages, one
row at a time. Ink-jet printers are inexpensive to
purchase (many under $100), but the real price
of an ink-jet printer comes in the replacement
cartridges.

Ink-jet printers usually come in two flavors:
regular and photo-quality. If you're doing photo
printing, most of the time you get better results
with a photo-quality printer. A photo-quality
printer usually costs a little more, but it's designed
especially for photographs and the high quality
required to print them. When shopping for an
ink-jet printer, pay attention to the resolution
advertised by the manufacturer, but also take
that resolution promise with a grain of salt.

On the other hand, while ink-jet printers usually
do a beautiful job on photographs, especially on
glossy paper, you'll often find that ink-jet printers
produce somewhat fuzzy, jagged text and graphics.

Some photo-quality ink-jets include extra features, such as a dedicated USB port for connecting your digital camera directly to the printer, built-in media card slots that let you plug in a storage card and press a button for instant prints, and a special menu for selecting prints. All those features mean you can bypass your computer. But if you use the printer's instant printing features, you don't get the option of first correcting and enhancing your image in PaintShop Pro. Where is the fun in that?

Laser Printers

You can purchase a black-and-white laser printer today for less than $200, but obviously a black-and-white printer won't work if you want a color print. So we look to color laser printers.

Designed for high-volume printing, color laser printers are among the most expensive printers you can purchase. Current prices average between $500 to $1,000, depending on the features offered, but like most electronics, that price will probably continue to drop. Less than ten years ago, the average color laser cost around $20,000! Per-page cost, however, is generally less than an ink-jet.

Laser printers don't use a wet ink process; instead, they use a dry toner, similar to a copy machine. The principal behind the laser printer is to apply the toner to the paper through a controlled electrostatic charge. Laser printers print razor-sharp text, color charts, and other two-dimensional graphics, and if you need to print images for a layout, they produce acceptable quality. But when it comes to color photographs, most color laser printers can't match an ink-jet printer's quality.

Printer Inks

The consumables cost of a printer plays a huge factor in image printing. With an ink-jet printer, a color photograph can cost between 6 and 18 cents to print. Some ink-jet manufacturers design printers that use a single ink cartridge containing all three colors. If you print a lot of images with red in them, you'll obviously run out of red ink faster, and even though you've hardly used the green ink, you'll have to throw it away and replace the entire cartridge. Other manufacturers, such as Canon, Epson, and HP, sell models with individual cartridges for each color instead of one cartridge for all three colors. The downside is that while you save ink by replacing cartridges one at a time, the individual color cartridges cost a few dollars more, so per page, they end up costing about the same.

Another option is a do-it-yourself refill kit for ink cartridges. Some people think they are great, but most people find them messy and time-consuming and feel that they produce a lower-quality print. If your vendor offers higher-capacity cartridges, you might want to take advantage of them as a better alternative. They cost more to purchase, but they contain twice the amount of ink, so they cost less per page.

On the other hand, color laser printers cost about 3 to 8 cents for a color page. Obviously, they are less expensive per page than ink-jets, but the cost increases because color lasers have separate toner cartridges for each color, which can cost as much as $250 apiece. Even with their high cost, however, in sufficient volume, the cost per page of a color laser's cartridges is still less than color from an ink-jet, because the yields are much higher, ranging from 6,000 to 12,000 pages.

Either way, with ink-jet or laser printers, whether you buy the manufacturer's brand of ink cartridge or toner or one from a third party is a matter of preference. Some people prefer companies such as Canon, Epson, and HP because they formulate their printers, ink, and paper as a complete system, and if you buy from a third party, you may not get the results you expect. Others find that the third-party producers are equally good and less pricey.

Paper Types

You'll find that the quality and cost of your print also is affected by the type of paper you use. For best results, use photo-quality paper, which is available in a number of sizes, such as 8.5 × 11 inches, 4 × 6 inches, 5 × 7 inches, and so forth. Photo paper costs more per page because the paper itself is more expensive. But hands down, using photo paper instead of regular paper produces a far better print.

Two other paper aspects you should consider because they also affect print quality are the brightness and the weight. The paper *brightness*, sometimes referred to as *whiteness*, is the measure of how much light is reflected from the paper. The whiteness depends on how evenly it reflects colors. For example, if the paper reflects more blue than red or yellow, it will have a cool hue to it, making it appear even brighter than white, sometimes creating an optical impression because cool white sheets tend to brighten colors. A bright white surface is perfect for high-resolution digital photos, as well as cherished family photos. You'll get realistic skin tones and true photo quality. Don't worry, though—you don't have to stand there and figure out the reflection value yourself. The paper manufacturers list the brightness levels on the packages. Most photo papers have a brightness level between 90 and 104.

Photo paper is available in two finishes: glossy and matte. Glossy finishes provide a reflective, vibrant look to your images, while matte paper is specially formulated so that light won't bounce off the photos, which reduces reflection and adds depth. Photo paper resists fading and is smear-proof and water resistant, so your photos never lose their brilliance, and your images have a more professional, photolab type of look.

Most people have a variety of paper sizes at their disposal. The smaller, individual sizes are per inch and are usually more expensive than the full-page size papers. But if you just want to print a single picture of your new puppy or your son in his football uniform, you will probably want a single sheet of 3 × 5- or 4 × 6-inch paper. If, however, you plan to print several copies to hand out to Aunt Martha, Cousin Jack, and Grandma Mary, you should consider using the larger 8.5 × 11 inch paper for speed and economic reasons. PaintShop Pro, as you will discover in the next section, makes it easy to print multiple images or multiple copies of an image on a single sheet. You can even print out a page of wallet sizes so that you can give one to each of your coworkers.

Paper weight is measured in pounds or mil. The higher the mil or the heavier the weight, the thicker and sturdier the paper is, making it more durable for framing, albums, and frequent handling than the standard paper you use for printing documents or making copies. Standard copy paper is usually a 20-pound paper, and cardstock is around 110 pounds. You'll find a pretty good range in photo papers running from around 45 pounds to 88 pounds. Keep the paper weight in mind when determining the final use for your image.

Printing with PaintShop Pro

NOW IT'S TIME TO PRINT your photographs. PaintShop Pro provides several printing methods for doing just that, and it all boils down to what you want to print.

- ▶ If you want to print images on nonstandard size paper, such as 4 × 6 or 5 × 7, you print through the standard Print menu.

- ▶ If you want to print multiple images or multiple copies of images on standard size paper, you use the PaintShop Pro Print Layout feature.

- ▶ If you want to print a contact sheet containing thumbnails of a group of pictures, you use the PaintShop Pro Manage workspace to print.

We will now take a look at all three printing methods, beginning with printing thumbnail-size images as a contact sheet.

Printing a Contact Sheet

In Chapter 3, you looked at the PaintShop Pro Manage workspace and how you could navigate among your folders and open, manage, or just view thumbnail sizes of your images visually rather than by filename. Another option in the Manage workspace is to print a contact sheet of images. You can print all the images in a folder or just the ones you select. You can only select images from a single folder; in other words, you cannot select some images from one folder and others from another folder.

If it's not already displayed, open the Manage workspace. In the Navigation palette, select the folder containing the images you want to print. The images then appear in the Organizer palette. Use one of the following methods to select the files you want to print:

- ▶ Click once on a single thumbnail if you want to print only that image. A gold border surrounds the selected image.

- ▶ Hold down the Ctrl key and click a nonsequential group of images. Selected images appear with a gold border surrounding the thumbnail (see Figure 14-6).

- ▶ Click the first image that you want to select; then hold down the Shift key and click the last image you want to select in a sequential group of images. The selected images will have a gold border around them.

After you select the files you want, from the Organizer palette, click the More Options button and choose Print Contact Sheet.

Because you access the Print option through the Organizer, the Print Contact Sheet dialog box appears instead of a standard Print dialog box. The Print Contact Sheet dialog box (see Figure 14-7) contains options relevant to printing thumbnail images.

More Options button   Selected images

Figure 14-6
Select the images you want to print.

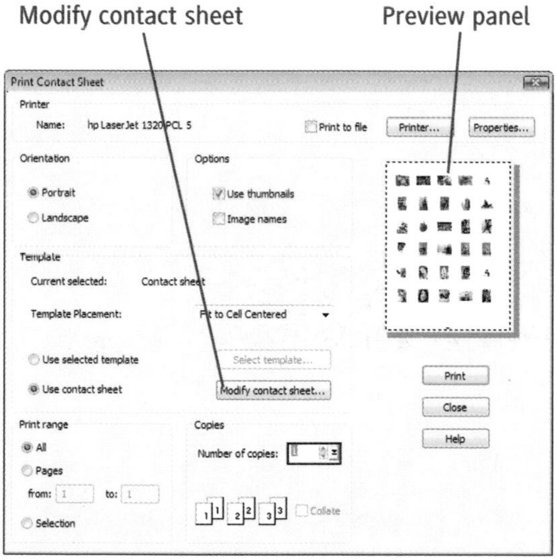

Modify contact sheet   Preview panel

Figure 14-7
Print a contact sheet through the Organizer window.

As you can see, this is a busy dialog box. The following list reviews each section of the Print Contact Sheet dialog box:

▶ The Printer section is where you choose the printer you want to use.

▶ The Preview panel shows you how your group of selected images will look based on the current settings.

▶ The Orientation setting allows you to print your contact sheet in landscape or portrait orientation. When printing in portrait orientation, the longest dimension is vertical, while in landscape orientation, the longest dimension is horizontal.

▶ Under the Options section, the Use Thumbnails option compresses the image for faster printing. Checking the Image Names option tells the printer to print the filename beneath each thumbnail image.

▶ The standard contact sheet has 6 rows of 5 images, for a total of 30 images per sheet. In the Template section, you'll find two important options. If you don't want the layout of 30 images per sheet, you can click the Modify Contact Sheet option, which displays the Custom Contact Sheet dialog box (see Figure 14-8). Here, you can specify the number of rows and columns you want for your thumbnails and optionally specify the individual cell height and width, as well as the spacing between each cell.

Figure 14-8

Create a customized contact sheet.

▶ Another option in the Template section that you should check is the Template Placement drop-down list. This option determines how the selected images are placed in their individual cells. For example, if your images are of different sizes, clicking the Fill Cell option makes them all the same size as the thumbnail cell. Be careful of this option, though. Using it can distort your images when printed.

Default
Free
Size and Center
Fill Cell
Fit to Cell Centered
Fit to Cell Left
Fit to Cell Right
Fit to Cell Top
Fit to Cell Bottom

▶ In the Print Range section in the lower-left corner of the Print dialog box, you can choose between printing all images in the window or clicking Selection to print only the images you selected from the Organizer window.

▶ Choose a number in the Copies box to set the number of copies you want to print.

After setting your options, click the Print button, and you'll see your images in a contact sheet thumbnail format.

Printing Through the Print Menu

Use the Print menu if you want to print images on nonstandard size paper, such as 4 × 6 or 5 × 7. You'll need to go through a couple of steps to tell your printer what you are doing:

1. From the Adjust workspace or the Edit workspace, open the image you want to print.

2. Click File ➤ Print or press Ctrl+P, which opens the Print dialog box.

3. If needed, click the Printer button to select the printer you are going to use.

4. PaintShop Pro assumes you want to print the image on standard 8.5 × 11-inch paper. Click the Properties button shown in Figure 14-9.

Properties button

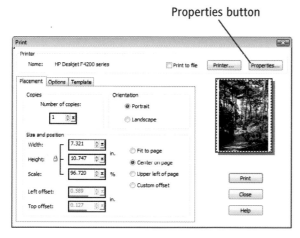

Figure 14-9
If you are printing on a nonstandard paper size, click the Properties button.

5. The Properties dialog box opens, but the options available and the appearance of the Properties dialog box varies depending on the printer you selected. Figure 14-10 shows two Properties dialog boxes for two different printers. From the Paper type (or Media type) drop-down list, select the paper type you want.

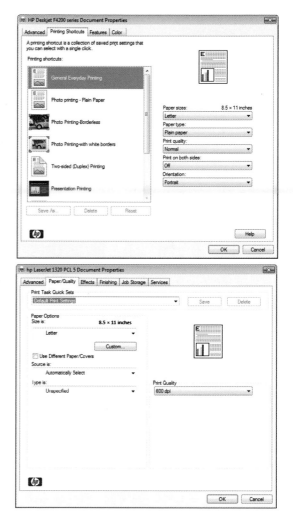

Figure 14-10
Available options vary depending on your selected printer.

6. Somewhere in the Properties dialog box, you'll find an option to select the paper size. In the example HP Deskjet 4200 printer, the Paper Size option is on the Printing Shortcuts tab, but on the HP Laserjet 1320 printer, the Paper Size option is under the Paper/Quality tab options. Select the paper size you want to use.

7. For the best results, make sure that the print quality is set to High. Again, the location of this option will vary, depending on the printer you are using.

8. Click OK to close the Properties dialog box; then click the Print button to print your image.

Working in Print Layout

You've already seen two ways to print your images, but the best is yet to come. PaintShop Pro includes a comprehensive range of choices in terms of image format and placement. These choices come in the form of Print Layout templates.

You can use the Print Layout templates, whether you want to print a single image, multiple images, or multiple copies of an image on a full-sized sheet of paper. The templates provided with PaintShop Pro cover the options most of us want, but if you need something else, you can create your own layout and save it for future use if you want to.

From the Manage or Edit workspaces, click File ➤ Print Layout, which displays the Print Layout window. The Print Layout window contains its own menu and toolbar, and any images you have open currently appear on the left side of the window (see Figure 14-11). By default, PaintShop Pro assumes that you want to print one image on the sheet.

Open Template button   Print Layout toolbar

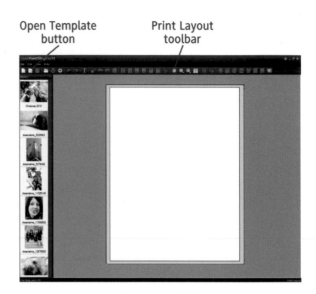

Figure 14-11
Currently open images appear on the left, but you can open additional images.

Click the File menu and choose Open Template (or click the Open Template button on the Print Layout toolbar), and the Templates dialog box shown in Figure 14-12 appears.

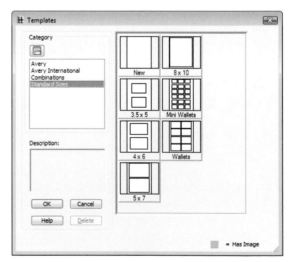

Figure 14-12
Select from a variety of printing templates.

The supplied templates are organized by vendor and by category, mostly based on standard image sizes such as 5 × 7s or wallet sizes. After you select a vendor and category, click the template you want to use and click OK. The Print Layout window now shows the template you selected.

Drag the image you want into each of the template frames (see Figure 14-13). Optionally, double-click an image to add it to the template frame. You can use any image more than once, and you don't have to use all the frames. If you want an image that does not appear in the Images area, click File ❯ Open to open additional images.

Figure 14-13
Drag and drop your images into the template.

Changes are made easily from the template. For example, if you place an image in the wrong holding space, simply drag it into the correct frame. If you place an image you don't want in a frame, click the image to select it and press the Delete key.

A number of options are available to help you adjust the image placements. If your images don't fit in the frame like you want, from the Edit menu, you can modify the cell placement, making choices such as Size and Center or Fill Cell. All the placement options are also available on the Print Layout toolbar. Pause your mouse over any tool to see its description. You'll also find options for rotating any framed image.

You'll probably need to select the appropriate paper type, so click the File menu and select Print Setup. You'll see the Print Setup dialog box (see Figure 14-14), which provides a number of options, including a Printer selection button and a Properties button, which is where you select the paper type if your printer supports that option. Refer to the previous section for a refresher on selecting paper type.

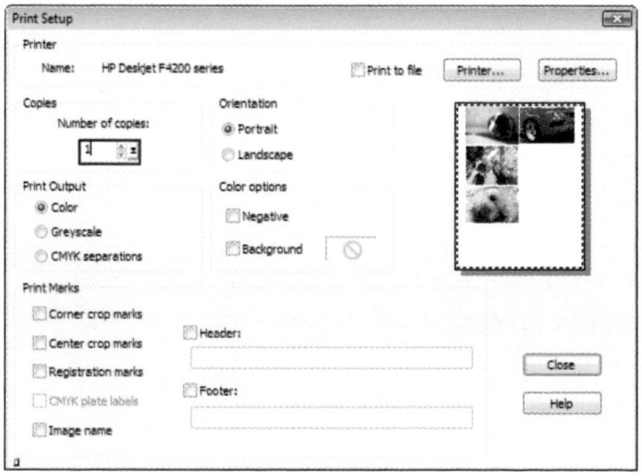

Figure 14-14
Set the options you want for this layout.

Other options on the Print Setup dialog box include the number of copies, the page orientation, and the Print Output, which is where you can print color, grayscale or CMYK separations if you want. (You learned about CMYK color in Chapter 7, "Understanding Color.")

You can also specify a header or footer to print on every page, and you can tell PaintShop Pro to print the image filename under every image. Make your choices and then click the Close button. Finally, when you're ready to print, click File ➤ Print.

You can close the Print Layout window by choosing File ➤ Close Print Layout. When you close the Print Layout box, a message box appears asking you if you want to save the layout (see Figure 14-15). If you think you want this layout for future use, such as if you need to go back and further edit an image, you should save it. Give it an easily identifiable name and check any other options in the Save dialog box. Upon closing the Print Layout window, the main PaintShop Pro window reappears.

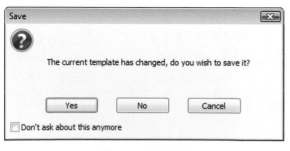

Figure 14-15
Optionally save the print layout options.

Setting Images as Your Computer Wallpaper

You probably already know how to change your desktop wallpaper using Windows, but just in case, here's a refresher. In Windows 7 or Vista, right-click a blank area of your desktop and choose Personalize.

Click Desktop Background and then click the Browse button to select your desired image. If you are using Windows XP, right-click a blank area of your desktop and choose Properties. From the Desktop tab, click the Browse button and locate the image you want to use. That's simple enough, right?

There's another way that you can make any photo the background picture on your computer screen. Simply follow these steps:

1. From the Manage or Edit workspaces, either open the photograph you want, or select it from the Organizer.

2. Choose File ❯ Export ❯ Set Wallpaper.
PaintShop Pro automatically applies your
image as your wallpaper. In Figure 14-16, you
see that my favorite picture is my computer
desktop wallpaper. Yes, that's a very tired
5-year-old with the grumpy face!

Figure 14-16
See your favorite photo all the time.

Emailing Images

BESIDES PRINTING IMAGES for yourself,
you might want to share them with friends and
family. Emailing images makes sharing easy
and free, and you can share your images from the
comfort of your own home. No more trekking to
the post office! You have the option of sending a
single image or a collection of images via your
email program.

Choose one of the following options to start the
email process:

▶ In the Edit workspace, open the image
you want to share, and then click File ❯
E-Mail ❯ Active Image.

▶ In the Edit workspace, open multiple
images you want to share, and then click
File ❯ E-Mail ❯ All Open Items.

▶ From the Manage workspace, select the
images you want to share, and then click
File ❯ E-Mail ❯ All Selected Items.

After choosing to email the images, you see an E-Mail dialog box like the one shown in Figure 14-17. You can send them as attachments to your email, or you can send them as embedded images where they will show up in the body of the email message. From the E-Mail As options, select the method you want.

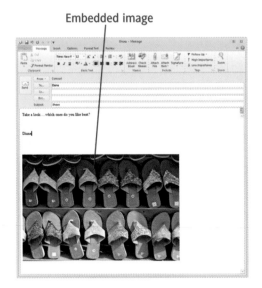

Embedded image

Figure 14-18
Send an embedded image in an email.

Click the OK button, and you see an email message. Enter the recipient, a subject line, and any desired text. Figure 14-18 shows the Microsoft Outlook email message with the embedded photo, and Figure 14-19 shows the email message with the image as an attachment.

Figure 14-17
Send an image via email.

Next, you must choose the image size. Choices include Small, Medium, Large, Original, and Cell Phone. The choice you make depends on how the recipients will use the image. If they are going to print it, you'll probably want to choose Large or Original. If they are only going to look at the image on their computer, Small or Medium will suffice. If you are sending it to their cell phone, choose the Cell Phone option, which sends the smallest size image. As you know, photos can be quite large; there's no need to send the image larger than necessary for its ultimate use.

Attachment icon

Figure 14-19
Send an image as an email attachment.

Posting Images

IF YOU HAVE A FACEBOOK or Flickr account, you can easily use PaintShop Pro to post your images directly to your Facebook or Flickr site. With your permission, people all around the world can see your photos in just a matter of seconds. If you don't already have an account with these sites, you may ask, "What are they?"

Let's take Facebook first. Facebook is a social networking site, which is a free online service that connects people who share interests. Your Facebook connections (called *Friends*) might include your family, friends, coworkers, old school chums, and many others. Millions of people share their lives either through comments they post to Facebook or through photographs they post there. If you don't have a Facebook account, you can get one free at www.facebook.com.

The second site supported by PaintShop Pro is Flickr. Flickr is a great way to store and share your photographs online. With Flickr you can organize your images, and it allows you and your family and friends to tell stories about the images. All you have to do is sign up for a free account at www.flickr.com. Once you have a Flickr account, you can then post images directly from PaintShop Pro to Flickr.

PaintShop Pro makes it easy to post your images. From any workspace, click File > Share > Facebook or File > Share > Flickr. If this is the first time you've accessed Facebook or Flickr through PaintShop Pro, a dialog box appears prompting you to give PaintShop Pro permission to access your Facebook or Flicker account. Click Allow.

Login

If you are not already logged into Facebook or Flickr, you'll be prompted for your login information.

The Social Sharing dialog box seen in Figure 14-20 appears. From here you can make a number of different choices:

- ▶ Click Log In as Another User to select a different Facebook or Flikr user.

- ▶ Click the Add File button and select the images you want to upload.

- ▶ Click the Save to Album button and choose an existing Facebook album in which to place the images.

- ▶ Click the New album button and create a new Facebook or Flickr album.

- ▶ Click the Quality arrow and choose the image size you want to post. Remember that the larger the number of pixels, the higher quality the image will be, but also that it takes larger disk space.

Add file　Save to　Quality　New　Change
　　　　　album　　　　album　user

Figure 14-20
Posting images to Facebook or Flickr.

Delete Images

If you have an image appearing that you don't want to upload, from the Social Sharing dialog box, click the image to select it and press the Delete key. You won't delete the image itself from your computer; only from the upload.

Once you finish selecting your options, click the Upload button. The images upload to Facebook and a dialog box shows you the progress. Click OK when the upload is finished.

Figure 14-21 shows my Facebook page after posting three images.

Figure 14-22 shows my Flicker page after posting two images.

Figure 14-21
My Facebook page.

Figure 14-22
My Flickr page.

Creating Panoramas
and 3-D Photos

PICTURE YOURSELF STANDING ATOP A HILL, overlooking a great city. You turn your head from side to side trying to take in the wide view of the majestic beauty, hoping you'll never forget the moment. Of course, you take pictures—lots of pictures—trying to capture the image. Your eyes see it as a panorama because you can view the entire width of the scene. You see the depth of each object in your view. Unfortunately, most camera lenses just can't capture what the human eye does.

Because the human eye can see depth and width, we are hungry to see it in our photographs. Even the television and movie industries are trying to feed our need for additional dimensions. The proliferation of advertising for wide screens and high definition is proof.

The camera still cannot come remotely close to what our eyes see, but with the help of PaintShop Pro, we can add a little bit more dimension to an otherwise square flat image.

Creating a Panorama

A *PANORAMA* IS A WIDE VIEW of a physical space. The word originated to describe paintings of an Irish painter named Robert Barker. Today, lots of things are in panoramic mode. Theme parks often construct theaters to show movies in a 360-degree setting, and most major cities now have an IMAX theater where you can watch movies in an *almost* 360-degree setting.

In the photography world, panoramic photography is a style that strives to create images with exceptionally wide fields of view. Some people used to say they had a wide-angle lens, and while there is no formal definition for the point at which wide-angle leaves off and panoramic begins, truly panoramic images are thought to capture a field of view comparable to, or greater than, that of the human eye. The resulting images offer an unobstructed or complete view of an area usually taking the form of a wide strip.

Some digital cameras come equipped with a built-in panorama feature that helps you overlap frames accurately, thus increasing the success rate in PaintShop Pro later. But, even if you don't have an expensive panoramic camera, you too, with the help of PaintShop Pro, can create panorama images. You need several pictures of the scene (which I'll discuss shortly) and, of course, PaintShop Pro. The process you use involves laying out multiple photographs with slightly overlapping fields of view to create a larger, panoramic image once assembled.

Preparing for a Panorama

When you take your photographs, you need to plan ahead if possible. Your source photographs play a large role in the success of your panoramic composition. Most methods require that all the images have been taken from the same point in space. You don't have to be perfect when you take your shots. PaintShop Pro can help with some correction, but you do need to take the best images you can. Here are a few guidelines to help you take the best shots for your panorama:

▶ Keep your subjects somewhat distant. Anything close to the camera could be distorted or may not line up properly in the final image.

▶ Take lots of shots with a liberal overlap of the photographed area. The overlap enables PaintShop Pro to choose the best position for the blending between the frames. Overlap images should overlap approximately 16% to 40%. Any more or less can make irregular blends in the merged images.

▶ Use a consistent focal length. Avoid using the zoom feature of your camera while taking your pictures.

▶ Keep the camera level with the horizon in every image. If your camera tilts up a little in some pictures but down in others, you'll end up with distortion in the final panorama. Use a tripod if you can, to help maintain camera alignment and viewpoint.

▶ Stay in the same position. Try not to change your location as you take a series of photographs, so that the pictures are from the same viewpoint.

▶ Maintain the same exposure. Don't use a flash in some pictures and not in others.

▶ Consider your lighting conditions. If it is toward early morning or mid evening, the horizon will be lighter than the rest of the scene. As you move away from the horizon, the scene becomes darker. Take the pictures quickly because you don't want the light to change between the images.

▶ Avoid using special distortion lenses.

▶ Avoid having moving people in the images.

Seeing the Whole Picture

Typically, creating a panorama involves joining anywhere from two to ten images. While most panoramas are based on a wide horizontal view, PaintShop Pro can also create a vertical panoramic image. The general principal in assembling a panorama is that you create an image with a transparent canvas large enough to display the panorama and then copy each photograph onto a separate layer. After you create the layers with the individual photographs, you align them and crop the overall image so that no transparency is showing.

Create a Tray

Create a tray for the images you will use in the panorama. See Chapter 3, "Becoming More Organized."

Let's look at an example. In Figure 15-1, you see five images that I pulled from the Organizer palette and opened in the Edit window to use for the panorama.

Figure 15-1
Select the images you want for your panorama.

As you build your panorama, it might be necessary to make some color adjustments to each layer, but I have found that it's easiest to make most color or tonal adjustments on the individual photograph before placing them in the master layer.

Determining Image Size

You need to determine the individual image's size and resolution so you can create a new transparent background that is wide enough for all the images.

Select one of your images and choose Image ›
Image Information, which displays the Current
Image Information dialog box that you see in
Figure 15-2. Make a note of the image dimensions and the number of pixels per inch. In
this example, the image is 1,824 pixels wide by
1,368 pixels tall. The Pixels per Inch value equals
72. Make a note of these pieces of information,
and then click the OK button.

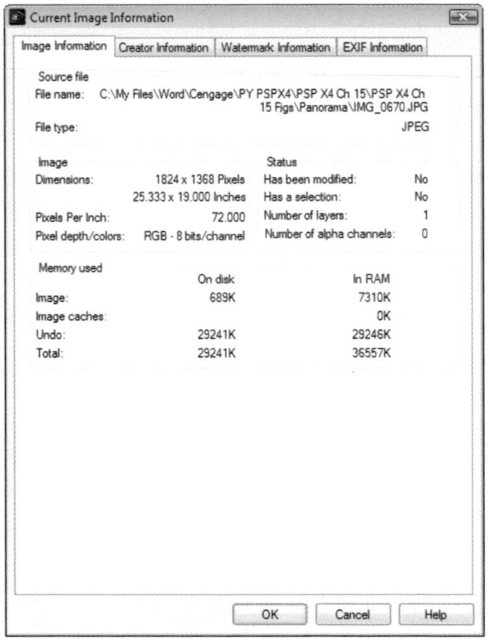

Figure 15-2
Determining image size.

Add together the widths of all the images
you are creating. If you are creating a vertical
panorama, add together the heights instead.
In the example I'm using, I have five images at
1,824 pixels wide each, making a total of 9,120
pixels wide. That's the minimum width I need
the background to be.

Creating the Background

Next, we need to create a new background on
which we'll layer all the images. Create a new file
by choosing File › New. The New Image dialog
box appears.

In the Image Dimensions section, specify the
total width plus a little extra for wiggle room.
In Figure 15-3, I'm creating an image 10,000
pixels wide and 1,500 pixels tall. It's better to
make it slightly wider and taller than you need
it so you can freely move the images into place.
You can crop the size to fit later. Set the
Resolution to match your other images, and
make sure the image is a raster background.
Click the Transparent option for a transparent
background, and then click OK.

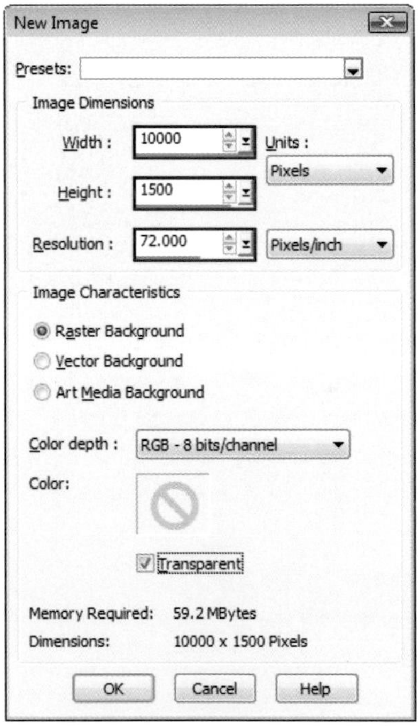

Figure 15-3
Creating a new image for the panorama.

348

Overlaying the Images

Now you are ready to begin laying out the images and overlapping them enough so they match up to each other. Make sure you have your Layers palette visible, because you're going to need it. If you don't see the Layers palette, choose View > Palettes > Layers or press the F8 key. The following steps show you how to begin the overlay process:

1. Select the first image for your panorama, and choose Selections > Select All. A marquee surrounds the entire image.

2. Choose Edit > Copy. It doesn't look like anything happened, but it did. Windows copies the image to the Windows Clipboard.

New Layer

Figure 15-4
Copying the first image.

Close Original Image

You can close the original image or minimize it to put it aside.

3. Activate the new blank image by clicking anywhere on the image.

4. Choose Edit > Paste As New Layer. The first image appears in the middle of the new image. See Figure 15-4. Notice that the Layers palette shows a new layer.

Name the Layers

Editing the images is easier if you name each layer according to its placement in the panorama.

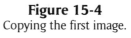

5. Select the Pick tool from the Tools toolbar. When you activate the Pick tool, the current layer displays a box with eight selection handles.

6. Click anywhere in the pasted image and drag to move it to the far left edge of the image. Do *not* drag by one of the selection handles.

7. Select the second image, and repeat steps 1 through 4. Again, a new layer appears on the image.

8. Again, using the Pick tool, move the second image close to the first image.

9. If necessary, zoom in on the image so you can clearly see both images.

10. Make sure the top raster image (Raster3) is selected, and lower the opacity to approximately 60% (see Figure 15-5). Lowering the opacity makes it easier to line up the two images.

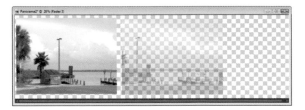

Figure 15-5
Changing layer opacity.

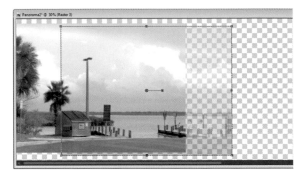

Figure 15-6
Aligning the images.

11. Using the Pick tool, move the second image so it overlaps the first image. Use the translucency to line up objects to each other (see Figure 15-6). Don't be surprised if the top image overlaps half of the first image. It depends on how much you turned as you took the photographs.

12. Return the layer opacity setting to 100%.

13. Continue copying each original image to a new layer on the panorama and lining them up to each other. Remember to reduce the opacity setting so you can align the images, and then change opacity back to 100% (see Figure 15-7).

Save Often

Don't forget to save your file often!

Figure 15-7
Aligning multiple layers.

Finishing the Panorama

Well, now that you see the panorama assembled, most likely, you'll have some seam lines appearing. Take advantage of the fact that the layers overlap each other, and use the Eraser tool at a fairly low opacity setting, which helps blend the photographs. Follow these steps:

1. Select the Eraser tool from the Tools toolbar.

2. Choose a low opacity setting (usually between 20 and 40), and make the size large enough to easily erase the lines but not too large to cut off the overlap (see Figure 15-8).

Figure 15-8
Erasing the seam lines.

3. Select the desired layer, and on the image, drag the Eraser over the overlap lines until the images blend and no seam lines appear. Make sure you select the top layer of the two layers you are trying to blend. In the previous figure, I was on the second of the five image layers.

4. When you are happy with the seam alignments, merge all the layers into a single layer. Choose Layers ❯ Merge All ❯ Flatten. Only one layer, the background layer, remains, and the transparent portion of the lowest layer turns into a solid white.

5. Finally, since the images probably didn't line up at the tops and bottoms evenly and there is extra white background on the image, crop the panorama to fit the actual image. Choose the Crop tool.

6. Drag the crop marks around the image, as you see in Figure 15-9.

Apply button

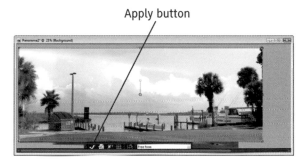

Figure 15-9
Crop extra space from the panorama.

7. Click the Apply button to accept the crop. Your panorama is complete.

Panoramas aren't limited to horizontal images. You can capture your images vertically and create great panoramas. Take a look at Figure 15-10, which shows three images of a spectacular waterfall. In Figure 15-11, you see the images combined to create a beautiful vertical panorama.

Figure 15-10
Create vertical panoramas using the same techniques
you used to create a horizontal one.

Figure 15-11
Create panoramas to see any large area.

Making 3-Dimensional Images

ONE IMAGINATIVE TRICK YOU can use on your scrapbooking pages is to make your images look 3-D. Great with action shots, 3-D can make a runner appear to jump out of the photograph, a fish appear to propel itself out of the water, or a bear appear to meander into your world. Check out the photographs in the scrapbook page seen in Figure 15-12.

> **Note**
>
> You'll learn more about creating scrapbook pages in Chapter 16, "Making Digital Scrapbooks."

3-D image

Figure 15-12
Add 3-D images to your scrapbook pages.

Follow these steps to learn how to make your images look alive.

1. Open your image, and create a duplicate copy. Choose Window ❯ Duplicate. Close the original image.

2. Convert the background of your image to a regular raster layer. Choose Layers > Promote Background Layer.

3. Create a new raster layer. Choose Layers > New Raster Layer, and click OK.

 4. From the Materials palette, choose the color black, and then select the Flood Fill tool. Fill the new layer with black.

5. Move the black layer down so it's underneath your image layer.

6. Create another new raster layer, and make it the top layer.

 7. Select the Rectangle tool, and draw a white *raster* rectangle on the new layer. (To make the rectangle a raster graphic, from the Tool Options palette, unclick the Create on Vector box before drawing.) Make the rectangle large enough to cover the portion of the image you want inside the frame, such as what you see in Figure 15-13.

Create on Vector option

Figure 15-13
Creating a raster rectangle.

8. Using the Pick tool, select the rectangle and shear it to distort it , giving the white rectangle a skewed perspective. To shear it, drag the corner handles while holding down the Shift key. See Figure 15-14 for an example.

Figure 15-14
Skew the rectangle to add depth perception.

9. Move the white rectangle layer down so it is below the photo layer but above the black layer.

10. Select the picture layer, and reduce opacity to 50% so you can clearly see the layer underneath the picture.

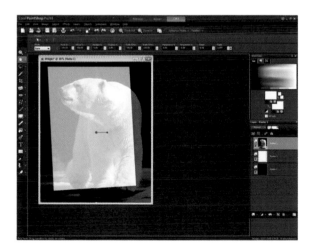

11. Using the Eraser tool, with hardness and opacity set at 100%; erase parts of the picture that you don't want. You should see the black layer showing through. Don't erase inside the white rectangle, and don't erase the part of the image you want to appear outside of the frame. In the example shown in Figure 15-15, I am erasing all the area outside the white rectangle, with the exception of the right side of the polar bear. I want that side to appear as though the polar bear is stepping out.

Zoom In for a Better View

This is a tedious and slow process. Zoom in closely, and use a small Eraser size to get the pixels close to your image.

Eraser tool mouse pointer

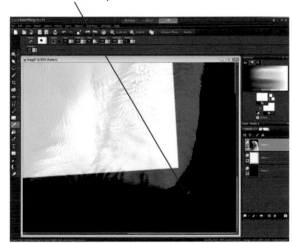

Figure 15-15
Erase unwanted areas.

12. Make sure the picture layer is still selected, and increase opacity back to 100%. You can now see the true image, and you'll see any pixels you missed during the erasing. Continue erasing until you remove any stray pixels you don't want.

13. Select the layer with the white rectangle.

14. Choose the Pick tool again, which selects the rectangle. Using the top, bottom, left, and right handles on the frame (not the corners), enlarge the white rectangle on all four sides to give the appearance of a frame around your picture.

15. Optionally, select the bottom black layer, and fill it with dark gray or whatever color you want for the "outside" area. Make sure this layer is on the bottom.

16. Choose the picture layer and, if desired, add a drop shadow by choosing Effects ❯ 3D Effects ❯ Drop Shadow. Click OK to accept the default settings.

17. Choose the picture frame layer (the one with the white rectangle), and apply a drop shadow to it. That's it! Figure 15-16 illustrates the final image.

Figure 15-16
The polar bear appears as if he's walking out of the photograph.

Making
Digital Scrapbooks

PICTURE YOURSELF SITTING ON THE SOFA, reminiscing about a special event in your life: a prom, a wedding, a vacation, your first home, a birth, or the home run you hit at the company softball game. You open your photo album and look through all the photographs and other memorabilia of that time and relive the day as though it were just yesterday. You come across the first card you ever received from your special someone and touch the front of the card as a gentle reminder and laugh at the funny message inside.

You can re-create and recapture some of those moments by creating scrapbook pages. Before we begin, you need to know there's no right or wrong creation. Each page is unique according to your subject, your personal taste, and the story you want to tell. Some creations will be very simple, while others can be quite elaborate. In this chapter, you'll learn more about the tools you need to add backgrounds, mats, embellishments, text, and other items you might want to appear on a scrapbook page. I'll give you the basics; the rest is up to your imagination.

Scrapbooking the Digital Way

ANSEL ADAMS once said, "A true photograph need not be explained, nor can it be contained in words." We've also heard that a picture is worth a thousand words, and PaintShop Pro has certainly proved that statement to be true over and over again. But, sometimes you just *have* to spell it out and want to tell a story about those pictures. Whether you create traditional or digital scrapbooks, you can combine the story and the photographs you've so painstakingly taken and then corrected and enhanced. *Scrapbooking*, which has been around as long as there have been photos, is the practice of combining photos, memorabilia, and stories in a scrapbook-style album.

Digital scrapbooking is the newest, hottest trend in the scrapbooking world. With digital scrapbooking, you can merge your passion for preserving precious memories with your love for working on the computer. Whether you add to or replace altogether your traditional scrapbook supplies and tools, you can use your computer, digital graphics, and PaintShop Pro in this exploding art form.

Scrapbooking has really come a long way from the days when your grandmother used to do it! With traditional scrapbooking, you end up with paper scattered throughout your house and ink and glue all over your hands, and you make many trips to the store, spending hundreds of dollars (or more) buying expensive paper and supplies. And what about the times you spend hours working on a layout, only to decide that you really wish you'd used a different color scheme or design? Sigh...you probably had to start all over again.

There's a lot to learn about digital scrapbooking, so just take it a little at a time, and don't expect perfection right away! Every layout you create will turn out better than the one before. And if you are really unhappy with the first layouts you do, you can always go back and redo them. That's something that's much harder to do with traditional scrapbooking. Digital scrapbooking provides you with complete freedom of design since you aren't limited to the supplies you have on hand. You'll find it affordable, convenient, efficient, and flexible.

Affordability

It's easy to see why digital scrapbooking is versatile and economical. As a digital scrapbooker, you don't have to purchase anything to start your scrapbook because you already have your computer and PaintShop Pro.

For traditional scrapbooking, you often buy a lot of different items because you aren't sure which things are going to work for the look you want to achieve. You end up spending a lot of money and then not using even half of what you buy.

However, with digital scrapbooking, once you have your backgrounds and graphics, which you can create yourself or purchase from other scrapbookers, you can use them over and over again, totally unlike the stickers or background papers you buy. You'll never run out of letters and other items.

Also, you always have just the right colors of whatever you need when you use PaintShop Pro, because you can change the color of anything instantly. You can design a layout and then print it as many times as you need it in just minutes so you can make identical scrapbooks for everyone in your family if you want to. With digital scrapbooking, your only consumables are your paper and ink if you plan to print your layouts.

Convenience

There are few full-time scrapbookers. Most scrapbookers work on their creations in their spare time. With traditional scrapbooking, unless you are fortunate enough to have a room devoted exclusively to scrapbooking, you end up with papers and supplies strewn all about a room or the dining room table. You find yourself constantly having to take out the supplies, work for a while, and then put them all back.

Whenever you have a free five minutes, you can work on your digital scrapbooking project without dragging out any supplies. This gives you a chance to tweak your layout, save it, and then come back to it whenever you have another few free minutes. There's no mess to drag out and put away.

Efficiency

When you work with digital scrapbooking, you never have to compromise your layout because you don't have the right color of materials. You can use PaintShop Pro to create your own exact, perfect color. With millions of colors to choose from, one of them is bound to be right for your layout.

Flexibility

Digital scrapbooking allows you to be creative and adventuresome when working with your designs. With traditional scrapbooking, you take your scissors and glue and manipulate your photograph into the shape and size you want. But once you've cut the image, you're stuck with the new smaller size and shape. Not so with digital scrapbooking. Because you don't use the original photographs in the layout page, you can let your creative side flow with virtually no risk to your precious photographs.

If you don't like something you did or you make a mistake, use the Undo or Delete commands and try something else.

General Design Rules

The elements and principles of design are the building blocks used to create any work of art. You'll find that many of the same guidelines used by professional photographers are used when designing scrapbook pages. Because design is a visual language and your goal is to tell a story with your visual images, everything you do to create the page should be done with a purpose. Let every item on the page guide you (or whomever is looking at the page) to remember and feel the story behind the page. Design your page for interest, and when you compose a scrapbook page, take a look at more than just the subject.

Become aware of shape, form, color, and light, all of which combine to make your page more interesting. Some designer theories say those are the four main elements of design; others say there are seven elements to design; and still others break the number of elements down into even more, smaller categories. Whichever theory you follow, the way you apply the basic principals of design determines how successful you are when creating your scrapbook page. As we take a look at some of these design principals, just remember that they all work together.

> ▶ **Subject**: Carefully arrange the page so it has one main topic or subject. Don't confuse the viewer with multiple topics on the same page. Relating the design elements to the idea being expressed reinforces the page unity.

▶ **Color**: In Chapter 7, "Understanding Color," you read about the color wheel and how different colors can project particular emotions, such as red suggesting danger and passion. When you're creating your scrapbook pages, your choice of color combinations can greatly influence the story you're telling. Color works best when you use strong contrasts such as dark accents on a light background and light accents on a dark background. Color gradients are good too, because they produce linear perspective and add movement.

▶ **Lines**: Lines represent order and give the eye explicit directions about where to look and how to interpret what it sees. Lines are used to group related objects and divide unrelated objects. Most often, lines are emotionally and physically functional rather than decorative. For example, horizontal lines tend to portray calmness, stability, and tranquility. Vertical lines provide a feeling of balance, formality, and alertness, and slanted lines suggest movement and action. Decide which part of your page is the most important, and direct attention to it by judicious use of lines. Do not scatter lines at random. Remember that margins are invisible lines.

▶ **Shape**: A *shape* is a defined area of geometric form. The main problem is to arrange all the different sizes and shaped items into larger and more important shapes, and then to relate them to the rest of the design. If you use background shapes, keep them simple and large. Any shape that overlaps another seems to be in front of it, and warm colors seem to be in front of cool ones. Anything that adds depth or the appearance of depth will enhance the display. And remember that size is simply the relationship of the area occupied by one shape to that of another.

▶ **Balance**: In scrapbook page design, balance is a critical element. Where you place your items can impact the emotions felt by those viewing your page. Balance, however, doesn't mean that everything is level and even. You could have a page where the central focus is centered and stable (symmetrical), or you could have a design that is off centered, which creates a sense of movement (asymmetrical). Another type of balance is *radial*, where the design has a pattern around the page, such as elements in all four corners, or a design that radiates from the center or swirls around the page. The main idea is that you can look at the scrapbook page and feel the story you're telling.

▶ **Texture**: *Texture* is the surface quality of a shape—rough, smooth, soft, hard, glossy, and so forth. Texture can be physical or visual. Surfaces can look or feel smooth, rough, soft, cool, or warm. Natural appearing fabric patterns are especially good for backgrounds, because you can sense how they would feel to the touch. Matte and shiny finishes also add texture.

▶ **Center**: Called the *Rule of Visual Center*, this guideline states that the most natural direction of your eyes when looking at a page is to focus first on an area on the page that's slightly to the right of and just above the actual center of the page. Designers say that placing an item exactly in the center of a page makes a demand on the viewers' eyes to stay at that point, resulting in a dull and uninteresting page. By placing the most important element or photo at this visual center, you're directing the viewer to use that as the starting point.

▶ **Thirds**: One of the basic rules used by photographers is the *Rule of Thirds*, where you imagine that your picture area is divided horizontally and vertically into thirds. Any of the four points where the lines intersect form a good line for a subject. Graphic designers use this same rule to make their designs more interesting. As important as the Rule of Thirds is, it's still just a guide to taking more interesting pictures and creating more attractive designs, so don't feel you have to use it all the time.

▶ **Space**: Less is more. How many times have you heard that statement? When you design a scrapbook page, you don't have to fill every inch of the page with some sort of decoration. Sure, most pages are busy, but some blank space is a good thing to have. These blank spaces, often referred to as *negative space* or *white space*, are simply areas on your page that aren't filled with elements. Blank space helps the balance of the page and enables the viewer to experience more of the idea behind the page—a memory. The blank space doesn't have to be black or white, but it should be only one color.

One more thing about design rules. It's all right to break them now and then. Once in a while, you have to bend the rules a little to emphasize your point!

Discovering Scrapbooking Components

So, BESIDES YOUR COMPUTER and PaintShop Pro, what do you need to begin scrapbooking? Most scrapbook pages use several types of elements, including backgrounds, text, photographs, mats, and embellishments. With the exception of the photographs, you can create all of these elements with PaintShop Pro, but if you don't feel that ambitious, you can use elements created by other digital scrapbook artists, many of which are free or available for a small charge.

Figure 16-1 shows a sample, very simple scrapbook page. Let's look at each type of element.

Background   Journaling   Mat   Embellishment

Figure 16-1
Not all scrapbook pages have to contain every element.

Photographs

Scrapbook pages don't *have* to have photographs, although most of them do. When planning your scrapbook page layout, determine which photographs you intend to use. Some pages contain multiple images, some contain a single image, and some contain a single image but also include smaller cutouts based on the original image, like the one you see in Figure 16-2. Even if the original photos are not digital, they can still be used in digital scrapbooking by scanning them, having a CD made from the negatives, or even taking a digital photograph of the original print.

Figure 16-2
Select the photographs that best tell your story.

Here are a few tips to keep in mind when working with your photographs:

- Choose a few pictures of a single event. Pick out the best photos. Get rid of the blurry ones and the ones that do not help tell the story or don't show anyone's face clearly. Look for themes in your photos, such as scenery, food, clothing, or activities. Choose one theme for your layout.

- You should have 3–5 photos of the event. A general rule of thumb in design is to use an odd number of images if you use multiple images (although this is not a requirement, just a tip). Crop the images as desired to remove unwanted portions.

- Try to select the one great photo that should be the focal point of the page. Often this image is larger than the remainder of the images.

Once you've chosen your photos, you'll have a sense of the colors, tone, and mood for the remainder of your layout.

Backgrounds

A scrapbook page background plays a crucial role in the overall layout of your page. It's the largest element you use and, typically, the other components are modeled, color-wise, after the background. Backgrounds can be solid, textured, gradients, patterned, or created from photos. Again, the choices are limitless, but let's take a brief look at how to create the backgrounds you see in Figure 16-3.

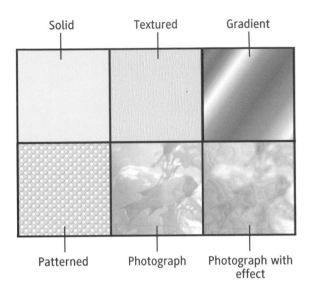

Solid   Textured   Gradient

Patterned   Photograph   Photograph with effect

Figure 16-3
Various background styles.

The following list describes how to create each of the effects listed:

▶ **Solid Color**: Use the Fill tool to fill a raster layer with a color of your choice.

▶ **Textured**: Use the Fill tool to fill a raster layer with color; then click Effects, Texture, Texture. Select the desired texture from the Texture dialog box.

▶ **Gradient**: Click the Foreground/Stroke color palette; click the Gradient tab and then select the desired gradient and gradient options. Use the Fill tool to fill a raster layer with the gradient.

▶ **Patterned**: Click the Foreground/Stroke color palette; then click the Pattern tab and select the desired pattern and pattern options. Use the Fill tool to fill a raster layer with the pattern.

▶ **Photograph**: Open the photograph you want to use and then copy the photograph as a new layer in the scrapbook page document.

▶ **Photograph with Effect**: Open the photograph you want to use and then copy the photograph as a new layer in the scrapbook page document. Next, apply the desired effect to the image layer.

Reduce Photograph Opacity

If you are using a photograph for a background, you may want to reduce the layer's opacity setting.

Titles

Another optional feature is a title for your page. Scrapbook page titles can help describe the moment or occasion. Typically, you create any text, including titles, on a vector layer. Figure 16-4 shows a scrapbook page with a title. You can use a single font or "mix them up." You can run the title across the page, vertically along the side, or have it repeat along all four sides. The choice is yours.

You'll learn later in this chapter how to manage text elements such as titles and journaling.

Title

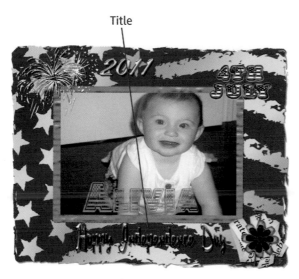

Figure 16-4
Titles help tell part of your story.

Journaling

Another type of text element is journaling. *Journaling* refers to text on a scrapbook page giving details about the photographs. The art of telling a story in print is what separates scrapbooks from photo albums. It is probably the most important part of memory albums. Your scrapbook page won't be complete until you tell the story behind the photos.

Some journaling consists of quotes or sayings to enhance the page (see Figure 16-5). Personal journaling lets you connect the page viewer with the actual event. Personal journaling records more than just titles, dates, and names. You can describe your reactions to what was happening, tell what the subject was doing and why, share how you feel when you look at the photos, or point out what you notice now that you didn't when the photo was taken.

Recollections may seem trivial at the time—the weather, what you ate, a travel situation, something funny that happened, for example—but these details will prove fascinating to those who read your scrapbook pages years from now.

Journaling

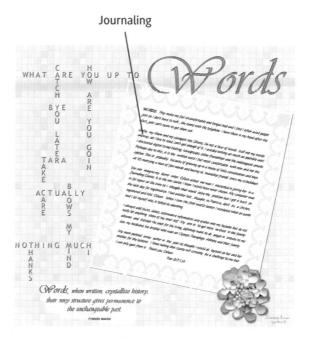

Figure 16-5
Use journaling to bring the viewer into the image event.

One journaling trick is to pull your five senses into your writing. Sight, touch, sound, smell, and taste—using your senses to describe things when you journal creates an interesting read as you pique the interest of your viewers and invite them to join in your world.

Mats

Use matting to make your photos, journaling, and memorabilia stand out on the page. You can coordinate matting colors and textures with your photographs, background, and memorabilia. For example, use a solid color mat to blend in with the layout or a patterned mat to make it stand out. Figure 16-6 shows a scrapbook page with two images on mats and one image without a mat.

Figure 16-6
Use mats to enhance the other elements
on your scrapbook page.

You create a mat by drawing a rectangle on its own layer, making it a coordinating color and slightly larger than the image that you are matting. The rectangle can be on a raster or vector layer, but you'll have much more control over the rectangle size and placement if you place it on a vector layer.

Embellishments

Use embellishments or decorations to personalize and further enhance your scrapbook pages by highlighting photos, drawing attention to journaling, or helping to set a theme. Nearly anything can work as an embellishment. In scrapbook pages, you might see buttons, rivets, shapes, tags, blocks, lines, or PaintShop Pro picture tubes. You can create the decorations yourself in PaintShop Pro, or you can purchase them online. You'll also find many free embellishments on the web. (See Appendix B, "Exploring Useful Websites.")

Fonts

Fonts, the typefaces used in text, are one of the most important pieces of digital scrapbooking. The title and journaling you place must be readable but still be creative. There are thousands of fonts available, but the ones you have available depend on the different software programs you have on your system. Many fonts come with Windows, but others are often provided with various software. Many fonts are available on the Internet, often for free. Once you get a font, you must install it on your computer before you can use it. Figure 16-7 displays some sample fonts that you can use in your scrapbook pages.

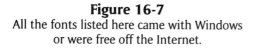

Figure 16-7
All the fonts listed here came with Windows
or were free off the Internet.

In the non-scrapbooker's world, such as in a letter or memo, mixing more than two fonts in a document is typically a no-no, and you should *never* mix fonts in a single sentence. But in scrapbooking, you can place great emphasis on your statements by mixing your fonts. Go ahead —get creative.

Layers

In Chapter 8, "Developing Layers," you learned how you can use layers to enhance your photographs, particularly with adjustment layers. You also created other raster layers so you could combine multiple photographs to make a single image, and you discovered mask layers so that you could hide portions of your image.

The flexibility of digital scrapbooking comes from using layers. You create a layer for each element on your scrapbook page so you can easily reposition, delete, angle, resize, or recolor the elements individually. In Figure 16-8, you see a scrapbook page that consists of thirteen layers, with the text and mats on vector layers and everything else on raster layers.

Figure 16-8
Using layers makes element manipulation easier.

Creating a Scrapbook Page

NOW THAT YOU UNDERSTAND the concepts behind scrapbook pages, it's time to put your creative cap on and put it to work. Remember that the examples you see in this chapter are just that—examples. Use your imagination!

When you begin planning your scrapbook page, you need to consider whether you will, upon completion, print it yourself, have a professional printer print it, or keep it only for computer or web viewing. If you plan to print it and place it in a scrapbook album, plan your page size accordingly. Some scrapbookers print at an 8×8-inch, 12×12-inch, or 8.5×11-inch size.

Begin by gathering the items you want to memorialize. Scan in memorabilia such as maps, ticket stubs, ribbons, stamps, or anything that is meaningful to the page you're creating. In the Manage workspace, place the photographs and scanned items you want to include in the Organizer palette's My Tray.

You'll find lots of scrapbooking items included with PaintShop Pro, such as backgrounds, frames, and embellishments. You can also use PaintShop Pro to create your own embellishments, but remember that you'll find lots of free scrapbooking stuff online. You'll also see some freebies and demos on the companion website for this book (www.courseptr.com/downloads). And, of course, you can gather your own photographs.

Starting the Page

Create a new PaintShop Pro canvas with a white background at the size you intend to use. While you can enlarge or reduce the canvas at any time, there's a possibility that resizing could distort your entire layout. Use a resolution of 180 to 200 DPI. Scrapbook pages tend to become quite large, especially if you use a high resolution and a large page size. Make sure you have *plenty* of hard disk storage space or the ability to write to CDs before you begin. I've seen individual scrapbook pages anywhere from 10MB up to 150MB!

From the Edit workspace, choose File ❯ New or press Ctrl+N. Select the image size and resolution you want and the background color you want to begin with. (I suggest white.) Click the OK button to display the blank layout canvas. For our example, I'm using a 12-inch by 12-inch canvas.

Save your file by choosing File ❯ Save. Because you're working with a new file, the Save As dialog box appears, where you can give your layout a name. In the Save as Type field, make sure PSPIMAGE is the file type. Click Save.

Save Often

Don't forget to save your layout often. Save the file as a PSPIMAGE file at least until you finish.

Placing Images

Display the Organizer palette in the Edit workspace by choosing View > Palettes > Organizer. If you don't already have them open, open the images that you are considering for your page. Duplicate the images, make any necessary edits or enhancements, and then close all unwanted images.

Now's the time to copy the images you want to use onto your layout canvas and move them around the page to determine the approximate arrangement you want. Copy each image onto its own raster layer on the layout canvas. After you copy and paste the images, you can close the remaining images. The following steps show you how to copy the images onto the layout canvas:

Downsize Images

If your images are larger than your layout canvas, you may want to downsize them before placing them on a scrap page layer. Resize the images by choosing Image > Resize.

1. Activate the first photo you want to copy and choose Selections > Select All or press Ctrl+A. A marching marquee appears around the entire image.

2. Choose Edit > Copy or press Ctrl+C.

3. Activate the scrap page canvas and choose Edit > Paste as New Layer. The image appears on the canvas on its own layer (see Figure 16-9).

Figure 16-9
Copying the images to the scrap page.

 4. Use the Pick tool to move, resize, and rotate the image layer as desired.

5. Repeat for each image that you want on the scrap page. Now that you have the images on the canvas, you can decide on a background.

Leave Extra Room

When adding and resizing images, be sure to leave room for the title and journaling.

Notice in Figure 16-10 that the Layers palette shows a layer for the background and a layer for each image.

Figure 16-10
Placing each image on its own layer.

Naming Layers

Scrapbook pages tend to have lots of layers, and it really helps you position elements if you name your layers according to their content. From the Layers palette, right-click any layer and choose Rename Layer. If you don't see the Layers palette, choose View > Palettes > Layers or press F8.

Deciding on a Background

Placing images on a plain white background can be the worst type of boring. If you want a quality scrap page, you need a little pizzazz for the page.

The background can set the tone for the entire layout.

Once your photographs are on the layout, you can use them as a color guide to coordinate with your background. You can create your own background by adding color and texture to the background layer, or you can use one of the thousands of predefined backgrounds available from the Internet or included with PaintShop Pro. In this example, we'll create our background from a pattern supplied with PaintShop Pro. Follow these steps:

1. Select the background layer.

 2. Click the Flood Fill tool.

3. On the Materials palette, click the Foreground and Stroke Properties box. The Material Properties dialog box appears.

4. Click the Pattern tab and the Pattern arrow, and then click the pattern you want. For this example, I'm choosing one with a dark red tile (see Figure 16-11).

5. Click OK; then with the Flood Fill tool, click anywhere in the background layer. The layer fills with the selected pattern. As I look at Figure 16-12, I think the red pattern is a bit too much for an entire background, so I'm going to make the pattern appear as a page border.

6. Create a new raster layer. If necessary, move the new layer so it's above the background layer.

Pattern arrow

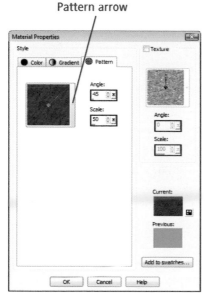

Figure 16-11
Choose a background fill.

Figure 16-12
Adding a pattern to the background.

7. By default, the background of a new raster layer is transparent. We need to set it to color mode. Click the Color option on the Background and Fill box.

8. Select the Dropper tool and right-click a color from the background pattern, which adds it to the Background and Fill color palette.

Choose Background Color

You could also click a different color from the background pattern or one of the images and make it the Foreground and Stroke color in the Materials palette.

9. On the Materials palette, click the Background and Fill box. The Material Properties dialog box appears.

10. From the Gradient tab, click the Gradient List arrow and choose a gradient. I'm choosing the Foreground option, which includes gradient colors from the color I selected from the background pattern (see Figure 16-13). Click OK.

11. Select the Rectangle tool and draw a rectangle on the new layer, making it smaller than the entire layer. A rectangle with the gradient fill appears, as you see in Figure 16-14.

12. Click the Apply button.

Gradient List arrow

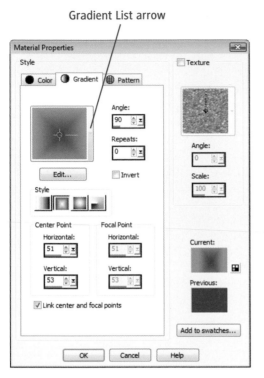

Figure 16-13
Selecting a gradient.

Figure 16-14
After adding a second background.

Adding Mats

For good design, you may want to add mats to complement the background. You use the vector drawing tools to create a mat to fit around the image. The following steps show you how to create your own image mat:

Create a Mat

You can also create a mat by adding a picture frame to your image. Picture frames are reviewed later in this chapter.

1. From the Tools toolbar, choose the Rectangle tool.

2. From the Tool Options palette, make sure Create on Vector is selected as well as the Anti-Alias option. Set the Line Width to 0.

3. Click the Background and Fill Properties swatch. The Material Properties dialog box appears.

4. Click the Color tab if it's not already selected; then, leaving the Material Properties dialog box open, use the mouse pointer to click the area of the photo containing the color you want to use in the mats.

5. Click OK.

6. Click and drag on the image layer (which automatically creates a new vector layer) to create a rectangle slightly larger than your photograph.

7. Click the Apply button.

8. If needed, using the Layers palette, drag the new layer so it is directly below the image you want matted. In Figure 16-15, I made the mat about one-eighth inch larger than the photograph. I also renamed the layer Blue Mat.

Image mat

Figure 16-15
Create a mat to surround your image.

9. Repeat steps 1 through 8 until each image you want matted has a mat around it (see Figure 16-16).

Give Depth to Images

Apply a drop shadow to each image to give the image a sense of depth against the mat. Select the photograph layer that you want to change and choose Effects > 3D Effects > Drop Shadow. Then click OK.

Figure 16-16
Matting your photographs.

Adding Text

Now you're ready to tell your story. It can be a short story (just a word or two) or something lengthy. To begin, think about what you really want to say. Who will view it? Is there something you want the viewer to know that the picture can't tell him? Scrapbook journaling is a personal process, and each person has his own style.

In Chapter 13, "Working with Text," you discovered working with vector text. The text you add to your scrap page layout is also vector text. As you discovered when adding images and mats, for easiest management, place each text object on its own vector layer.

ADDING A TITLE

Consider that your title is a prominent element in the layout, so you want to make it really special. You can place a title in any part of the layout, such as the top, bottom, left, or right side, and you can make it vertical or horizontal. Typically, a title is a much larger font size than you use for journaling text, and most often, it uses a different font face.

T To add a title, select the Text tool and click the mouse where you want the text to begin. From the Tool Options toolbar, choose a font type, size, color, and alignment. Take a guess if you don't know what you want. You can change the font later if you need to. Make sure the Create on Vector option is selected.

Type the text you want, and then click the Apply button. Apply any desired effects to the text. In Figure 16-17, I used a 48-point font called Horrormaster to create the horizontal title. After creating the text, I resized and stretched it and then applied a Drop Shadow effect. When adding the Drop Shadow effect, PaintShop Pro first needed to convert the text vector layer to a raster layer.

Figure 16-17
Creating a title for the layout.

JOURNALING

Journaling fills your scrapbook page with meaning. You can be personal, expressing your feelings about the people and events in your life and expressing your love, hopes, and values. And for those times that you can't find just the right words or you don't want to draw on a personal experience, you can turn to poems and quotes for beautifully phrased, meaningful words.

For example, a photo of a beautiful sunset may not have much history behind it, but the image may still suggest strong feelings. Adding a quote helps create mood and convey your emotions. Sharing your favorite quotes reveals who you are and what's important to you.

You may not have rooms filled with books to help you find the perfect citation, but the Internet is an invaluable resource. You can find poems and quotes on every imaginable topic either by using a search engine such as Google or by looking at the numerous online scrapbooking sites, which often have resource areas dedicated to poems and quotes.

You add your journaling text in the same manner that you add a title. You select the Text tool and, after choosing a location and font options, type the text you want. See Figure 16-18, where I added a journaling comment to my layout.

Figure 16-18
Add journaling to express your thoughts, emotions, and memories.

Effective Journaling

Our brains store our life experiences through the sensory information we receive. As children, we learned about our five senses. We learned that our eyes see colors and shapes; our fingers and toes feel textures; and our ears hear sounds. When our noses smell aromas, we can almost taste with our tongues the various flavors accompanying the scents. Effective journaling requires drawing attention to what our senses tell us. We can use words that build the senses to reflect things we can see, hear, smell, taste, and touch.

To enliven your text, use words that suggest action, such as jumping, soaring, reaching, or stomping. For better visualization, try using words that accentuate size, such as huge, miniscule, dozens, scant, or multitudes. When you want to provide a sense of touch, use words that describe textures or temperatures.

For example, do you say, "Mom baked an apple pie" or "The entire neighborhood detected the wafting scent from Mom's apple pie cooling on the window sill"? You could say, "I donned my white sweater" or "I felt the evening chill leave my arms as I wrapped myself in the soft cashmere fabric of my favorite sweater." Which sentence produces a sense of calmness and comfort? Experiment with different phrases and see which leaves you yearning for more information.

Journaling is a means of presenting facts in a way that gets to the core of why you created the scrapbook page in the first place.

Add the Date

Many scrapbookers like to add the date to their layout. Create a separate text entry for that.

Embellishing the Story

When someone is telling a story and he adds a little extra to it without changing the plot, he is said to be *embellishing* it. An artistic embellishment is anything that adds design interest or enhances the appearance of something (such as a scrapbook layout) without having a functional purpose. Embellishments are a lot of fun in traditional paper scrapbooking, and they are equally fun in digital scrapbooking.

You can add a little extra to your layout by adding embellishing elements ranging from the simple, such as small gold dots or brass-looking brads, to the fancy, like leaves, shiny ribbons, dangly trinkets, and the like.

The embellishments can be in the form of other graphics files that you create yourself, that you open and then copy and paste onto your image, or that involve using the PaintShop Pro picture tubes. Put each embellishment on its own layer, and give the layer a name that describes what it contains.

You'll also find many additional tubes on the Internet. In Figure 16-19, I added some gold buttons from the picture tubes included with PaintShop Pro 4x, and some Halloween-themed tubes that I downloaded from the Corel.com website. Go to www.corel.com and search "free tubes".

Figure 16-19
Add picture tubes and other embellishments.

A well-placed drop shadow makes an embellishment item appear three-dimensional. Experiment with adding embellishments and different effects.

More Than Scrapbook Pages

Once you have the basic concepts of scrapbooking, you can apply the same measure to creating greeting cards. Create Christmas cards, birthday cards, get-well cards, thank-you cards, or thinking-of-you cards. You manage greeting cards in the same way you manage a scrapbook page.

Working with Picture Frames

ANOTHER VARIATION often used when creating scrapbook pages or just with images in general includes placing a picture frame around the images. PaintShop Pro contains a variety of picture frames, which are raster images, ranging from wood to metal, stone, and other decorative surfaces. Lots of additional frames are available over the Internet, many of them free.

PaintShop Pro includes a Picture Frame dialog box that takes all the work out of adding a frame to your image. You can add a picture frame to an entire scrapbook page or to an individual image on the page.

Note

PaintShop Pro cannot properly frame rotated images.

Open the image that you want a picture frame on, and click Image ❯ Picture Frame. You'll see the Picture Frame dialog box similar to the one in Figure 16-20.

Click here to choose a frame

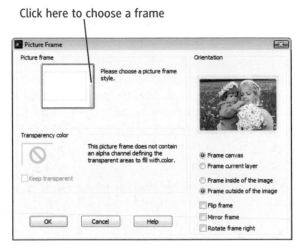

Figure 16-20
Add a picture frame to highlight your image.

Click the Picture Frame arrow and select the picture frame you'd like to try. You can preview your image in the frame as you select any desired frame options (see Figure 16-21).

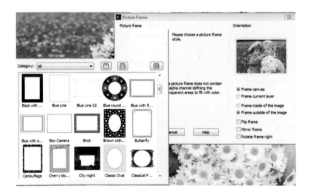

Figure 16-21
See the picture frame around your image.

Note

It doesn't matter whether the frame is tall or wide. The Picture Frame Wizard can fit the frame to your image.

Depending on the shape of the frame you selected, you may need to select a color to fill the transparent areas outside the frame. Odd-shaped frames usually have a transparent area. Here are some other picture frame options:

▶ **Frame canvas**: The frame fits around the canvas size. This gives the appearance of a picture frame around the entire image.

▶ **Frame current layer**: The frame fits around the current layer which, in the case of scrapbooking, may contain a photograph smaller than the overall canvas. This gives the appearance of only one photograph having a frame, not a frame around the entire image.

▶ **Frame inside the image**: PaintShop Pro resizes the frame to fit within the edges of the image. Part of the image is covered by the picture frame, and the dimensions of the image are not altered.

▶ **Frame outside the image**: PaintShop Pro increases the canvas size to accommodate the frame. The original image is not covered, and the dimensions of the image are increased by the size of the frame.

Here are a few examples of images in PaintShop Pro's picture frames.

Use a Frame as a Mat

To use a picture frame as a photograph mat, select the layer you want to frame, and choose Image > Picture Frame. From the dialog box, select the frame you want, and select the Frame Current Layer option. Only the photograph on the selected layer will have the frame.

In Figure 16-22, you see where I placed a picture frame around the center image on a scrapbook page.

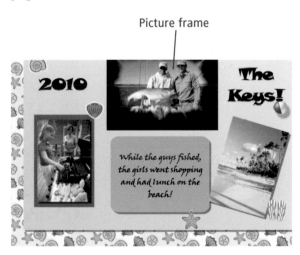

Figure 16-22
Apply a picture frame around individual scrapbook images.

A

Keyboard Shortcuts

LIKE MOST WINDOWS APPLICATIONS, there's usually more than one way to accomplish a single task or access a particular feature. Included with PaintShop Pro are a number of shortcut keystrokes you can use to access tools or menu options without having to reach for your mouse.

> **Note**
>
> These keyboard shortcuts work only in the Edit workspace.

Tool and Menu Shortcuts

Tool Menu Shortcuts

Shortcut	Function
A	Pan tool
B	Paint Brush tool
C	Clone tool
D	Raster Deform tool
E	Tool
F	Flood Fill tool
G	Rectangle tool
H	Symmetric Shape tool
I	Picture Tube tool
J	Dodge Brush tool
K	Pick tool
L	Lighten/Darken Brush tool
M	Move tool
O	Vector Object Selector tool
P	Preset Shapes tool
Q	Ellipse tool
R	Crop tool
S	Selection tool
T	Text tool
V	Pen tool
X	Eraser tool
Z	Zoom tool
Ctrl+Shift+F6	Reset Materials Palette

MOST COMMONLY ACCESSED MENU functions include a shortcut key combination you can use instead of clicking the top-level menu and selecting options under that menu. These shortcuts are organized by the different top-level menu items.

File Menu Shortcuts

Shortcut	Function
F12	File ❯ Save As
Ctrl+N	File ❯ New
Ctrl+O	File ❯ Open
Ctrl+P	File ❯ Print
Ctrl+S	File ❯ Save
Ctrl+F12	File ❯ Save Copy As
Ctrl+Delete	File ❯ Delete
Shift+F12	File ❯ Save for Office

Edit Menu Shortcuts

Shortcut	Function
Delete	Edit > Clear
Ctrl+C	Edit > Copy
Ctrl+E	Edit > Paste as New Selection
Ctrl+G	Edit > Paste as New Vector Selection
Ctrl+L	Edit > Paste as New Layer
Ctrl+V	Edit > Paste as New Layer
Ctrl+X	Edit > Cut
Ctrl+Y	Edit > Repeat
Ctrl+Z	Edit > Undo
Ctrl+Shift+E	Edit > Paste as Transparent Selection
Ctrl+Shift+L	Edit > Paste into Selection
Ctrl+Shift+V	Edit > Paste as New Image
Ctrl+Alt+Z	Edit > Redo

View Menu Shortcuts

Shortcut	Function
Num+	View > Zoom In by One Step
Num−	View > Zoom Out by One Step
F3	View > Palettes > History
F4	View > Palettes > Tool Options
F6	View > Palettes > Materials
F7	View > Palettes > Histogram
F8	View > Palettes > Layers
F9	View > Palettes > Overview
F10	View > Palettes > Learning Center
F11	View > Palettes > Brush Variance
Ctrl+Shift+A	View > Full Screen Preview
Ctrl+Shift+G	View > Snap to Grid
Ctrl+Alt+G	View > Grid
Ctrl+Alt+N	View > Zoom to 100%
Ctrl+Alt+R	View > Rulers
Ctrl+Alt+M	View > Magnifier
Shift+F3	View > Palettes > Script Output
Shift+F6	View > Palettes > Mixer
Shift+F9	View > Palettes > Organizer
Ctrl+Shift+A	View > Full Screen Edit
Shift+Alt+G	View > Snap to Guides

Image Menu Shortcuts

Shortcut	Function
Ctrl+I	Image > Flip Vertical
Ctrl+M	Image > Flip Horizontal
Ctrl+R	Image > Free Rotate
Shift+I	Image > Image Information
Shift+O	Image > Palette > Load Palette
Shift+P	Image > Palette > Edit Palette
Shift+R	Image > Crop to Selection
Shift+S	Image > Resize
Shift+V	Image > Palette > View Palette Transparency
Ctrl+Shift+1	Image > Decrease Color Depth > 2 Color Palette
Ctrl+Shift+2	Image > Decrease Color Depth > 16 Color Palette
Ctrl+Shift+3	Image > Decrease Color Depth > 256 Color Palette
Ctrl+Shift+4	Image > Decrease Color Depth > 32K Color Palette
Ctrl+Shift+5	Image > Decrease Color Depth > 64K Color Palette
Ctrl+Shift+6	Image > Decrease Color Depth > x Colors
Ctrl+Shift+7	Image > Increase Color Depth > RGB-8 Bits/Channel
Ctrl+Shift+8	Image > Increase Color Depth > 16 Color Palette
Ctrl+Shift+9	Image > Increase Color Depth > 256 Color Palette

Adjust Menu Shortcuts

Shortcut	Function
Shift+B	Adjust > Brightness and Contrast > Brightness and Contrast
Shift+E	Adjust > Brightness and Contrast > Histogram Equalize
Shift+H	Adjust > Hue and Saturation > Hue/Saturation/Lightness
Shift+L	Adjust > Hue and Saturation > Colorize
Shift+M	Adjust > Brightness and Contrast > Highlight/Midtone/Shadow
Shift+T	Adjust > Brightness and Contrast > Histogram Stretch
Shift+U	Adjust > Color > Red/Green/Blue
Ctrl+Shift+H	Adjust > Brightness and Contrast > Histogram Adjustment

Layers Menu Shortcuts

Shortcut	Function
Shift+K	Layers ❯ Invert Mask/ Adjustment
Shift+Y	Layers ❯ New Mask Layer ❯ Hide All
Ctrl+Alt+V	Layers ❯ View Overlay

Selections Menu Shortcuts

Shortcut	Function
Ctrl+A	Selections ❯ Select All
Ctrl+D	Selections ❯ Select None
Ctrl+F	Selections ❯ Float
Ctrl+H	Selections ❯ Modify ❯ Feather
Ctrl+Shift+B	Selections ❯ From Vector Object
Ctrl+Shift+F	Selections ❯ Defloat
Ctrl+Shift+I	Selections ❯ Invert
Ctrl+Shift+M	Selections ❯ Hide Marquee
Ctrl+Shift+P	Selections ❯ Promote Selection to Layer
Ctrl+Shift+S	Selections ❯ From Mask

Window Menu Shortcuts

Shortcut	Function
Ctrl+W	Window ❯ Fit to Image
Shift+D	Window ❯ Duplicate
Shift+W	Window ❯ New Window

Help Menu Shortcuts

Shortcut	Function
F1	Help ❯ Help Topics
F10	Learning Center

B

Exploring Useful Websites

THE WORLD WIDE WEB HAS THOUSANDS of sites dedicated to using PaintShop Pro. If you have Internet access, take some time to check out some of the links listed in this Appendix. Some provide general PaintShop Pro help information, whereas others offer step-by-step tutorials on special tasks you can accomplish with PaintShop Pro. Still others are links to lots of free or mostly free things you can download to use with PaintShop Pro—things like picture tubes, masks, filters, frames, and other goodies.

Many of these sites refer to prior versions of PaintShop Pro, but you'll find most of the information they offer works with PaintShop Pro X4 as well. Some of these sites offer help specifically designed for new users, while others have lots of tutorials to guide you step by step through various PaintShop Pro processes.

I apologize in advance if any listed site closes or modifies its content. While at the time of publication these links were active and accurate, remember that websites change frequently. Also, always make sure your antivirus software is up-to-date before you download anything from the Internet. You cannot be too safe! The references are in no particular order.

http://groups.google.com/group/comp.graphics.apps.paint-shop-pro/topics

www.corel.com

http://digitalscrapdesigns.com/digitalscrapstore/index.php?main_page=index&cPath=19

http://graphicssoft.about.com/od/paintshopprodownloads/Free_Paint_Shop_Pro_Downloads_Brushes_Patterns_Presets_Tubes_Etc_.htm

http://hem.passagen.se/grafoman/plugtool/plugs.html

http://htmlhelp.rootsweb.com/imagehelp

www.psptoybox.com

www.lvsonline.com

http://loriweb.pair.com

http://mardiweb.com/web

http://members.home.nl/j.a.c.backer/gif-index.html

http://millerfg.home.mindspring.com/wpf2.htm

http://moonsdesigns.com

http://nansons-place.com

http://pspimaginarium.com

http://store.scrapgirls.com/category/75/Paint-Shop-Pro-Tools

www.alienskin.com

www.avbros.com

www.campratty.com/search.html

www.dizteq.com

www.extenuation.net/psp

www.flamingpear.com/blade.html

www.flashpowdergraphics.com

www.fortunecity.com/westwood/idea/909/index.html

www.freefoto.com/index.jsp

www.graphicallusions.com

www.jaguarwoman.com/store/index.php?main_page=index&cPath=61

www.pspug.org

www.sheilsoft.com/psp.htm

www.state-of-entropy.com

www.suzsplace.com

www.the-graphics-tablet.com/paint-shop-pro-videos.html

www.xanthic.net/tutorials.php

Glossary

1-bit image: An image that contains a maximum of two colors (black and white).

4-bit image: An image that contains a maximum of 16 colors.

8-bit image: An image that contains a maximum of 256 colors.

15-bit image: An image that contains a maximum of 32,768 colors.

16-bit image: An image that contains a maximum of 65,536 colors.

24-bit image: An image that contains a maximum of 16,777,216 colors.

adjustment layer: A layer that is used to apply color and tonal adjustments to the layers below it.

anti-alias: The smoothing and blending of pixel edges to eliminate jagged edges on curved and slanted lines.

aspect ratio: The ratio of width to height.

attribute: An item that determines the appearance of text, such as bold, underline, italic, font, or size.

automatic rollups: Floating objects that open automatically as you hover your mouse in their area but then close up again when you move your mouse out of their vicinity.

AutoSave: A feature that periodically saves a temporary version of your document.

AVI: Abbreviation for Audio Video Interleave. A Windows multimedia file format used for video and audio.

background: The canvas on which graphics display.

background color: The canvas color on which graphics display.

background layer: The bottom layer in many images.

bevel: A three-dimensional edge on an object.

bit: The smallest unit of digital information with which a computer can work.

bit depth: *See* color depth.

bitmapped image: An image that is composed of small squares, called pixels, that are arranged in columns and rows. Each pixel has a specific color and location.

blend: To combine two layers or areas of an image.

blur: An effect that reduces areas of high contrast and softens the appearance of an image.

BMP: File format abbreviation for a bitmapped image.

brightness: The amount of light or white color in an image.

canvas: The area on which an image is displayed.

canvas size: The size of the area within an image window.

clone: To duplicate a portion of an image.

CMYK: Abbreviation for Cyan/Magenta/Yellow/Black, which are the four standard ink colors used in printing.

color depth: The number of bits of color information available for each pixel.

Color palette: Contains a selection of available colors, styles, and textures and displays the current foreground and background colors and styles.

Color wheel: The circular color area from which you can create a custom color.

colorize: An effect that converts an image or selection to a uniform hue and saturation while retaining its lightness.

compression: A process that is applied to certain file formats of saved images to reduce file size.

Contract command: Shrinks a selection by a specific number of pixels.

contrast: The difference between the light and dark areas of an image.

crop: To remove part of an image outside a selection.

defloat: To merge a floating selection into a layer.

deformation: To change an image's appearance by moving data from one area to another.

defringe: To clean the edges of a selection by removing pixels of the background color.

digital: Information that a computer reads and processes.

digital camera: A camera that takes pictures and stores them on its memory card.

dithering: When a computer monitor substitutes a color that it cannot display with a similar color.

DPI: Abbreviation for dots per inch. A unit of measurement that measures the number of dots that fit horizontally and vertically into a one-inch measure.

Edit workspace: The workspace where you can apply detailed modifications to images.

effect: A graphics function that modifies an image in a predetermined manner.

emboss: An effect that causes the foreground of an image to appear raised from the background.

expand a selection: Increases the size of a selection by a specified number of pixels.

export: The process of saving data into a different format.

Express lab: The workspace area for applying quick edits to images.

feather: The process of fading an area on all edges of a selection. Measured in pixels.

file associations: A method of determining which files your computer opens automatically using PaintShop Pro.

file format: The structure of a file that defines the way it is stored.

filter: A tool that applies special effects to an image.

Flip command: The command that reverses an image vertically.

Float command: The command that temporarily separates a selection from an image or layer.

floating objects: Screen elements appearing in the middle of the PaintShop Pro window that can be moved to other areas of the window. Floating objects have automatic rollup.

foreground color: The primary color for the painting and drawing tools.

format: The shape and size of an image or text. Also, the method that a browser uses to display an image.

GIF: File format abbreviation for a Graphic Interchange Format image. GIF images support transparency but only 8-bit (256) color. Commonly used with web graphics.

gradient fill: A fill that is created by the gradual blending of colors.

grayscale image: An image that uses up to 256 shades of gray.

grid: An equally spaced series of vertical and horizontal lines used to help align objects.

handles: Control points on objects that are used to edit the object.

highlight: The lightest part of an image.

histogram: A graphics representation showing the distribution of color and light in an image.

HSL: Abbreviation for Hue/Saturation/Lightness. A method of defining colors in an image.

HTML: Abbreviation for Hypertext Markup Language. A programming language that is used to create webpages.

hue: A color.

Image window: The area in which you work on your image.

Internet: A global network of computers used to transfer information.

JPEG: Abbreviation for Joint Photographic Experts Group. Same as JPG file format.

JPG file format: A file format that supports 24-bit (16,777,216) color but not transparency. Commonly used with web graphics.

kerning: The distance between characters of text.

layer: A level of an image that can be edited independently from the rest of the image.

Layers palette: Lists each layer in the current image.

leading: The distance between lines of text.

line art: An image that consists of distinct straight and curved lines usually placed against a plain background.

logo: A name or symbol used, often by businesses, for easy recognition.

luminance: A physical measurement of the brightness information in an image.

Magic Wand: A selection tool that works by selecting content rather than defining edges.

marquee: A selection area that is represented by "marching ants."

mask: A feature that allows some portion of an image to be hidden.

mirror: An exact copy of an image that is placed in reverse of the copied image.

negative image: A photographic image in reversed form where the light areas become dark and the dark areas become light.

node: A control point on a vector object.

noise: The grainy appearance in some images.

object: A single element in an image.

opacity: The density of a color or layer.

Organizer: The palette that allows you to manage your images.

Overview palette: Displays entire image when zooming in to a small area.

path: The guiding line for a vector object.

picture tubes: Fun little pictures that you paint with your brush.

pixel: The smallest element in an image.

PNG: Abbreviation for Portable Network Graphics. A file format designed for web graphics that supports both transparency and 24-bit (16,777,216) color.

posterize: Effect that replaces areas of continuous color tone with single colors.

Preferences: The area in which each user maintains customized settings for the PaintShop Pro application.

Print Preview: The feature that allows you to view an image onscreen prior to printing it on paper.

PSPIMAGE format: A proprietary image file format used by Corel PaintShop Pro that allows for layers and other PaintShop Pro features.

raster image: A bitmapped image made up of pixels.

rasterize: To convert a vector image to raster.

red-eye: A photographic effect that frequently occurs in photographs of humans and animals, giving a shiny or red appearance to eyes.

Replace Color command: The PaintShop Pro feature that allows you to pick a specific color and replace it with any other color.

resize: The ability to make an image or object larger or smaller.

resolution: The measurement of the detail in an image.

RGB (Red/Green/Blue): The three primary colors that compose most images.

rotate: To turn an image or object.

saturation: The measure of strength of an image's color.

scanner: A hardware device used to translate pictures and text into digital language that a computer can interpret.

selection: The outline that appears around an area to be modified.

shadow: The darkest area of an image. Sometimes applied as an effect.

sharpen: An effect that increases the contrast in an image.

skew: A deformation that tilts an image along its horizontal or vertical axis.

solarize: An effect that inverts all colors above a selected value.

Standard toolbar: Displays tools to manage files and commonly used menu functions.

status bar: The line at the bottom of an application window that displays help and image details.

stroke: An outline of text.

thumbnail: A miniature version of an image.

TIFF: Abbreviation for Tagged Image File Format. A format that scanners commonly use.

title bar: The bar at the top of the application that displays the PaintShop Pro application name; the Manage, Adjust, and Edit workspace tabs; the Corel Guide button; and the standard Minimize, Restore Down, and Close buttons found in the upper-right corner of every Windows program.

toggle: To switch an item back and forth from one state to another. Frequently used to turn the display of layers on and off.

Tool Options palette: Displays options for the currently selected Tools toolbar tool.

Tools toolbar: Contains the image-editing tools.

transparency: An area that lacks color.

TWAIN: A common computer interface among scanners, digital cameras, and computers.

undo: The ability to reverse actions.

vector graphic: An object that uses mathematics to create images. Vector graphics can be edited, moved, and resized easily with little or no loss of quality.

watermark: Embedded information in an image that is used to mark an image with copyright and author information.

web browser: A software program that is designed specifically to view web pages on the Internet.

workspaces: The portions of the PaintShop Pro window where you work on your image.

zoom: The process of viewing an image in a larger or smaller magnification.

Index

3D effects, 223
3D images, 353–356

A

acutance (sharpness), 130–133
adding. *See* creating
Adjust menu keyboard shortcuts, 386
Adjust workspace, 7
adjusting
  Adjust workspace, 7
  adjustment layers, 184, 186, 196–198
  color
    cast, 119–120
    hue, 123
    images, 118–120
    saturation, 123–124
    temperature, 118–119
  images
    Adjust menu keyboard shortcuts, 386
    Blemish Fixer, 87–88
    Clone Brush, 98–100
    Color Changer, 95–96
    Crop tool. *See* cropping
    Eye Drop, 87, 89–90
    Object Extractor, 100–102
    One Step Photo Fix, 80
    panoramas, 351
    red-eye, 82–87
    rotating, 110

Scratch Remover, 93–95
size, 324–327
Skin Smoothing, 92–93
Smart Carver, 96–97
Straighten tool, 108–109
Suntan, 90–91
Thinify, 91
Toothbrush, 88–89
text (shapes), 317
adjustment layers, 184, 186, 196–198
Airbrush, 244
Alien Skin website, 230
alignment
  text, 304
  vector objects, 282–284
Andromeda website, 230
anti-aliasing (selections), 67
applying filters, 222
arranging
  layers, 189
  vector objects, 281–285
art media effects, 224
art media layers, 184
art media tools, 239, 244–245
artistic effects, 224–225
assigning tags, 51–52
asymmetric nodes (vector objects), 290
Auto Action, 16
Auto FX website, 231
Auto-Preserve, 29–30, 79
AutoSave, 30

AV Bros. website, 231
Average Blur filter, 215

B

background layers, 183, 192
backgrounds
  background layers, 183, 192
  color, 24
  eraser tools, 258–259
  images, 338–339
  panoramas, 348
  scrapbooks, 365–366, 372–374
  selections, 23
backlighting, 141–142
backups (images), 61
balance (scrapbooks), 363
balancing color, 167–168
barrel distortion, 138
batches, 56–61
Bézier curves
  shape tools, 251
  vector object lines, 272–273
bitmaps (raster graphics)
  overview, 27
  raster layers, 183
    eraser tools, 256, 258
    vector layers, converting, 299
  vector objects comparison, 266–267
black-and-white images, 143–146
Blemish Fixer, 87–88
blending layers, 205–209